60 Years
of Notable Children's Books

Compiled by Sally Anne Thompson

Association for Library Service to Children

BOOKLIST PUBLICATIONS
AMERICAN LIBRARY ASSOCIATION
2003

Dedication

For William C. Morris,
in gratitude for his tireless dedication
to excellence in children's literature.

Table of Contents

Preface

The Association for Library Service to Children (ALSC) and Booklist Publications are very pleased to present *60 Years of Notable Children's Books*. Over the past 65 years, members of the ALSC Notable Children's Books Committees have read thousands of books for children in order to select those they deemed truly "notable." Though the lists are published each year in *Booklist*, this volume represents the first compendium of Notable Children's Books ALSC has produced since 1970. The annotated lists included here represent the dedication and diligence of the past members of the Notable Children's Books Committees and symbolize a powerful and ongoing commitment to children and to the quality of children's literature.

A division of the American Library Association, The Association for Library Service to Children is the world's largest organization dedicated to the support and enhancement of services to children from birth through age 14 in all types of libraries. ALSC sets the agenda for the future of children's library service and acts as a children's advocate, urging policy makers to support library service for children. To fulfill its mission, ALSC partners with government institutions, publishers, teachers, and a wide range of organizations serving children and their families.

The annual development of the Notable Children's Books lists is one way in which ALSC develops and supports the profession of children's librarianship by enabling and encouraging its practitioners to provide the best library service to our nation's children. Both school and public librarians have come to rely on these lists of outstanding children's books in their work with children from birth to age 14.

ALSC is dedicated to the improvement and extension of library services to children in all types of libraries. To that end, we believe that this compilation of the Notable Children's Books of the last six decades will aid children's librarians, parents, and educators in the preselection and acquisition of high-quality children's books for young readers. To ensure that the annual lists include only the most distinguished titles published each year, members of ALSC book-selection committees work carefully to evaluate, select, and annotate books for designation as Notable Children's Books.

ALSC is committed both to ensuring that children have high-quality literature to read and to promoting a love of reading in all children. We firmly believe that the annual selection of Notable Children's Books has served to enhance the quality of literature published for children. The Notables lists reflect the thoughtful and informed judgments of educators and librarians who work with children daily. As such, they provide a benchmark of literary merit for authors, illustrators, and producers of children's literature.

ALSC is grateful to Sally Anne Thompson, librarian at Pope John XXIII School Library in Scottsdale, Arizona, for beginning this compilation of Notable Children's Books some five years ago. Culling materials from almost 60 years of committee work, she compiled and edited the lists from 1940 to 1998 for this volume. Since then, the compilation has grown and expanded. In addition, ALSC acknowledges the work of the immediate past chair of the Notable Children's Books Committee, Toni Bernardi of the San Francisco Public Library, who explains the purpose, definition, selection criteria, and committee makeup of the Notable Children's Books in her foreword to this book. The foreword thoroughly explains the painstaking process each committee undertakes to create these spectacular lists.

ALSC Board member and professor at Kent State University's School of Library and Information Science Dr. Carolyn S. Brodie, along with Cuyahoga County Public Library Children's Librarian and ALSC Priority Group Chair Leslie M. Molnar, created 20 theme lists, which appear as an appendix to this book. These theme lists are intended to help individuals who may wish to use the book in conjunction with themed units in libraries, classrooms, day-care centers, or other venues. The lists include Notable Children's Books that fit within a variety of thematic units. This addition to the book has expanded the scope of the work beyond an annotated bibliography, providing an invaluable bibliographic and interactive tool for readers.

It is our hope that you will use *60 Years of Notable Children's Books* to foster a love of reading in children within your community and beyond. ALSC's commitment to high-quality reading materials and to the joy of reading extends beyond this publication, and it is our wish that you use this book to enhance your own commitment to children's literacy and love of learning. We know that you will find this book useful in reader's-advisory work, program development, and the creation of bibliographies to meet the needs of your community, students, and patrons. Happy reading and programming!

—*Malore I. Brown*
Executive Director
Association for Library Service to Children

Foreword

S erving on the Notable Children's Books Committee is one of the most challenging and rewarding opportunities that anyone working with children's books could have. It requires a major commitment of time and effort over the period of the appointment. The lists produced in this compilation are the result of countless hours of reading, evaluation, and discussion by professionals who dedicated their personal time to the goal of selecting the very best out of the many wonderful books published for children in the United States each year. I had the privilege of serving on the committee for four years and am delighted that I was asked to provide a brief foreword to this book.

Purpose

The Notable Children's Books list has been compiled annually since 1940. Its purpose is to assist children in selecting books to read and to encourage them to seek out "notable titles" among the many books available in bookstores and libraries. It also encourages libraries and bookstores to make these books accessible to children.

Definition of Notable

For the purpose of the list, *notable* is defined as worthy of note or notice, important, distinguished, outstanding. As applied to children's books, notable encompasses books of especially commendable quality, books that exhibit venturesome creativity, and books of fiction, information, poetry, and pictures for all age levels (through age 14) that reflect and encourage children's interests in exemplary ways.

Selection Criteria and Eligibility

The Notable Children's Books Committee uses the following evaluative criteria to select books for inclusion on the list:
- literary quality
- originality of text and illustration
- clarity and style of language
- excellence of illustration
- excellence of design and format

- subject matter of interest and value to children
- the likelihood of acceptance by children

For a book to be eligible for consideration, its potential audience must include children through age 14, and it must have been published in the United States during the year preceding the Midwinter Meeting of the American Library Association at which the selection is made. This means that eligible books must have been available for purchase in that year and have a copyright date no later than that year. A book might have a copyright date prior to the year under consideration if it was not, for various reasons, published until the year under consideration.

There is no limitation as to format. A book may be in hard or paper covers, spiral bound, in portfolio, etc. It is expected that books will have a collective unity of story line, theme, or concept developed through text or pictures or a combination thereof.

Inclusion of Other Award Titles

Newbery, Caldecott, Belpré, and Sibert Medal and Honor Books and the Batchelder Award Book are automatically included in the Notable Children's Books list.

Committee Makeup

The Notable Children's Books Committee is made up of 11 members appointed by the vice-president of ALSC in November each year. Members serve a two-year term. The chair is appointed annually, at the same time, from among the members who have served for at least one year.

Publication of Notables Lists

The list of Notable Children's Books is published annually in *Children and Libraries: The Journal of the Association for Library Service to Children* and on the ALSC Web site at www.ala.org/alsc. Previous lists, back to 1996, are also posted on the Web site. *Booklist* also publishes the list annually in its March 15 issue.

Not everyone is expected to agree with the committee's decisions on the Notable Books. However, examination of this compilation will show that the majority of titles have displayed remarkable longevity, relevance, and overall quality. In short, they have proven themselves notable. This publication provides an exceptional list of titles to be read, enjoyed, and examined in the light of 60 years of change.

—*Toni Bernardi*
San Francisco Public Library
Notable Children's Books Committee Chair, 2002–03

Introduction

From 1940 through 1999, the Notable Children's Books Committee of the Association for Library Service to Children has affixed the label "notable" to more than 6,000 books. The purpose of this volume is to take an appreciative look backward at a selection of those 6,000 notable children's books. Why a selection? Space demands it, for starters. In addition, our goal has been to isolate those books that have most successfully stood the test of time and can still be enjoyed by young readers today. We hope, as well, that this volume will be of help to youth services librarians involved in both collection development and weeding. In order to include as many notable authors and illustrators as possible in our selections, we have not always listed *all* the notable works of well-known writers, but among the 1,504 titles, there are multiple listings for many revered figures in the history of children's literature (Arnold Lobel, Virginia Hamilton, and Maurice Sendak, among them).

The text is organized chronologically, with chapters sorted by decade, from the 1940s through the 1990s. Entries within each chapter are listed alphabetically. Bibliographic information for each title includes author or editor, title, illustrator (when different from the author), original publication date, and in-print hardcover and paper editions (when available), with publisher, price, and ISBN listed for each. Out-of-print titles are listed as [o.p.], and the original hardcover publisher is included.

A note about those dreaded words *out of print*: the relationship between a book's in-print status and its availability has undergone a transformation in recent years. Print-on-demand technology threatens eventually to make an anachronism of the very idea of a book being out of print, and in the meantime, the relative ease with which out-of-print titles can be purchased from Internet book dealers means that both libraries and individuals should be able to acquire many of the o.p. titles listed here with very little effort and at reasonable expense. Even in the pre-electronic era, out-of-print status was an always-fluctuating phenomenon, with titles constantly moving from one designation to the other. That continues to be the case today, of course, and it should be remembered that the bibliographic information included here reflects in-print status as of fall 2003.

In the 1970s, the Children's Notable Book Committee began dividing its list into age-designated groups: Younger Readers, Middle Readers, Older Readers, and All Ages. Our chapters on the 1970s through the 1990s appear alphabetically, but each title carries an identifying letter—**Y, M, O,** or **A**—at the end of the bibliographic imprint that reflects the age designation selected by the committee.

Annotations for each title are based on the original text as written by members of the committee in the year the books were honored as notable. Information has been added to identify winners of the following children's literature awards: Newbery Medal, awarded annually to the author of the most distinguished contribution to American literature for children published in the United States during the preceding year; Caldecott Medal, awarded annually to the artist of the most distinguished American picture book for children published in the United States during the preceding year; and Batchelder Award, given annually to the American publisher of the most outstanding children's book originally published in a foreign language in a foreign country and subsequently published in English in the United States during the preceding year.

Following the decade-by-decade listings is an appendix comprising theme lists made up of notable titles selected from those included in the body of the book. The titles in the theme lists include brief bibliographic imprints in which author, title, illustrator (if different from the author), original year of publication, and age designation are included.

The book concludes with author-illustrator and title indexes to the material included in the decade-by-decade chapters.

1

Notable Children's Books
of the 1940s

Adshead, Gladys L. and **Duff, Annis,** eds. An Inheritance of Poetry. Illus. by Nora S. Unwin. 1948. Houghton [o.p.].
   Poems selected from a broad variety of sources and on a wide range of subjects make this an inviting anthology.

Bailey, Carolyn S. Miss Hickory. Illus. by Ruth Gannett. 1946. Viking, $16.99 (0-670-47940-3); paper, $5.99 (0-14-030956-X).
   Delightful humor abounds in the adventures of a doll with an applewood twig body and a hickory nut head. A Newbery Medal winner.

Benson, Sally. Stories of the Gods and Heroes. Illus. by Steele Savage. 1940. Dial [o.p.].
   A selection of classic stories based on Bulfinch's *The Age of Fable.*

Brenner, Anita. The Boy Who Could Do Anything and Other Mexican Folk Tales. Illus. by Jean Charlot. 1942. Addison-Wesley [o.p.].
   Stories of magic and of everyday life, legends, and myths are retold with insight and humor.

Brown, Marcia. Stone Soup: An Old Tale. 1947. illus. Simon & Schuster/Atheneum, paper, $16 (0-684-92296-7).
   A lively, simple retelling is enriched by the author's charming illustrations, which carry the flavor and underlying wit of the old folktale. A Caldecott Honor Book.

Buff, Mary and **Buff, Conrad.** Big Tree. 1946. illus. Viking [o.p.].
   Poetic text and elegant illustrations depict the grandeur and antiquity of a majestic sequoia. A Newbery Honor Book.

Burton, Virginia Lee. The Little House. 1942. illus. Houghton, $14.95 (0-395-18156-9); paper, $5.95 (0-395-25938-X).
   A little house watches the seasonal cycles and the encroaching growth of the city. Reflected in Burton's artwork is the joy of viewing the sun by day and at night. A Caldecott Medal winner.

Caudill, Rebecca. The Tree of Freedom. Illus. by Dorothy Bayley Morse. 1949. Viking [o.p.].
The struggles of a frontier family settling in the Kentucky wilderness of the 1780s provide drama, suspense, and excitement. A Newbery Honor Book.

Chase, Richard, ed. The Jack Tales. Illus. by Berkeley Williams, Jr. 1943. Houghton, $17 (0-618-34693-7); paper, $7.95 (0-618-34692-9).
Jack tales variants of European folktales are reflected in the native humor and speech patterns of the people of the Appalachian Mountains.

Clark, Ann Nolan. In My Mother's House. Illus. by Velino Herrera. 1941. Viking, $15.95 (0-670-83917-5).
This day-by-day account of the life of a Native American child, written for the most part by Pueblo children, presents an accurate depiction of life in the southwest desert. A Caldecott Honor Book.

Coblentz, Catherine C. The Blue Cat of Castle Town. Illus. by Janice Holland. 1949. Longmans [o.p.].
Set in Vermont in the 1800s, this is a beautifully told fantasy in which magic and goodness triumph over the forces of greed and power. A Newbery Honor Book.

Courlander, Harold and **Herzog, George.** The Cow-Tail Switch and Other West African Stories. Illus. by Madye Lee Chastain. 1947. Holt, paper, $12.95 (0-8050-0298-7).
Originality and humor permeate these 17 folktales reflecting the philosophy and customs of the West Africans. Illustrated with black-and-white drawings. A Newbery Honor Book.

Daugherty, James. Poor Richard. 1941. illus. Viking [o.p.].
Daugherty's text and lithographs combine to produce an excellent picture of the many-faceted Ben Franklin, focusing on his political life.

d'Aulaire, Ingri and **d'Aulaire, Edgar P.** Leif the Lucky. 1941. illus. Doubleday [o.p.].
The authors' dramatic illustrations combined with the sense of vigor and hardihood of Leif and the others conveyed in the narrative result in a strong read.

DeAngeli, Marguerite. The Door in the Wall. 1949. illus. Doubleday [o.p.].
In medieval England, Robin, crippled son of a nobleman, overcomes his disabilities by craftsmanship and wins knighthood by an act of courage. A Newbery Medal winner.

DeAngeli, Marguerite. Thee, Hannah! 1940. illus. Doubleday [o.p.].
Hannah found it difficult to control her love of fine things and to fit into her Philadelphia Quaker family's conservative pattern during the 1850s.

De la Mare, Walter. Rhymes and Verses: Collected Poems for Children. Illus. by Elinore Blaisdell. 1947. Holt [o.p.].
   This stunning single volume of rhymes culled from 11 collections by De la Mare is very attractively illustrated.

Deutsch, Babette. Heroes of the Kalevala: Finland's Saga. Illus. by Fritz Eichenberg. 1940. Messner [o.p.].
   A zestful retelling of the great Finnish epic, in fluent rhythmic prose.

Downer, Marion. Discovering Design. 1947. illus. Lothrop [o.p.].
   Excellent nature photographs and reproductions of art are used to demonstrate the characteristics and types of design.

Du Bois, William Pené. The Twenty-One Balloons. 1947. illus. Viking, $16.99 (0-670-73441-1); Penguin/Puffin, paper, $5.99 (0-14-032097-0).
   The fantastic adventures of a professor who sailed from San Francisco in one balloon and was found weeks later in the Atlantic with the wreckage of 20 balloons. A Newbery Medal winner.

Duvoisin, Roger. They Put Out to Sea: The Story of the Map. 1943. illus. Knopf [o.p.].
   Direct, graphic text works together complete with the author's illustrations to record the development of maps, showing how traders and explorers used cartography to traverse the globe.

Eaton, Jeanette. Lone Journey: The Life of Roger Williams. Illus. by Woodi Ishmael. 1944. Harcourt [o.p.].
   Williams is presented in this fictionalized biography as a fighter for freedom of speech and religious expression.

Edmonds, Walter. The Matchlock Gun. Illus. by Paul Lantz. 1941. Putnam, $16.99 (0-399-21911-0); paper, $4.99 (0-698-11680-1).
   Ten-year-old Edward and his mother manage to protect themselves from marauding Native Americans in their colonial New York homestead in the mid-eighteenth century. A Newbery Medal winner.

Enright, Elizabeth. The Saturdays. 1941. illus. Holt, $16.95 (0-8050-7060-5).
   Four unique, lively city children pool their allowances to plan and enjoy each Saturday in an eventful manner.

Estes, Eleanor. The Moffats. Illus. by Louis Slobodkin. 1941. Harcourt, $17 (0-15-255095-X); paper, $6 (0-15-202541-3).
   Nine-year-old Janey cheerfully details the experiences of her warm family of four children and a courageous mother.

Ets, Marie Hall. In the Forest. 1944. illus. Viking [o.p.].

A tiny child is joined by a variety of animals on a spirited, fanciful walk through the forest. A Caldecott Honor Book.

Field, Rachel L. Prayer for a Child. Illus. by Elizabeth Orton Jones. 1944. Simon & Schuster/Macmillan, $14 (0-02-735190-4); Simon & Schuster/Aladdin, paper, $6.99 (0-689-81319-8).

The meaning of everyday childhood experiences is enriched in this beautifully illustrated prayer. A Caldecott Medal winner.

Forbes, Esther. America's Paul Revere. Illus. by Lynd Ward. 1946. Houghton [o.p.]; paper, $9.95 (0-395-24907-4).

This picture biography recreates the world of Paul Revere and gives an authentic picture of life and social customs during the American Revolutionary era.

Forbes, Esther. Johnny Tremain: A Novel for Old and Young. Illus. by Lynd Ward. 1943. Houghton, $16 (0-395-06766-9); Dell/Yearling, paper, $6.50 (0-440-44250-8).

An apprentice to Paul Revere becomes involved in the struggle for freedom in this dramatic presentation of our nation's beginnings. A Newbery Medal winner.

Foster, Genevieve. Abraham Lincoln's World (1809–1865). 1944. illus. Scribner [o.p.].

A panorama of worldwide events parallels the life of Abraham Lincoln. A Newbery Honor Book.

Gannett, Ruth S. My Father's Dragon. Illus. by Ruth Chrisman Gannett. 1948. Random, $17.99 (0-679-98911-0); Knopf, paper, $5.99 (0-394-89048-5).

A highly original nonsense tale in which a small boy rescues a baby dragon from wild beasts on a jungle island. A Newbery Honor Book.

Gates, Doris. Blue Willow. Illus. by Paul Lantz. 1940. Viking [o.p.]; paper, $5.99 (0-14-030924-1).

In this heart-warming tale, Janey, daughter of a migrant worker, prizes a blue willow plate that seems to symbolize the security she seeks. A Newbery Honor Book.

George, John and **George, Jean.** Vulpes, the Red Fox. Illus. by Jean George. 1948. Dutton [o.p.]; Penguin/Puffin, paper, $6.99 (0-14-037623-2).

Sensitive wash drawings add to the beauty of a brave and cunning Maryland Red Fox.

Goudge, Elizabeth. The Little White Horse. Illus. by C. Walter Hodges. 1947. Coward [o.p.]; Penguin/Puffin, paper, $5.99 (0-14-230027-6).

Goudge's skillful blend of fantasy and reality features clear, vivid characterizations in a mystery set in nineteenth-century England.

Graham, Shirley and **Lipscomb, George.** Dr. George Washington Carver: Scientist. Illus. by Elton C. Fax. 1944. Messner [o.p.].

The great dignity and tremendous accomplishments of this scientist of humble beginnings are honestly portrayed.

Gray, Elizabeth Janet. Adam of the Road. Illus. by Robert Lawson. 1942. Viking, $18.99 (0-670-10435-3); paper, $5.99 (0-14-032464-X).

Set in thirteenth-century England, Adam's adventures in search of his minstrel father are rich in medieval lore. A Newbery Medal winner.

Hader, Berta and **Hader, Elmer.** The Big Snow. 1948. illus. Macmillan [o.p.].

The interrelationship between various birds and animals as they prepare for the first snowfall of the season is depicted in the authors' text and illustrations. A Caldecott Medal winner.

Hatch, Mary C. 13 Danish Tales. Illus. by Edgun. 1947. Harcourt [o.p.].

This retelling of Danish stories of enchantment and magic is both fresh and entertaining.

Henry, Marguerite. King of the Wind. Illus. by Wesley Dennis. 1948. Rand McNally [o.p.]; Simon & Schuster, $17.95 (0-02-743629-2); $15 (0-02-74362902); Aladdin, paper, $4.99 (0-689-71486-6).

An enthralling portrait of a mute stable boy's fierce devotion to his horse. A Newbery Medal winner.

Holbrook, Stewart. America's Ethan Allen. Illus. by Lynd Ward. 1949. Houghton [o.p.].

Spirited black-and-white and full-color illustrations complement a rousing tale of the tempestuous New England frontiersman and the rugged life he led in the early 1800s.

Holling, Holling C. Paddle-to-the-Sea. 1941. illus. Houghton, $20 (0-395-15082-5); paper, $11.95 (0-395-29203-4).

Holling's words and art trace the journey of a little carved Native American figure in a canoe as it travels the length of many waters, from Canadian country to the Atlantic Ocean. A Caldecott Honor Book.

Kelsey, Alice. Once the Hodja. Illus. by Frank Dobias. 1943. McKay [o.p.].

In this series of humorous tales from Turkish folklore, the Hodja says and does foolish things but is always wise enough to get out of any trouble.

Lawson, Robert. Rabbit Hill. 1944. illus. Viking, $16.99 (0-670-58675-7); paper, $5.99 (0-14-031010-X).

New folks are coming to live in the big house on Rabbit Hill, and the small animals are truly elated. Lawson conveys the animals' excitement with humor and love in this kindly tale. A Newbery Medal winner.

Lenski, Lois. Indian Captive: The Story of Mary Jemison. 1941. illus. HarperCollins, $17.89 (0-397-30076-X).

Known as the "White Woman of the Genesee," Mary Jemison lived out her entire life with the Seneca tribe of the Iroquois Indians after her capture in 1758. A Newbery Honor Book.

Lenski, Lois. The Little Fire Engine. 1946. illus. Walck [o.p.].

Simple text and pictures of firemen and fire engines in action made this a favorite of small children.

Lum, Peter. The Stars in Our Heavens: Myths and Fables. Illus. by Anne Marie Jauss. 1948. Pantheon [o.p.].

The lore and old beliefs that Greeks, Romans, Babylonians, Norsemen, Chinese, and Native Americans connected with the stars are presented in story and illustrated with scientific and imaginative star maps.

Malcolmson, Anne, ed. Song of Robin Hood. Illus. by Virginia Lee Burton. 1947. Houghton, $20 (0-618-07186-5).

The story of Robin Hood is told in 18 ballads, 15 of which are accompanied by original music arranged by Grace Castagnetta. Detail in the illustrations and in the margin and page decoration makes this an outstanding creative endeavor. A Caldecott Honor Book.

McCloskey, Robert. Blueberries for Sal. 1948. illus. Viking. $16.99 (0-670-17591-9); paper, $6.99 (0-14-050169-X).

A captivating adventure of a small girl, a baby bear, and their mothers in search of blueberries. Beautiful drawings capture the Maine countryside and the color and delight of a bright summer day. A Caldecott Honor Book.

McCloskey, Robert. Homer Price. 1943. illus. Viking, $15.99 (0-670-37729-5); Penguin/Puffin, paper, $5.99 (0-14-030927-6).

Six episodic stories of young Homer's preposterous adventures stand as classics, and Centerburg, where the doughnuts were made, will long be remembered.

McCloskey, Robert. Make Way for Ducklings. 1941. illus. Viking, $16.95 (0-670-45149-5); paper, $4.99 (0-14-050171-1).

Mr. and Mrs. Mallard are not discouraged about finding the perfect habitat in which to raise their large family in Boston. How they do it is a delight for all in this oversize picture book. A Caldecott Medal winner.

McGinley, Phyllis. The Plain Princess. Illus. by Helen Stone. 1945. Lippincott [o.p.].

With a bit of humor and common sense, Princess Esmeralda is transformed into a beautiful princess in this modern, endearing fairy tale.

Politi, Leo. Song of the Swallows. 1949. illus. Simon & Schuster/Atheneum, $16.95 (0-684-18831-7); Aladdin, paper, $5.99 (0-689-71140-9).

Muted tones of gray, pink, green, and yellow provide a peaceful backdrop for a tale of the time of year when the swallows return annually to the mission church at Capistrano. A Caldecott Medal winner.

Rankin, Louise S. Daughter of the Mountains. Illus. by Kurt Wiese. 1948. Viking [o.p.]; Penguin/Puffin, paper, $6.99 (0-14-036335-1).

In this dramatic inspiring tale, a young girl makes a difficult journey alone from her home in Tibet to Calcutta in search of her beloved dog, which has been stolen. A Newbery Honor Book.

Reyher, Rebecca. My Mother Is the Most Beautiful Woman in the World: A Russian Folktale. Illus. by Ruth Gannett. 1945. HarperCollins, $16.93 (0-688-51251-8).

Varya, lost in the wheat fields of the Ukraine, can only identify her mother as "the most beautiful woman in the world." A Caldecott Honor Book.

Sauer, Julia L. Fog Magic. 1943. Viking [o.p.]; Penguin/Puffin, paper, $5.99 (0-14-032163-2).

The magic and mystery of the fog transports Greta in and out of the past and present and into a secret village. A Newbery Honor Book.

Seeger, Ruth. American Folk Songs for Children. Illus. by Barbara Cooney. 1948. Doubleday [o.p.].

An attractive collection of American folk songs, complete with suggestions for rhythmic play, improvisations, and piano and guitar accompaniments.

Seuss, Dr. Horton Hatches the Egg. 1940. illus. Random, $14 (0-394-80077-X).

Horton, the faithful elephant, sits on an egg for a vacationing bird through storms and threats to his life in this rollicking, fantastic story told in verse and hilarious drawings.

Shippen, Katherine B. The Great Heritage. Illus. by C. B. Falls. 1947. Viking [o.p.].

Eloquent prose makes this combination of history and legend a living story of the discovery and development of the treasures of the American earth.

Slobodkina, Esphyr. Caps for Sale. 1947. illus. Addison-Wesley [o.p.]; Harper-Trophy, paper, $5.99 (0-06-443143-6).

The classic folktale of a cap peddler who takes a nap under a tree and wakes up to find his caps stolen by a band of playful monkeys.

Sperry, Armstrong. Call It Courage. 1940. illus. Simon & Schuster/Aladdin, paper, $4.99 (0-689-71391-6).

In a story based on a dramatic Polynesian legend of heroism, an island boy deemed a coward by his people sails off alone to a sacred island to overcome his fear of the sea. A Newbery Medal winner.

Swift, Hildegarde. The Little Red Lighthouse and the Great Gray Bridge. Illus. by Lynd Ward. 1942. Harcourt, $16.95 (0-15-204574-0); paper, $8 (0-15-204573-2).

The great George Washington Bridge over the Hudson River must not overpower the little red lighthouse. They both have their place! So think the children.

Thurber, James. Many Moons. Illus. by Louis Slobodkin. 1943. Harcourt, $16 (0-15-251873-8); paper, $7 (0-15-656980-9).

When Princess Lenore falls ill after eating too many tarts, she declares that if she can have the moon she will be well again. But neither the King nor all his men could get it for her. A Caldecott Medal winner.

Tresselt, Alvin. Rain Drop Splash. Illus. by Leonard Weisgard. 1946. HarperCollins, $7.60 (0-688-04352-3).

With appropriate visual extensions, terse, poetic text follows falling raindrops making their way from puddle to pond to lake to river and into the sea. A Caldecott Honor Book.

Untermeyer, Louis, ed. Stars to Steer By. Illus. by Dorothy Bayley. 1941. Harcourt [o.p.].

More than 150 poems are arranged under several broad headings and include pleasant bits of explanatory prose.

White, Anne T. Lost Worlds: Adventures in Archaeology. 1941. illus. Random [o.p.].

White conveys the thrill and excitement of discovering four long-lost civilizations in this absorbing book.

Wilder, Laura Ingalls. The Long Winter. 1940. HarperCollins, $16.99 (0-06-026460-8); paper, $6.99 (0-06-440006-9).
- Little Town on the Prairie. 1941. HarperCollins, $16.99 (0-06-026450-0); paper, $6.99 (0-06-440007-7).
- These Happy Golden Years. 1943. HarperCollins, $16.99 (0-06-026481-0); paper, $6.99 (0-06-44008-5).

An outstanding series that scans decades in the generational lives of the author's pioneer family. All three are Newbery Honor Books.

Withers, Carl, ed. A Rocket in My Pocket: The Rhymes and Chants of Young Americans. Illus. by Susanne Suba. 1948. Holt [o.p.]; paper, $9.95 (0-8050-0804-7).

The rhythm of more than 400 chants, songs, rhymes, and riddles used by children in different regions of the U.S. is expressed equally well in the illustrations.

2

Notable Children's Books of the 1950s

Andersen, Hans Christian. Seven Tales. Tr. by Eva Le Gallienne. Illus. by Maurice Sendak. 1959. Harper [o.p.].

An extraordinary combination of writer and artist for some of Andersen's best-known tales. The fresh, colloquial style of the text is perfect for reading aloud, and the handsome drawings, medieval in flavor, are distinguished.

Andersen, Hans Christian. The Swineherd. Tr. and illus. by Erik Blegvad. 1958. Harcourt [o.p.].

Enchanting illustrations complement this fresh retelling of the well-loved tale about the foolish princess who prizes artificiality, fails to recognize true love, and gets what she deserves.

Asbjörnsen, P. C. The Three Billy Goats Gruff. Illus. by Marcia Brown. 1957. Harcourt [o.p.]; paper, $7 (0-15-690150-1).

Delightful pictures that convey perfectly the terrible nature of the troll and the impudent courage and gaiety of the goats complement this favorite folktale.

Baumann, Hans. Sons of the Steppe.Tr. by Isabel and Florence McHugh. Illus. by Heiner Rothfuchs. 1958. Walck [o.p.].

The life and character of the Mongol warrior hordes are remarkably well pictured in a stirring tale of two unique grandsons of Ghenghis Khan.

Behn, Harry. The Two Uncles of Pablo. Illus. by Mel Silverman. 1959. Harcourt [o.p.].

A richly humorous, perceptive character study of a young Mexican boy and his two dissimilar, feuding uncles.

Bemelmans, Ludwig. Madeline's Rescue. 1953. illus. Viking, $16.99 (0-670-44716-1); Penguin/Puffin, paper, $7.99 (0-14-056651-1).

After she saves Madeline from drowning, a dog dubbed Genevieve becomes mascot of the orphanage until snobbish trustees put her out. She returns with enough pups to satisfy all 12 orphans. A Caldecott Medal winner.

Benary-Isbert, Margot. The Ark. Tr. by Clara and Richard Winston. 1953. Harcourt [o.p.].

A West German refugee family struggles to begin life anew in the aftermath of World War II. This is a study in courage and warm human relationships.

Berna, Paul. The Horse without a Head. Tr. by John Buchanan-Brown. Illus. by Richard Kennedy. 1958. Pantheon [o.p.].

Paris is the colorful setting for a memorable story of a gang of children who find mystery and adventures in a derelict neighborhood through their headless, iron-wheeled wooden horse.

Boston, Lucy M. The Children of Green Knowe. 1955. Harcourt, $17 (0-15-202462-X); paper, $6 (0-15-202468-9).
- Treasure of Green Knowe. 1958. Harcourt, $17 (0-15-202595-2); paper, $6 (0-15-202601-0).
- River at Green Knowe. 1959. Harcourt, $17 (0-15-202613-4); paper, $6 (0-15-202607-X).

At his great-grandmother's lovely English mansion, Green Knowe, three children of an earlier century come alive for a lonely boy. Though each story is uniquely different in plot, fantasy and realism are charmingly blended in this series.

Brown, Margaret Wise. Wheel on the Chimney. Illus. by Tibor Gergely. 1954. HarperCollins, $15 (0-06-024247-7).

Richly colored drawings enhance this life cycle story that follows a pair of storks through a year, from nesting in Hungary to migrating to Africa and returning again to Hungary. A Caldecott Honor Book.

Buff, Mary and **Buff, Conrad.** Elf Owl. Illus. by Conrad Buff. 1958. Viking [o.p.].

Sensitive, verselike prose and lovely sepia drawings reflect the beauty and moods of the desert, conveying the drama of life around a water hole.

Carlson, Natalie S. Alphonse, That Bearded One. Illus. by Nicolas. 1954. Harcourt [o.p.].

Told in French Canadian folk fashion, this is a diverting tall tale of a bear posing as a man who, when conscripted into the army, effects peace with the Iroquois Indians.

Carlson, Natalie S. The Family under the Bridge. Illus. by Garth Williams. 1958. HarperCollins, $15.89 (0-06-020991-7); paper, $5.99 (0-06-440250-9).

A warm and flavorsome story of an old hobo in Paris, whose heart and life become entangled, against his will, with a fatherless family in search of a home. A Newbery Honor Book.

Carlson, Natalie S. The Talking Cat and Other Stories of French Canada. Illus. by Roger Duvoisin. 1952. Harper [o.p.].

These seven zesty and easily read French Canadian tales were handed down to the author by her great-great-uncle.

Chaucer, Geoffrey. Chanticleer and the Fox. Adapted and illus. by Barbara Cooney. 1958. HarperCollins/Crowell, $16.99 (0-690-18561-8); HarperTrophy, paper, $6.99 (0-06-443087-1).
Handsome, accurately detailed drawings in brilliant colors and black-and-white illustrate a well-told version of the proud cock and the sly fox. A Caldecott Medal winner.

Chubb, Thomas Caldecot. The Byzantines. Illus. by Richard M. Powers. 1959. World [o.p.].
The author vividly reconstructs the Byzantine civilization and makes clear its influences on the Western world.

Church, Richard. Five Boys in a Cave. 1951. Day [o.p.].
When John and his four friends in the Tomahawk Club investigate an old cave and become lost, the danger tests their mettle and proves the character of each.

Chute, Marchette. Stories from Shakespeare. 1956. Collins/World [o.p.].
Designed to give the reader "a preliminary idea of the 36 plays by telling the stories and explaining in a general way the intentions and points of view of the characters," this is an illuminating guide for a young person reading Shakespeare for the first time.

Ciardi, John. The Reason for the Pelican. Illus. by Madeleine Gekiere. 1959. Lippincott [o.p.].
An inviting collection of laughable verse, imaginatively illustrated.

Clark, Ann Nolan. Blue Canyon Horse. Illus. by Allan Houser. 1954. Viking [o.p.].
When his young mare joins the herd of wild horses in the Blue Canyon, a Native American boy is disconsolate, but his joy is unbounded when she returns in the spring with her colt. Pictures capture the stark beauty of Utah mesas and canyons.

Clark, Ann Nolan. Santiago. Illus. by Lynd Ward. 1955. Viking [o.p.].
An introspective story of a Guatemalan Indian boy, foster son of a Spanish aristocrat, who was claimed at the age of 12 by his Indian relatives. With later maturity he has his choice of worlds and decides to return as a teacher to his father's village.

Clark, Ann Nolan. Secret of the Andes. Illus. by Jean Charlot. 1952. Viking [o.p.]; Penguin/Puffin, paper, $4.99 (0-14-030926-8).
Leading a solitary life high in a Peruvian mountain valley, young Cusi tends a precious llama herd and ponders his future. The text has a mystical quality that enchants perceptive readers. A Newbery Medal winner.

Cleary, Beverly. Henry Huggins. Illus. by Louis Darling. 1950. Morrow, $15.89 (0-688-31385-X); Avon, paper, $4.50 (0-380-72800-1).

Henry Huggins is a typical small boy who quite innocently gets himself into all sorts of funny predicaments. Amusing drawings enhance this tale of everyday life.

Dalgliesh, Alice. The Bears on Hemlock Mountain. Illus. by Helen Sewell. 1952. Scribner, $15 (0-684-19169-5); Aladdin, paper, $4.99 (0-689-71604-4).

Eight-year-old Jonathan crosses Hemlock Mountain to borrow a large iron pot from his aunt. The return trip demonstrates his bravery when he discovers there ARE bears out there. A Newbery Honor Book.

Dalgliesh, Alice. The Courage of Sarah Noble. Illus. by Leonard Weisgard. 1954. Atheneum, $15.99 (0-684-18830-9); Aladdin, paper, $4.99 (0-689-71540-4).

Young Sarah helps her father build a homestead in the Connecticut wilderness in 1702, proving her courage when she remains with friendly Native Americans while her father returns to Massachusetts for Sarah's mother and baby sister. A Newbery Honor Book.

Dalgliesh, Alice. The Thanksgiving Story. Illus. by Helen Sewell. 1954. Atheneum, $16 (0-684-18999-2); Aladdin, paper, $5.99 (0-689-71053-4).

A story of one family's journey on the Mayflower, their settling in Plymouth Colony, and their celebration in thanksgiving for their first harvest. Full-color, stylized illustrations complement the simple text. A Caldecott Honor Book.

Daugherty, James. Of Courage Undaunted: Across the Continent with Lewis and Clark. 1951. illus. Viking [o.p.].

Based on the explorers' records and vigorous illustrations, this forceful text brings an exciting expedition to life for junior-high history buffs.

d'Aulaire, Ingri and **d'Aulaire, Edgar P.** Benjamin Franklin. 1950. illus. Doubleday. [o.p].

Well-chosen incidents from Franklin's varied career are told with liveliness and humor in this simple biography. Full-page lithographs in color and sepia and decorative page borders provide a view of pre-Revolutionary America.

d'Aulaire, Ingri and **d'Aulaire, Edgar P.** Columbus. 1955. illus. Doubleday [o.p.].

The explorer's life from boyhood through four voyages to his old age in Spain is presented in dramatic text and illustrated with brilliant lithographs.

DeAngeli, Marguerite, ed. Book of Nursery and Mother Goose Rhymes. 1954. illus. Doubleday [o.p.].

Here is an abundance of nearly four-hundred familiar and not so familiar rhymes, collected and illustrated with loving care in soft black, white, and glowing colors. A Caldecott Honor Book.

DeJong, Meindert. The Wheel on the School. Illus. by Maurice Sendak. 1954. HarperCollins, $16.99 (0-06-021585-2); paper, $5.99 (0-06-440021-2).

In the Dutch town of Shora the enthusiasm of six school children to bring good luck storks spreads until their efforts are crowned with success. A Newbery Medal winner.

Eager, Edward. Half Magic. Illus. by N. M. Bodecker. 1954. Harcourt, $17 (0-15-202069-1); paper, $6 (0-15-202068-3).

Marvelous things happen on a summer day when four siblings find a magic silver talisman granting them half of every wish. Entertaining, suspenseful adventures in time and space follow.

Eaton, Jeanette. Gandhi: Fighter without a Sword. Illus. by Ralph Ray. 1950. Morrow [o.p.].

A finely written, readable biography of the great leader who gave humanity a lesson in brotherhood and peace. A Newbery Honor Book.

Eichenberg, Fritz. Dancing in the Moon: Counting Rhymes. 1955. illus. Harcourt [o.p.].

Rollicking animals abound in this picture book, which introduces the numbers from one to twenty with nonsense rhymes.

Enright, Elizabeth. Gone-away Lake. Illus. by Beth Krush and Joe Krush. 1957. Harcourt, $17 (0-15-202274-0); paper, $6 (0-15-202272-4).

Vivid descriptions and realistic dialogue give freshness and verve to a story of summer holiday fun. A Newbery Honor Book.

Ets, Marie Hall. Play with Me. 1955. illus. Viking, paper, $15.95 (0-670-55985-7).

In a walk through the meadow, a little girl searches out small wild creatures and discovers the secret of making friends. Simple childlike text is augmented with softly colored line drawings. A Caldecott Honor Book.

Ets, Marie Hall and **Labastida, Aurora.** Nine Days to Christmas. Illus. by Marie Hall Ets. 1959. Viking, $16.99 (0-670-51350-4); Penguin/Puffin, paper, $5.99 (0-14-05442-9).

An enjoyable story of a small Mexican girl and her first posada is illustrated with detailed drawings effectively capturing the color and charm of Mexico. A Caldecott Medal winner.

Farjeon, Eleanor. The Little Bookroom: Short Stories for Children. Illus. by Edward Ardizzone. 1956. Walck [o.p.].

Twenty-seven tales reflect the fine qualities of fantasy characteristic of this author.

Farjeon, Eleanor. The Silver Curlew. Illus. by Ernest H. Shepard. 1954. Viking [o.p.].

An expansion and embroidering of the story of "Tom Tit Tot" and the old rhyme of the man in the moon in Norwich are skillfully woven into a delightful fantastic tale.

Fatio, Louise. The Happy Lion. Illus. by Roger Duvoisin. 1954. McGraw-Hill [o.p.].

Some unexpected adventures transpire when an affable French lion finds his zoo cage open. He takes advantage of the situation to walk through his village in search of friends.

Fischer, Hans. Pitschi. 1953. illus. Harcourt [o.p.]; North-South, $16.95 (1-55858-644-X).

Discontented Pitschi, an engaging kitten, tries living as a rooster, a goat, a duck and a rabbit before finally deciding that life as a cat is best.

Flora, James. The Fabulous Firework Family. 1955. illus. Harcourt, $14.95 (0-689-50596-5).

Humorous text and brilliant illustrations portray the excitement of the Mexican fiesta, for which the firework family build a magnificent firework castle that turns out to be the most marvelous ever constructed.

Françoise. Jeanne-Marie Counts Her Sheep. 1951. illus. Scribner [o.p.].

Jeanne-Marie tells her sheep, Patapon, what she will buy when the latter has lambs in this colorful counting book.

Frasconi, Antonio. See and Say. 1955. illus. Harcourt [o.p.].

Colorful woodcuts add humor as each page depicts familiar objects with the word for each given in English, Italian, French, and Spanish.

Freeman, Don. Fly High, Fly Low. 1957. illus. Viking [o.p.].

Dramatic pictures that give a bird's-eye view of San Francisco are the outstanding feature in this tale of two pigeons in search of a place to nest. A Caldecott Honor Book.

Freuchen, Pipaluk. Eskimo Boy. Illus. by Ingrid Vang Nyman. 1951. Lothrop [o.p.].

When his father is killed by a walrus, a Greenland Eskimo lad's heroic courage and daring lead him to become his family's provider in this understated, starkly realistic story.

Frost, Robert. You Come Too: Favorite Poems for Young Readers. Illus. by Thomas W. Nason. 1959. Holt, $18 (0-8050-0299-5); paper, $7.95 (0-8050-0316-9).

Tastefully designed and illustrated, this excellent selection of poems will appeal to all ages.

Gaer, Joseph. The Adventures of Rama. Illus. by Randy Monk. 1954. Little [o.p.].
   This spirited retelling uses the Valmiki version of the Hindu epic and is divided into six sections telling of Rama's banishment, his wanderings with Sita, Sita's capture and rescue, and Rama's ascent to his rightful throne.

George, Jean Craighead. My Side of the Mountain. 1959. illus. Dutton, $15.99 (0-525-46346-1); Penguin/Puffin, paper, $6.99 (0-14-131242-4).
   An engrossing chronicle of a young boy who runs away to live off the land in the Catskills. A Newbery Honor Book.

Gipson, Fred. Old Yeller. Illus. by Carl Burger. 1956. HarperCollins, $23 (0-06-011545-9); paper, $5.99 (0-06-080971-X).
   Set in the Texas frontier territory, this is a skillfully written, simple, moving story of a boy's love for a mongrel dog. A Newbery Honor Book.

Godden, Rumer. Impunity Jane: The Story of a Pocket Doll. Illus. by Adrienne Adams. 1954. Viking. [o.p].
   Relegated to sitting on a bead cushion in a dusty doll's house for 50 years, Impunity longs to be a "pocket" doll. Her ambition is realized when she becomes seven-year-old Gideon's mascot and shares his lively adventures.

Goudey, Alice E. Houses from the Sea. Illus. by Adrienne Adams. 1959. Scribner [o.p.].
   Rhythmic prose and softly colored drawings convey the wonder and beauty of the seashore and the shells that two children find there.

Grimm, Jakob and **Grimm, Wilhelm.** The Wolf and the Seven Little Kits. Illus. by Felix Hoffmann. 1959. Harcourt [o.p.].
   The well-loved household tale is freshly interpreted in beautiful lithographs, strong and simple in line and restrained in color.

Haviland, Virginia. Favorite Fairy Tales Told in England. Retold from Joseph Jacobs. Illus. by Bettina. 1959. Little [o.p.].
   One title of many in an excellent series of carefully selected tales from the folklore of the world. Each volume is illustrated by an artist familiar with the country.

Homer. The Odyssey of Homer. Retold by Barbara L. Picard. Illus. by Joan Kiddell-Monroe. 1952. Oxford. [o.p].
   The exciting, wonderful adventures of the Greek hero are retold in their entirety in clean, forceful prose.

Hosford, Dorothy G. Thunder of the Gods. Illus. by Claire Louden and George Louden. 1952. Holt [o.p.].
   Fifteen Norse myths are retold with simplicity and dignity.

Ipcar, Dahlov. Brown Cow Farm: A Counting Book. 1959. illus. Doubleday [o.p.].

Rhyming text and eye-catching drawings in pleasing colors add up to a delightful counting book.

Ipcar, Dahlov. World Full of Horses. 1955. illus. Doubleday [o.p.].

This bit of social history offered with brisk, detailed pictures in warm colors introduces the place of horses in the world before mechanization took place, and to their present role.

Jewett, Eleanore M. Which Was Witch? Tales of Ghosts and Magic from Korea. Illus. by Taro Yashima. 1953. Viking [o.p.].

Ghosts and magic abound in this skillfully narrated collection of 14 stories from Korea.

Judson, Clara. Benjamin Franklin. Illus. by Robert Frankenberg. 1957. Follett [o.p.].

A discerning biography of Franklin that brings him to life as a person and sets him against a well-drawn historical background.

Keith, Harold. Rifles for Watie. 1957. HarperCollins/Crowell, $16.89 (0-690-04907-2); paper, $5.99 (0-06-447030-X).

Especially good for its fair treatment of both sides of the conflict, this is an unusually mature, objective telling of the Civil War as it was fought in the Missouri-Oklahoma area. A Newbery Medal winner.

Kendall, Carol. The Gammage Cup. Illus. by Erik Blegvad. 1959. Harcourt [o.p.].

An original, skillfully fashioned, humorous fantasy of a colony of small people who come to appreciate the four nonconformists they have outlawed. A Newbery Honor Book.

Krumgold, Joseph. And Now Miguel. Illus. by Jean Charlot. 1953. HarperCollins/Crowell, $16.95 (0-690-09118-4); HarperCollins/Trophy, paper, $5.95 (0-06-440143-X).

Twelve-year-old Miguel's great longing to accompany his family to pasture their sheep on the Sangre de Christo Mountains is finally realized in this moving and perceptive tale. A Newbery Medal winner.

Krumgold, Joseph. Onion John. Illus. by Symeon Shimin. 1959. HarperCollins/Crowell, $16.89 (0-690-04698-7); HarperCollins/Trophy, paper, $5.99 (0-06-440144-8).

The foibles of a small town are brought into sharp focus in this account of a young boy whose friendship with the town eccentric leads eventually to a better understanding between the boy and his father. A Newbery Medal winner.

Langstaff, John. Frog Went A-Courtin'. Illus. by Feodor Rojankovsky. 1955. Harcourt, $16 (0-15-230214-X); paper, $7 (0-15-633900-5).

An Americana version of an old Scottish ballad imaginatively interpreted in humorously detailed, colored pictures that bring the characters to vivid realization. A Caldecott Medal winner.

Latham, Jean Lee. Carry On, Mr. Bowditch. Illus. by John O'Hara Cosgrave. 1955. Houghton, $16 (0-395-06881-9); paper, $6.95 (0-395-25074-3).

Mathematical and navigational data, plus a lively story of sailing ships and the romance of old Salem, are interestingly combined in this fictionalized biography of the great American navigator, Nathaniel Bowditch. A Newbery Medal winner.

Lawson, Robert. Mr. Revere and I. 1953. illus. Little [o.p.].

The subtitle of this delightful tale reveals it as "Being an account of certain episodes in the career of Paul Revere, Esq. as recently revealed by his horse Schererazade, late pride of his Royal Majesty's 14th Regiment of Foot. Set down and embellished with humorous drawings by Robert Lawson."

Lewis, Clive S. The Lion, the Witch, and the Wardrobe: A Story for Children. Illus. by Pauline Baynes. 1950. HarperCollins, $16.99 (0-06-023481-4); paper, $5.99 (0-06-447104-7).

Four English children have strange and frightening adventures in the magical land of Narnia, where they aid Aslan, the lion ruler, in freeing his land from an evil spell. This beautifully written, modern fairy tale is the first in a series of seven books about the mystical world of Narnia.

Lindgren, Astrid. Pippi Longstocking. Tr. by Florence Lamborn. Illus. by Louis S. Glanzman. 1950. Viking, $15.99 (0-670-55745-5); Penguin/Puffin, paper, $4.99 (0-14-030957-8).

Nine-year-old Pippi is a child of remarkable strength and prodigious imagination in this exaggerated, fantastic, and funny story with amusing illustrations.

Lindquist, Willis. Burma Boy. Illus. by Nicolas Mordvinoff. 1953. McGraw [o.p.].

Haji, son of a famous Burmese elephant trainer, proves his ability as an elephant rider while saving the life of a renegade elephant.

Lindquist, Jennie D. The Golden Name Day. Illus. by Garth Williams. 1955. Harper [o.p.].

When her mother becomes ill, Nancy comes to stay with her Swedish American grandparents, arriving on Grandmother Benson's name day. Enchanted with this Swedish custom, Nancy longs to celebrate her own name day. A Newbery Honor Book.

McCloskey, Robert. One Morning in Maine. 1952. illus. Viking, $17.99 (0-670-52627-4); Penguin/Puffin, paper, $6.99 (0-14-050174-6).

Though quite disappointed when she can't find her baby tooth to place under her pillow, Sal is cheered when her wish comes true anyway. Detailed lithographs capture the spirit of childhood and the beauty of the sea. A Caldecott Honor Book.

McCloskey, Robert. Time of Wonder. 1957. illus. Viking, $19.99 (0-670-71512-3); Penguin/Puffin, paper, $6.99 (0-14-050201-7).

Distinctive, full-color pictures and rhythmic, poetic text perfectly complement each other to capture the feeling of summer on the Maine coast. A Caldecott Medal winner.

McLean, Allan C. Storm over Skye. Illus. by Shirley Hughes. 1957. Harcourt [o.p.].

A forceful, exciting tale of mystery and murder on the Isle of Skye. Action-packed and suspenseful without ever becoming melodramatic.

Mead, Margaret. People and Places. Illus. by W. T. Mars and Jan Fairservis. 1959. Collins/World [o.p.].

Handsome, accurately detailed drawings and photographs add to the effectiveness of this provocative, objective introduction to anthropology.

Milhous, Katherine. The Egg Tree. 1950. illus. Atheneum, $16 (0-684-12716-4); Aladdin, paper, $5.99 (0-689-71568-4).

Full-page illustrations, rich in design and color, and simple text catch the holiday spirit of a Pennsylvania Dutch family as they make an Easter egg tree. A Caldecott Medal winner.

Minarik, Else H. Little Bear. Illus. by Maurice Sendak. 1957. HarperCollins, $15.99 (0-06-024241-8); paper, $3.95 (0-06-444004-4).
• Father Bear Comes Home. Illus. by Maurice Sendak. 1959. HarperCollins, $15.95 (0-06-024230-2); paper, $3.95 (0-06-444014-1).

Easy texts and gently humorous pictures depict events in the life of Little Bear, his family, and his friends.

Nankivell, Joice Mary. Tales of Christophilos. Illus. by Panos Ghikas. 1954. Houghton [o.p].

Stories of Christophilos, a young Greek goatherd living near Mount Athos after World War I, are told with simplicity and humor.

Norton, Mary. The Borrowers. Illus. by Beth Krush and Joe Krush. 1953. Harcourt, $17 (0-15-204768-9).
• The Borrowers Afield. 1955. Harcourt, $17 (0-15-210166-7); paper, $6 (0-15-210535-2).
• The Borrowers Afloat. 1959. Harcourt, $17 (0-15-210345-7); paper, $6 (0-15-210534-4).

Diminutive Pod, Homily, and Arietty convincingly exist in a miniature world in this delightful series by a noted English author.

Pearce, Philippa. Tom's Midnight Garden. Illus. by Susan Einzig. 1959. Harper-Collins/Lippincott, $14.89 (0-397-30477-3); HarperCollins/Trophy, paper, $5.95 (0-06-440445-5).

Realism and fantasy are perfectly blended in this highly original, evocative tale of a young boy's adventuring into the past.

Perrault, Charles. Cinderella; or, The Little Glass Slipper. Illus. by Marcia Brown. 1954. Atheneum, $16 (0-684-12676-1); Aladdin, paper, $5.99 (0-689-81474-7).

Blending a free translation from the French with delicate, graceful full-color drawings, Brown has done full justice to Perrault's classic. A Caldecott Medal winner.

Perrault, Charles. Puss in Boots. Illus. by Marcia Brown. 1952. Scribner [o.p.].

Perrault's sly but loyal cat who turns his poor master into a marquis is Brown's jaunty hero. A free translation with rich coral pink, yellow, and gray illustrations. A Caldecott Honor Book.

Petry, Ann. Harriet Tubman: Conductor on the Underground Railroad. 1955. Crowell [o.p.]; HarperCollins/Trophy, paper, $5.95 (0-06-446181-5).

A dramatic and moving portrait of an indomitable woman that also puts this historic period and the growth of the abolition movement into perspective.

Pope, Elizabeth M. The Sherwood Ring. Illus. by Evaline Ness. 1958. Houghton, $18 (0-618-17737-X); paper, $5.95 (0-618-15074-9).

Twentieth-century mystery and eighteenth-century intrigue, deftly interwoven, set the stage for an original and amusing romantic adventure.

Prishvin, Mikhail. The Treasure Trove of the Sun. Tr. by T. Balkoff-Drowne. Illus. by Feodor Rojankovsky. 1952. Viking [o.p.].

Searching for cranberries in a forbidding swamp near a Russian village, Anna and Peterkin become lost and must depend on their resourcefulness and courage to get back to safety. Rich, colorful drawings are among Rojankovsky's best.

Rand, Ann and **Rand, Paul.** I Know a Lot of Things. 1956. illus. Harcourt [o.p.].

A picture book of strong design presents imaginative concepts and successfully conveys the little child's sense of wonder and delight in his increasing knowledge of the world about him.

Ravielli, Anthony. Wonders of the Human Body. 1954. illus. Viking [o.p.].

Arguing that the body is a machine whose parts are interdependent, Ravielli presents an imaginative, anatomically accurate introduction to anatomy.

Rawlings, Marjorie Kinnan. The Secret River. Illus. by Leonard Weisgard. 1955. Scribner [o.p.].

Discovering a magic river in the Florida pinewoods, Calpurnia is able to catch enough catfish to change her family's luck, but she is never able to retrace her steps to the river. Sensitive illustrations capture the charm and enchantment of this adventure in imagination. A Newbery Honor Book.

Read, Herbert Edward, ed. This Way Delight: A Book of Poetry for the Young. Illus. by Juliet Kepes. 1956. Pantheon [o.p.].

In this unusual anthology the selection has been made with definite discrimination; modern as well as older poets are represented. An inspiring final chapter not only illuminates poetry but also encourages aspiring writers.

Robertson, Keith. Henry Reed, Inc. Illus. by Robert McCloskey. 1958. Viking [o.p.]; Penguin/Puffin, paper, $4.99 (0-14-034144-7).

Illustrations exactly match the straight-faced, first-person narrative of a truly funny story and the summer enterprises of an inventive boy and neighborhood girl.

Rugh, Belle Dorman. Crystal Mountain. Illus. by Ernest H. Shepard. 1955. Houghton [o.p.].

Lebanon is the setting for the summer adventures of three children who discover a cave and a tumble-down house near their home.

Sandoz, Mari. The Horsecatcher. 1957. Westminster [o.p.]; Univ. of Nebraska Press, paper, $9.95 (0-8032-9160-4).

A young boy's attempt to assert his individuality at the expense of social acceptance forms the theme for a perceptive story of early Native American life. A Newbery Honor Book.

Sasek, Miroslav. This Is London. 1959. illus. Macmillan [o.p.].
• This Is Paris. 1959. illus. Macmillan [o.p.].

Expressive, colored drawings and captioned text bring to life these two cities, perfectly conveying the spirit of each.

Sawyer, Ruth. Journey Cake, Ho! Illus. by Robert McCloskey. 1953. Viking [o.p.].

In this version of the Johnnycake tale, a boundout boy leaves the mountain farm because of hard times, and is given a crusty cake as a parting gift. Escaping the boy's knapsack, the cake leads him on a merry chase crowned by a triumphant return to the farm. A Caldecott Honor Book.

Sharp, Edith. Nkwala. Illus. by William Winter. 1958. Little [o.p.].

A gripping and beautifully written tale of a Salish Native American's quest for manhood and his peace-loving tribe's migration from a drought-stricken land.

Sharp, Margery. The Rescuers. Illus. by Garth Williams. 1959. Little [o.p.].

The hazardous adventures of three courageous, resourceful mice are written with a light, sure touch and humor that is child appealing. Enchanting drawings capture the mood of the telling.

Sherlock, Philip M. Anansi, the Spider Man: Jamaican Folktales. Illus. by Marcia Brown. 1954. Crowell [o.p.].

Probably African in origin, these 15 humorous stories feature Anansi, the folk character who often assumes the form of a spider.

Shippen, Katherine B. Men, Microscopes, and Living Things. Illus. by Anthony Ravielli. 1955. Viking [o.p.].

Tracing the work of great biologists through the ages, Shippen records the theories and experiments that have led to a clearer understanding of nature's way. A Newbery Honor Book.

Sojo, Toba. Animal Frolic. Text by Velma Varner. 1954. Putnam [o.p.].

Varner's brief story line gives a sense of continuity to the pictures from Toba Sojo's twelfth-century Japanese masterpiece, Scroll of Animals.

Sorensen, Virginia. Miracles on Maple Hill. Illus. by Beth Krush and Joe Krush. 1956. Harcourt, $17 (0-15-204719-0); paper, $5.95 (0-15-204718-2).

Excellent characterization, spirited values, and vivid delineation of nature and the changing seasons in a memorable story of a troubled city family drawn together again in love and happiness during a year of country living. A Newbery Medal winner.

Speare, Elizabeth George. The Witch of Blackbird Pond. 1958. Houghton, $22 (0-395-91367-5); Dell/Yearling, paper, $5.99 (0-440-49596-2).

Strong plot, fully realized characters, and convincing atmosphere distinguish this historic narrative of a girl whose rebellion against bigotry and her Puritan surroundings culminates in a witch hunt and trial. A Newbery Medal winner.

Steele, William O. The Perilous Road. Illus. by Paul Galdone. 1958. Harcourt [o.p.]; paper, $6 (0-15-260647-5).

A confused Yankee-hating Tennessee mountain boy learns by experience the senselessness of war, the true meaning of courage, and the importance of understanding in a perceptive, swiftly-paced story. A Newbery Honor Book.

Steele, William O. Winter Danger. Illus. by Paul Galdone. 1954. Harcourt [o.p.]; paper, $6 (0-15-260647-5).

Winter sets in suddenly, and 11-year-old Caje and his father leave the forests of Kentucky and head for the home of kinfolk. Left with them, Caje must adjust by contributing what he can and accepting what help he needs.

Sterne, Emma G. Mary McLeod Bethune. Illus. by Raymond Lufkin. 1957. Knopf [o.p.].
A warmly sympathetic yet penetrating biography of a great Black educator.

Sutcliff, Rosemary. The Lantern Bearers. Illus. by Charles Keeping. 1959. Walck [o.p.]; Farrar, paper, $6.95 (0-374-44302-5).
Aquila, a young Roman officer, deserts the legion, choosing to remain in Britain. Mature, thoroughly researched historical fiction with intensely realistic characterization and swift-paced action.

Sutcliff, Rosemary. The Shield Ring. Illus. by C. Walter Hodges. 1959. Walck [o.p.].
A vigorous tale of early England when the Norsemen were making a last valiant stand against the Normans.

Swift, Hildegarde. The Edge of April: A Biography of John Burroughs. Illus. by Lynd Ward. 1957. Morrow [o.p.].
This intriguing biography does much to re-create the period in which Burroughs lived, and the many famous people of that era.

Udry, Janice. The Moon Jumpers. Illus. by Maurice Sendak. 1959. HarperCollins, $15.95 (0-06-028460-9).
The magic of moonlight and the delight children find in it are sensitively conveyed in both text and drawings. A Caldecott Honor Book.

Udry, Janice. A Tree Is Nice. Illus. by Marc Simont. 1956. HarperCollins, $16.99 (0-06-026155-2); paper, $6.95 (0-06-443147-9).
In this picture book about trees, the simple childlike text is much enhanced by the brilliant illustrations done in strong lines that combine a poetic quality with a certain modern sophistication. A Caldecott Medal winner.

Ullman, James. Banner in the Sky. 1954. HarperCollins, $12.95 (0-397-32141-4); HarperTrophy, paper, $5.99 (0-06-447048-2).
To conquer the unclimbed Citadel Mountain and follow in his famous father's footsteps as an alpine guide are the overwhelming ambitions of young Rudi. His success in the wake of failure provides a gripping tale of courage and heroism.

Vipont, Elfrida, ed. Bless This Day: A Book of Prayer for Children. Illus. by Harold Jones. 1958. Harcourt [o.p.].
A rich and varied collection of Christian prayers, traditional and modern, prose and poetry, combined with interpretive, reverent illustrations.

Ward, Lynd. The Biggest Bear. 1952. illus. Houghton, $16 (0-395-14806-5); paper, $6.95 (0-395-15024-8).

Johnny's bear grows and grows to become a trial and tribulation to the whole valley. Action and mood are magnificently portrayed in the simple text and the dramatic monochromatic illustrations. A Caldecott Medal winner.

Weisgard, Leonard. Treasure to See: A Museum Picture Book. 1956. illus. Harcourt [o.p.].
A stimulating introduction to a fine arts museum for the very young. Striking illustrations are not actual reproductions, but the author's own representation of famous works of art.

White, E. B. Charlotte's Web. Illus. by Garth Williams. 1952. HarperCollins, $16.99 (0-06-026385-7); paper, $6.99 (0-06-440055-7).
In a story that blends fantasy and realism, a young girl's compassion and a spider's ingenuity save a pig from the butcher's knife. A classic tale of loyalty and friendship in which the pictures happily complement the text. A Newbery Honor Book.

Yashima, Taro. Crow Boy. 1955. illus. Viking, $17.99 (0-670-24931-9); Penguin/ Puffin, paper, $5.99 (0-14-050172-X).
Until an understanding teacher arrives, a shy, lonely mountain boy is ridiculed and ignored by his Japanese village schoolmates. Full-page impressionistic illustrations are vibrant and colorful, yet retain a simplicity of form. A Caldecott Honor Book.

Yashima, Taro. Umbrella. 1958. illus. Viking [o.p.]; Penguin/Puffin, paper, $6.99 (0-14-050240-8).
The anticipation, impatience, and joy of a little girl who waits for a rainy day to use her birthday umbrella are sensitively portrayed in this beautiful picture book. A Caldecott Honor Book.

Adoff, Arnold, ed. I Am the Darker Brother: An Anthology of Modern Poems by Negro Americans. Illus. by Benny Andrews. 1968. Simon & Schuster, $17 (0-689-81241-8); paper, $4.99 (0-689-80869-0).

The black experience in America is expressed with vitality in this handsome anthology.

Aiken, Conrad. Cats and Bats and Things with Wings: Poems. Illus. by Milton Glaser. 1965. Atheneum [o.p.].

Sixteen sprightly, colorfully illustrated poems are included in this collection about creatures of the animal world that appeal to children.

Aiken, Joan. The Wolves of Willoughby Chase. Illus. by Pat Marriott.
1963. Delacorte, $16.95 (0-385-32790-0); Dell, paper, $5.50 (0-440-49603-9).

Two girls are at the mercy of a mean, scheming governess trying to secure their estate while their parents are away, in this Gothic page-turner.

Alexander, Lloyd. The Book of Three. 1964. Holt, $19.95 (0-8050-6132-0); Dell/Yearling, paper, $5.99 (0-440-40702-8).
* The Black Cauldron. 1965. Holt, $17.95 (0-8050-0992-2); Dell/Yearling, paper, $5.99 (0-440-40649-8).
* The Castle of Llyr. 1966. Holt. $19.95 (0-8050-6133-9); Dell/Yearling, paper, $5.99 (0-440-41125-4).
* Taran Wanderer. 1967. Holt, $18.95 (0-8050-6134-7); Dell/Yearling, paper, $5.99 (0-440-48483-9).
* The High King. 1968. Holt, $19.95 (0-8050-6135-5); Dell/Yearling, paper, $5.99 (0-440-43574-9).

The adventures of Taran, Assistant Pig-Keeper, and his friends in the mythical kingdom of Prydain are chronicled in these five volumes of fantasy, excellently written in the best of Welsh tradition. *The High King* is a Newbery Medal winner; *The Black Cauldron* is a Newbery Honor Book.

Almedingen, E. M. Young Mark: The Study of a Venture. Illus. by Victor G. Ambrus. 1968. Farrar [o.p.].

Czarist Russia is the setting for the compelling story of Mark Poltoratzky, who ran away from home to become a singer against his father's wishes.

Andersen, Hans Christian. The Nightingale. Tr. by Eva La Gallienne. Illus. by Nancy E. Burkert. 1965. HarperCollins, $13.95 (0-06-023780-5).
Decorated pages and double-spreads in color evoke the Chinese flavor of this finely honed classic tale.

Armstrong, William H. Sounder. Illus. by James Barkley. 1969. HarperCollins, $14.95 (0-06-020143-6); paper, $6 (0-06-080975-2).
An African American sharecropper and his family endure cruel injustice with courage and dignity in a stark, deeply moving story. A Newbery Medal winner.

Baity, Elizabeth C. Americans before Columbus. Rev. ed. Illus. by C. B. Falls. 1961. Viking [o.p.].
People and their culture, from the Ice Age to the colonization of the Americas, are included in this historical panorama. Maps, drawings, and photographs are included in the well-designed book.

Baker, Betty. Walk the World's Rim. 1965. Harper [o.p.].
A shared belief in human dignity binds together an Avavare Indian boy and a Black slave in a tautly written historical novel set in the sixteenth-century southwestern U.S.

Baron, Virginia O., ed. The Seasons of Time: Tanka Poetry of Ancient Japan. Illus. by Yasuhide Hobashi. 1968. Dial [o.p.].
Nature poems from the eighth and tenth centuries, beautifully decorated with brush-and-ink drawings.

Baumann, Hans. The Caves of the Great Hunters. Rev. ed. Tr. by Isabel McHugh and Florence McHugh. 1962. Pantheon [o.p.].
On September 12, 1940, four boys seeking a lost dog in an oak forest south of Montignac in France discovered the Lascaux Cave. Paintings on the walls therein have provided insights into the everyday life of prehistoric people.

Baumann, Hans. I Marched with Hannibal. Tr. by Katharine Potts. Illus. by Ulrick Schramm. 1962. Walck [o.p.].
A first-person, action-packed narrative by an old man who relives his adventures as a 12-year-old elephant driver with Hannibal's march across the Alps to Italy in 218 B.C.

Baylor, Byrd. Before You Came This Way. Illus. by Tom Bahti. 1969. Dutton [o.p.].
Southwest Native American petroglyphs and the prehistoric way of life suggested by them are strikingly illustrated.

Behn, Harry. The Faraway Lurs. 1963. Collins/World [o.p.].

In the Bronze Age, 3,000 years ago, Heather of the Forest People falls in love with Wolf Stone of the Sun People. Tragedy follows because their people are enemies.

Belting, Natalia M. The Sun Is a Golden Earring. Illus. by Bernarda Bryson. 1962. Holt [o.p.].

Folk sayings about the sun, wind, and other celestial bodies or phenomena are accompanied by handsome drawings highlighting the text. A Caldecott Honor Book.

Bernard, Jacqueline. Journey toward Freedom: The Story of Sojourner Truth. 1967. illus. Norton [o.p.]; Feminist Press, paper, $14.95 (1-55861-024-3).

Born into slavery, Sojourner became a dynamic spokeswoman for social reform, as presented in this strong, moving biography.

Blishen, Edward, ed. The Oxford Book of Poetry for Children. Illus. by Brian Wildsmith. 1964. Oxford [o.p.].

One-hundred-sixty English poems, arranged by subjects with intriguing headings, are brightly illustrated in an appealing anthology.

Bontemps, Arna. Hold Fast to Dreams: Poems Old & New. 1969. Follett [o.p.].

Personal poetry preferences of a notable African American writer are stunningly presented.

Braymer, Marjorie. The Walls of Windy Troy: A Biography of Heinrich Schliemann. 1960. illus. Harcourt [o.p.].

Absorbing biography of the German archaeologist who realized his lifelong dream of finding Homer's Troy.

Brown, Marcia. Once a Mouse: A Fable. 1961. illus. Atheneum, $16.95 (0-684-12662-1); Aladdin, paper, $6.99 (0-689-71343-6).

Woodcuts, distinguished for their strength and fluidity, illustrate this vigorous retelling of an ancient Indian fable about the ungrateful mouse and the hermit who saves his life. A Caldecott Medal winner.

Bryson, Bernarda. Gilgamesh: Man's First Story. 1967. illus. Holt [o.p.].

In text and handsome illustrations a Sumerian hero tale is effectively retold.

Burch, Robert. Queenie Peavy. Illus. by Jerry Lazare. 1966. Viking [o.p.]; Penguin/Puffin, paper, $5.99 (0-14-032305-8).

Queenie hides the unhappiness caused by her father's imprisonment behind defiance and indifference, until she learns to face reality.

Burnford, Sheila. The Incredible Journey. Illus. by Carl Burger. 1961. Dell, $15.95 (0-385-32279-8); paper, $4.99 (0-440-22670-8).

Three animals—a Labrador retriever, a terrier, and a Siamese cat—share an adventurous journey homeward for 250 miles through the wilderness of northwestern Ontario.

Carlson, Natalie S. The Empty Schoolhouse. Illus. by John Kaufmann. 1965. Harper [o.p.].
Desegregation of a school in a small Louisiana parish creates personal and community problems for 10-year-old Lullah Royal and her family, as hatred and friendships are tested in an emotional situation.

Caudill, Rebecca. A Certain Small Shepherd. Illus. by William Pené Du Bois. 1965. Holt, $9.95 (0-03-089755-6); paper, $6.95 (0-8050-5392-1).
A small mute boy's innocent act toward a stranded couple on Christmas Eve is the catalyst for a touching miracle in Appalachia.

Caudill, Rebecca. Did You Carry the Flag Today, Charley? Illus. by Nancy Grossman. 1966. Holt, $16.95 (0-8050-1201-X); Dell/Yearling, paper, $4.50 (0-440-40092-9).
School in the Appalachian Mountains for a five-year-old independent, precocious boy provides many tender and laugh-out-loud happenings.

Chase, Alice Elizabeth. Looking at Art. 1966. illus. Crowell [o.p.].
More than 100 reproductions in color and black-and-white provide a provocative guide to art appreciation.

Chase, Richard, ed. Billy Boy. Illus. by Glen Rounds. 1966. Golden Gate/ Children's [o.p.].
The humor and folk quality of the old song are perfectly mirrored in drawings that capture the tough, independent spirit of the pioneer woman.

Chaucer, Geoffrey. A Taste of Chaucer: Selections from the Canterbury Tales. Ed. by Anne Malcomson. Illus. by Enrico Arno. 1964. Harcourt [o.p.].
A brief, inviting introduction to Chaucer, his times, and his tales. Includes selections from the prologue, nine child-appealing tales, a few lines of the Middle English text, background notes, and a glossary of names and words.

Christopher, John. The White Mountains. 1967. Simon & Schuster, $16.95 (0-689-85504-4); Aladdin, paper, $4.99 (0-02-042711-5).
The harrowing escape of a young boy from a futuristically mechanized tyranny is compellingly described in this first volume of a science fiction trilogy.

Ciardi, John. I Met a Man. Illus. by Robert Osborn. 1961. Houghton [o.p.].
Humorous verses, rhymes, riddles, and games emphasize the fun of words. Cartoonlike drawings heighten the nonsense of the imaginative verses.

Clark, Mavis Thorpe. The Min-Min. 1969. Macmillan [o.p.].

In present-day Australia, a girl and her brother, overwhelmed by daily personal problems, run away across desolate country to find guidance.

Clarke, Pauline. The Return of the Twelves. Illus. by Bernarda Bryson. 1963. Coward [o.p.]; Akadine, $24.95 (1-58579-021-4).

Twelve wooden soldiers, which once belonged to the Brontë children, come alive and seek help from three children to return to their home at Haworth, now the Brontë Museum.

Cleaver, Vera and **Cleaver, Bill.** Where the Lilies Bloom. Illus. by Jim Spanfeller. 1969. HarperCollins/Lippincott, $15.95 (0-397-31111-7); HarperCollins/Trophy, paper, $5.99 (0-06-447005-9).

In order to keep her orphaned family together, a determined, resourceful Appalachian girl conceals her father's death.

Coolidge, Olivia E. The King of Men. Illus. by Ellen Raskin. 1966. Houghton [o.p.].

Based on Greek mythology, a deftly written, engrossing narrative about Agamemnon.

Coolidge, Olivia E. Tom Paine, Revolutionary. 1969. Scribner [o.p.].

An objective view of the life and writings of a controversial eighteenth-century political radical and reformer.

Cricket Songs: Japanese Haiku. Ed. and tr. by Harry Behn. Illus. by Sesshu and others. 1964. Harcourt [o.p.].

Illustrated with reproductions of paintings by Japanese masters, the delightful haiku about frogs, butterflies, fog, and rain have great appeal.

A Crocodile Has Me by the Leg: African Poems. Illus. by Solomon Irein Wangboje. 1967. Walker [o.p.].

Bold illustrations accompany a varied selection of verses, whose rhythms, color, and sensitivity to emotion reflect a life lived close to the earth.

Cullen, Countee. The Lost Zoo: Rhymes by Christopher Cat and the Author. Illus. by Joseph Low. 1968. Follett [o.p.].

Humorous illustrations complement the poet's explanations in verse about the animals who missed Noah's ark.

Darling, Louis. The Gull's Way. 1965. illus. Morrow [o.p.].

The life cycle of a family of herring gulls is observed on an uninhabited island off the coast of Maine, with accompanying black-and-white illustrations and stunning photographs.

d'Aulaire, Ingri and **d'Aulaire, Edgar P.** Norse Gods and Giants. 1967. illus. Doubleday [o.p.].
Spirited, colorful lithographs illustrate a vigorous retelling of the Norse myths.

Davis, Katherine and others. The Little Drummer Boy. Illus. by Ezra Jack Keats. 1968. Viking, $15.99 (0-670-89226-2); Aladdin, paper, $4.95 (0-689-71158-1).
Lyrics of a modern Christmas song form the text of this lovely, richly colored picture book.

Dayrell, Elphinstone. Why the Sun and the Moon Live in the Sky: An African Folktale. Illus. by Blair Lent. 1968. Houghton, $16 (0-395-29609-9); paper, $6.95 (0-395-53963-3).
Original, stylized illustrations use colors and motifs in harmony with the nature and national origin of the tale. A Caldecott Honor Book.

De Jong, Meindert. Journey from Peppermint Street. Illus. by Emily Arnold McCully. 1968. Harper [o.p.].
A little Dutch boy's first venture with his grandfather into the world beyond his home is recounted with rare perception and warmth.

De la Mare, Walter. The Magic Jacket. Illus. by Paul Kennedy. 1962. Knopf [o.p.].
Ten beautifully written tales, including "Broomsticks," "The Riddle," and "Alice's Godmother." Mood rather than plot sustains the stories.

Denny, Norman and **Filmer-Sankey, Josephine.** The Bayeux Tapestry: The Story of the Norman Conquest, 1066. 1966. illus. Atheneum [o.p.].
Stunning photographic reproductions of the entire 900-year-old work of art, accompanied by a brief explanatory text.

De Regniers, Beatrice. May I Bring a Friend? Illus. by Beni Montresor. 1964. Atheneum $16 (0-689-20615-1).
A brightly illustrated tale with rhyming text that relates the humorous adventures of a small boy invited to tea by the King and Queen, and of the animal "friends" who accompany him. A Caldecott Medal winner.

de Treviño, Elizabeth Borton. I, Juan de Pareja. 1965. Farrar, $17 (0-374-33531-1); paper, $5.95 (0-374-43525-1).
Velasquez, the great painter, is ably assisted by his faithful slave Juan. Secretly though, the assistant practices his art alone until he becomes as famous as his master. A Newbery Medal winner.

Dillon, Eilis. The Singing Cave. Illus. by Stan Campbell. 1960. Funk [o.p.].
Set on the coast of Ireland, a suspenseful and strongly atmospheric tale of the discovery and disappearance of a Viking treasure.

Douglass, Frederick. Life and Times of Frederick Douglass. Adapted by Barbara Ritchie. 1966. Crowell [o.p.].
An eloquent account, skillfully abridged from Douglass' autobiography.

Dowden, Anne. Look at a Flower. 1963. illus. Crowell [o.p.].
The parts of a flower and the general characteristics and representatives of 10 of the most common families are described by a botanical artist.

Downer, Marion. Roofs over America. 1967. illus. Lothrop [o.p.].
Simple but striking illustrations and accompanying text focus on roof tops to give a panoramic view of American domestic architecture from colonial days to the present.

Downer, Marion. The Story of Design. 1964. illus. Lothrop [o.p.].
Excellent photographs of well-chosen examples of design in art and household items detail the historical development from prehistoric to modern times.

Duggan, Alfred. Growing Up in 13th Century England. Illus. by C. Walter Hodges. 1962. Pantheon [o.p.].
A lively and informative description of everyday life in the homes of an earl, a country knight, a peasant, a rich merchant, and a craftsman in the 1270s.

Dunning, Stephen and others, eds. Reflections on a Gift of Watermelon Pickle . . . and Other Modern Verse. 1967. illus. HarperCollins, $19.99 (0-688-41231-9).
Striking photographs capture the varied moods of a lively selection of poetry for today's young readers. The artwork set a new touchstone for poetry selections.

Dunning, Stephen and others, eds. Some Haystacks Don't Even Have Any Needle and Other Complete Modern Poems. 1969. illus. Lothrop [o.p.].
Poetry illuminated by color reproductions of modern art—fresh, contemporary, relevant.

Ellis, Ella Thorpe. Roam the Wild Country. Illus. by Bret Schlesinger. 1967. Atheneum [o.p.].
In Argentina, three boys and an old gaucho drive a herd of horses across two treacherous mountain ranges to save them from the drought.

Emberley, Barbara. Drummer Hoff. Illus. by Ed Emberley. 1967. Simon & Schuster, $16 (0-671-66248-1); Aladdin, paper, $5.95 (0-671-66240-X).
Brilliant color and stylized design interpret a rollicking cumulative verse about the building of a cannon. A Caldecott Medal winner.

Emberley, Barbara, ed. One Wide River to Cross. Illus. by Ed Emberley. 1966. Prentice-Hall [o.p.].

A folk song about Noah's ark, presented in a strikingly designed book with black woodcuts on colored pages. A Caldecott Honor Book.

Ets, Marie Hall. Gilberto and the Wind. 1963. illus. Viking, $15.99 (0-670-34025-1); paper, $5.99 (0-14-050276-9).
A sensitive, childlike picture book that tells how a small Mexican boy learns to play with and understand the various moods of the wind.

Fisher, Aileen. Valley of the Smallest: The Life Story of a Shrew. Illus. by Jean Zallinger. 1966. Crowell [o.p.].
A creature scarcely more than two inches long is the subject of a dramatic, scientifically accurate, and beautifully illustrated book.

Fitzhugh, Louise. Harriet the Spy. 1964. illus. Delacorte, $15.95 (0-385-32783-8); Dell/Yearling, paper, $5.99 (0-440-41679-5).
Precocious, overprivileged Harriet darts around her Manhattan neighborhood ferreting out the "scoop" on the moving scene.

Forman, James. Ring the Judas Bell. 1965. Farrar [o.p.].
Fifteen-year-old Nicholas, his sister, and a group of younger children are kidnapped and taken into a prison camp in Albania. They struggle to escape and return home in this stark, powerful novel set amid post–World War II civil conflict in Greece.

Foster, Genevieve. The World of Columbus and Sons. 1965. illus. Scribner [o.p.].
The world of the Renaissance and the Reformation, 1451-1539, is thoughtfully and colorfully presented through events and persons that made the period historically significant.

Fox, Paula. How Many Miles to Babylon? Illus. by Paul Giovanopoulos. 1967. Bradbury, $13.95 (0-02-735590-X).
In a Brooklyn ghetto 10-year-old James is kidnapped by three tough boys and used in their dog-stealing racket.

Fox, Paula. Portrait of Ivan. Illus. by Saul Lambert. 1969. Bradbury [o.p.].
A sensitive, perceptive portrait of a lonely boy whose awareness develops as his ordered world is enlarged by new acquaintances and situations.

Fox, Paula. The Stone-Faced Boy. Illus. by Donald A. MacKay. 1968. Bradbury, $13.95 (0-02-735570-5).
The timid, middle child in a family of self-assured individualists masks his fears and doubts behind an expressionless face.

The Fox Went Out on a Chilly Night. Illus. by Peter Spier. 1961. Doubleday [o.p.]; Dell/Yearling, paper, $6.99 (0-440-40829-6).

Colorful, detailed paintings of a moonlit New England country-side harvest night are the background for this sprightly interpretation of a popular old folk song. A Caldecott Honor Book.

Frasconi, Antonio. The Snow and the Sun/La Nieve y el Sol: A South American Folk Rhyme in Two Languages. 1961. illus. Harcourt [o.p.].

Brilliant three-color woodcuts interpret a South American folk rhyme told in simple repetitive dual-language text.

Friis-Baastad, Babbis. Don't Take Teddy. Tr. by Lise Somme McKinnon. 1967. Scribner [o.p.].

Mikkel, fiercely protective of his mentally challenged older brother, is frightened when Teddy accidentally hurts someone; he runs away with him to keep him from being institutionalized. A Mildred L. Batchelder Award winner.

Fritz, Jean. Brady. Illus. by Lynd Ward. 1960. Coward [o.p.]; Penguin/Puffin, paper, $5.99 (0-698-11937-1).

In a believable and satisfying narrative, the son of an underground railroad agent learns to control his tongue, forms his own opinion about slavery, and acts with judgment when the need arises.

Gage, Wilson. Big Blue Island. Illus. by Glen Rounds. 1964. Collins/World [o.p.].

A wild crane helps a motherless, unhappy 11-year-old city boy understand and respect the life on his old great-uncle's Tennessee River island.

Gard, Joyce. The Mermaid's Daughter. 1969. Holt [o.p.].

Roman Britain and the Scilly Isles are the backdrop for an intense novel of a peaceful matriarchal society in conflict with a more aggressive world.

Gard, Joyce. Talargain. 1965. Holt [o.p.].

Talargain, a youth of early Britain, appears in the guise of a seal to a young girl in modern England and tells her the dramatic story of his life. The seventh-century struggle between the tribal Britons and Scots is recreated vividly in this well-written fantasy.

Garfield, Leon. Smith. Illus. by Antony Maitland. 1967. Farrar, $18 (0-374-30827-6).

A lusty, Dickensian tale of a young pickpocket in eighteenth-century London's underworld.

Garner, Alan. The Owl Service. 1968. Walck [o.p.].

Three young people are drawn into a reenactment of a tragic Welsh legend in this haunting story.

Glubok, Shirley. The Art of Ancient Greece. 1963. Atheneum [o.p.].
- The Art of the Eskimo. 1964. Harper [o.p.].
- The Art of Africa. 1965. Harper [o.p.].
- The Art of Ancient Peru. 1966. Harper [o.p.].

An excellent, inviting series that, through photographs and concise, informative text, provides an insight into the art and creativity of the people of a period or country.

Goble, Paul and **Goble, Dorothy.** Red Hawk's Account of Custer's Last Battle: The Battle of the Little Bighorn, 25 June 1876. Illus. by Paul Goble. 1989. Pantheon [o.p.].

Handsome stylized illustrations reminiscent of Sioux tipi decorations accompany this account, told by a young Ogalala Sioux participant as it might have been.

Godden, Rumer. The Doll's House. Illus. by Tasha Tudor. 1962. Viking [o.p.]; Penguin/Puffin, paper, $4.99 (0-14-030942-X).

An enchanting doll family residing in an old Victorian doll house influence the behavior of the children who give them life.

Goodall, John S. The Adventures of Paddy Pork. 1968. illus. Harcourt [o.p.].

Detailed drawings tell the story of a young pig who runs away from his mother to follow a circus in this enchanting wordless picture book

Goudge, Elizabeth. Linnets and Valerians. Illus. by Ian Ribbons. 1964. Coward [o.p.]; Penguin/Puffin, paper, $5.99 (0-14-230026-8).

A mystery filled with fantasy and witchcraft set in an English village, where four children and their stern uncle try to unravel the Valerian family secret.

Greene, Constance C. A Girl Called Al. Illus. by Byron Barton. 1969. Viking [o.p.]; Penguin/Puffin, paper, $5.99 (0-14-034786-0).

Deft characterization and sparkling dialogue in a story of the friendship between two girls and their apartment building superintendent.

Grimm, Jakob and **Grimm, Wilhelm.** Jorinda and Joringel. Tr. by Elizabeth Shub. Illus. by Adrienne Adams. 1968. Scribner [o.p.].

Strong, stylized illustrations accompany the traditional tale of Jorinda, who's transformed into a nightingale, and Joringel, who rescues her from the witch's spell.

Guilcher, Jean and **Noailles, Robert H.** A Fruit Is Born. 1960. illus. Sterling [o.p.].

Scientific information on the life cycle of fruit is lucidly presented in brief text, captions, and remarkable close-up photography.

Guillot, Rene. Grishka and the Bear. Tr. by Gwen Marsh. Illus. by Joan Kiddell-Monroe. 1960. Abelard [o.p.].

Primitive village life and superstitions are revealed in the haunting story of a Siberian boy and his bear cub.

Hamilton, Virginia. The House of Dies Drear. Illus. by Eros Keith. 1968. Simon & Schuster, $17 (0-02-74500-2); Aladdin, paper, $5.99 (0-02-043520-7).

Ghosts from the Underground Railway inhabit the house into which Thomas and his family move in this richly peopled tale of suspense.

Hamilton, Virginia. Zeely. Illus. by Symeon Shimin. 1967. Simon & Schuster [o.p.]; Aladdin, paper, $3.95 (0-87628-345-8).

Zeely, a young Black girl, learns to distinguish between fantasy and reality when she finally meets the majestic woman she has imagined to be a princess.

Harnett, Cynthia. Caxton's Challenge. 1960. illus. Collins/World [o.p.].

Fifteenth-century London comes alive in the engrossing tale of a young apprentice embroiled in the conflict between two conniving scriveners and William Caxton.

Harris, Christie. Raven's Cry. Illus. by Bill Reid. 1966. Atheneum [o.p.]; Univ. of Washington Press, paper, $17.95 (0-295-97221-1).

The efforts of the last three Haida Native American chieftains to preserve their rich, highly artistic culture against the encroachment of white "civilization."

Hauff, Wilhelm. Dwarf Long-Nose. Illus. by Maurice Sendak. Tr. by Doris Orgel. 1960. Random [o.p.].

Delightfully illustrated with sturdy, humorous drawings that match exactly the folk quality of the German fairy tale about a shoemaker's son transformed into a misshappen dwarf.

Haugaard, Erik Christian. Hakon of Rogen's Saga. Illus. by Leo and Diane Dillon. 1963. Houghton [o.p.].
• A Slave's Tale. Illus. by Leo and Diane Dillon. 1965. Houghton [o.p.].

Two powerfully written tales tell of the struggle of Hakon, a teen-age Viking chieftain, to regain his birthright, the rocky island of Rogen. In the sequel, Helga, formerly his slave, secretly accompanies Hakon on a perilous voyage to France. The stories vividly portray the stark and cruel life of Norsemen in Viking times.

Haugaard, Erik Christian. The Little Fishes. Illus. by Milton Johnson. 1967. Houghton [o.p.]; Peter Smith, $18 (0-8446-6245-3).

A deeply moving story of the grim struggle of three Italian war orphans to survive the horrors of World War II.

Hautzig, Esther. The Endless Steppe: Growing Up in Siberia. 1968. Crowell [o.p.]; Turtleback, $11 (0-606-03343-2).

Based on the author's recollections of her five years between the ages of ten and fifteen as a Polish deportee in Siberia.

Hentoff, Nat. Jazz Country. 1965. HarperCollins [o.p.].

A realistic portrayal of the Black jazz world as seen through the eyes of a teen-age white boy whose great desire is to become a trumpet player.

Hill, Elizabeth S. Evan's Corner. Illus. by Nancy Grossman. 1967. Holt [o.p.].
The need of a place of one's own and the joy of sharing are warmly conveyed in the story of a boy in an overcrowded slum apartment.

Hirsch, S. Carl. Printing from a Stone: The Story of Lithography. 1967. Viking [o.p.].
A pleasingly presented history of lithography as an art medium and as a printing technique.

Hitchcock, Patricia. The King Who Rides a Tiger and Other Folk Tales from Nepal. Illus. by Lillian Sader. 1966. Parnassus [o.p.].
Twelve Nepalese folktales told and illustrated with distinction.

Hoban, Russell. Bedtime for Frances. Illus. by Garth Williams. 1960. Harper-Collins, $15.89 (0-06-027107-8); paper, $5.99 (0-06-443451-6).
The familiar bedtime-delaying tactics of small children are mirrored with gentle humor in a beguiling picture story of a little badger.

Hodges, C. Walter. The Namesake. 1964. illus. Coward [o.p.].
• The Marsh King. 1967. Coward [o.p.].
The stirring tale of one-legged Alfred who becomes the student of and scribe to his namesake, Alfred of Wessex, King of England. In the sequel, King Alfred, driven into the marshes by the invading Danes, battles to regain his full kingdom.

Hodges, Margaret. The Wave. Illus. by Blair Lent. 1964. Houghton [o.p.].
In order to save the villagers from a tidal wave, an old Japanese man burns his rice fields. This version is adapted from Lafcadio Hearn's *Gleanings in Buddha-Fields*. A Caldecott Honor Book.

Holm, Anne. North to Freedom. Tr. by L. W. Kingsland. 1965. Harcourt [o.p.]; paper, $6 (0-15-257553-7).
The moving chronicle of 12-year-old David's search for his inner and outer identity as he wanders through Europe after his escape from a concentration camp.

Houston, James. Akavak: An Eskimo Journey. 1968. illus. Harcourt [o.p.].
Menaced by cold and hunger, an Eskimo boy and his grandfather fight their way across treacherous glacial mountains in this stark narrative.

Houston, James. The White Archer: An Eskimo Legend. 1967. illus. Harcourt [o.p.].
A vividly written story of an Eskimo boy's personal triumph over hatred reflects the author's knowledge and appreciation of Eskimo character and culture.

Hughes, Langston. Don't Turn Your Back: Poems. Ed. by Lee Bennett Hopkins. Illus. by Ann Grifalconi. 1969. Knopf [o.p.].

Sensitive woodcuts emphasize the expressiveness of these poems.

Hunt, Irene. Across Five Aprils. 1964. Follett [o.p.]; Berkley, paper, $4.99 (0-425-10241-6).

The author weaves a memorable story, based on family records, of a young boy's experiences in the backwoods of southern Illinois during the tragic Civil War period. His brothers go off to war, two joining the Union forces and one the Confederacy's, dad has a heart attack, and the boy becomes the head of the family. A Newbery Honor Book.

Hunt, Irene. Up a Road Slowly. 1966. Follett [o.p.]; Berkley, paper, $4.99 (0-425-18817-5).

Characters drawn from life give substance to a gracefully written, perceptive story of a girl growing up. A Newbery Medal winner.

Hunter, Kristin. The Soul Brothers and Sister Lou. 1968. Scribner [o.p.].

Louretta Hawkins, 14, and her friends succeed in creating soul music despite the frustrations and violence surrounding them in this honest story of life in an urban ghetto.

Hutchins, Pat. Rosie's Walk. 1968. illus. Simon & Schuster, $16 (0-02-745850-4); Aladdin, paper, $6.99 (0-02-043750-1).

Highly animated, stylized pictures enliven this picture-book comedy in which a hen, unaware that she is being stalked, unwittingly foils the fox at every turn.

Hutchins, Ross E. The Amazing Seeds. 1965. illus. Dodd [o.p.].

A fascinating and informative study of the variety and wonder of seeds, illustrated with excellent, unusual photographs.

Hutchins, Ross E. This Is a Tree. 1964. illus. Dodd [o.p.].

An excellent introduction to the life processes of a tree, its leaves, flowers, and seeds. A well-organized presentation of fact and lore.

Ish-Kishor, Sulamith. A Boy of Old Prague. Illus. by Ben Shahn. 1963. Pantheon [o.p.].

Tomas, a young serf, given in partial payment of a debt by his master to an old Jew of the ghetto, learns for the first time about kindness and human dignity.

Ish-Kishor, Sulamith. Our Eddie. 1969. Pantheon [o.p.].

An honest, incisive story of the effect of an egotistic, fanatic Jewish father on his family, particularly his son Eddie. A Newbery Honor Book.

Janson, Horst W. and **Janson, Dora J.** The Story of Painting for Young People, from Cave Paintings to Modern Times. 1962. Abrams [o.p.].

A panoramic view of art using 245 reproductions, 32 in full color, and a lively text to describe styles, meaning, and history.

Jarrell, Randall. The Animal Family. Illus. by Maurice Sendak. 1965. Harper-Collins, $14.89 (0-06-205089-3); paper, $7.99 (0-06-205904-1).

This lovely, sensitive allegory tells about a lonely hunter who finds companionship with a mermaid, a bear cub, a baby lynx, and a small boy washed ashore from a shipwreck. A Newbery Honor Book.

Johnson, Annabel and **Johnson, Edgar.** Wilderness Bride. 1962. HarperCollins [o.p.]; Green Mansions, $12.95 (0-9714612-7-9).

Fifteen-year-old Corey Tremaine is bound by her father to a Mormon, as the promised wife for his stepson. Independent, wilderness-reared Corey has trouble adjusting to the strict life and the forced trek west from Illinois in search of the new Zion.

Jones, Weyman B. Edge of Two Worlds. Illus. by J. C. Kocsis. 1968. Dial [o.p.].

A lost boy and an ancient Cherokee searching for his people, linked by chance in unlikely companionship on the prairie, grow to mutual understanding and respect.

Keats, Ezra Jack. The Snowy Day. 1962. illus. Viking, $15.99 (0-670-65400-0); paper, $5.99 (0-14-050182-7).

The feel and sound of snow are conveyed in text and colorful pictures, as Peter adventures out in the snow leaving tracks and making snowballs, angels, and snowmen. A Caldecott Medal winner.

Keats, Ezra Jack. Whistle for Willie. 1964. illus. Viking, $15.99 (0-670-76240-7); paper, $5.99 (0-14-050202-5).

Peter is frustrated but ultimately successful in learning to call his dog, Willie, by whistling like the big boys. A handsome book full of color and movement.

Kelly, Eric P. The Trumpeter of Krakow. Illus. by Janina Domanska. 1966. Simon & Schuster, $17.95 (0-02-750140-X); Aladdin, paper, $4.50 (0-689-71571-4).

A stirring tale in which courage in fifteenth-century Poland saves the lives of a family two centuries later. A reissue of a book first published in 1928, in a new, handsomely designed and illustrated format.

Kijima, Hajime. Little White Hen: A Folk Tale. Ed. and illus. by Setsuko Hane. 1969. Harcourt [o.p.].

How the hen outwits the hungry fox is dramatized in captivating colored pictures.

Kingman, Lee. The Year of the Raccoon. 1966. Houghton [o.p.].

With two talented brothers and a dynamic father, the middle boy Joey has difficulty in realizing his own worth.

Konigsburg, E. L. From the Mixed-up Files of Mrs. Basil E. Frankweiler. 1967. illus. Simon & Schuster/Atheneum, $17 (0-689-20586-4); Aladdin, paper, $5.99 (0-689-71181-6).

A runaway sister and brother live undiscovered for one wonderful week in the Metropolitan Museum of Art. An uncommonly fresh and vital story. A Newbery Medal winner.

Konigsburg, E. L. Jennifer, Hecate, Macbeth, William McKinley, and Me, Elizabeth. 1967. illus. Simon & Schuster/Atheneum, $16 (0-689-30007-7); Aladdin, paper, $4.99 (0-689-84625-8).

Crisply told and original, the story of two lonely girls whose friendship evolves from imaginative play in which one is a witch and the other her eager apprentice. A Newbery Honor Book.

Kroeber, Theodora. Ishi, Last of His Tribe. Illus. by Ruth Robbins. 1964. Houghton [o.p.]; Bantam, paper, $5.99 (0-553-24898-7).

The compelling true story of a California Yahi Native American, the last of his tribe, who leaves his primitive life in 1911 and enters the modern world. An excellent combination of historical fact and anthropological background.

Krumgold, Joseph. Henry 3. Illus. by Alvin Smith. 1967. Atheneum [o.p.].

Being too bright isn't popular, as Henry has long since discovered. His struggle to come to terms with his intelligence is sensitively chronicled in this story set in present-day suburbia.

Lear, Edward. The Scroobius Pip. Illus. by Nancy Ekholm Burkert. 1968. Harper [o.p.].

Fine craftsmanship and delicate coloring give distinction to the intricately drawn pictures in an illustrated version of Lear's nonsense poem, completed by Ogden Nash.

Lee, Mildred. The Rock and the Willow. 1963. Lothrop [o.p.].

Realistic depiction of the life of a teen-ager growing up in rural Alabama in the 1930's, the oldest girl in a large family. Coping with everyday poverty and learning about sex, love, and grief, her dreams of becoming a teacher and writer seem remote.

Le Guin, Ursula K. A Wizard of Earthsea. Illus. by Ruth Robbins. 1968. Simon & Schuster/Atheneum, $18 (0-689-31720-4); Bantam, paper, $7.50 (0-553-26250-5).

An overzealous student of wizardry unleashes a malevolent creature that endangers the world of Earthsea in this detailed, skillfully conceived fantasy.

Leodhas, Sorche Nic. Heather and Broom: Tales of the Scottish Highlands. Illus. by Consuelo Joerns. 1960. Holt [o.p.].

* Thistle and Thyme: Tales and Legends from Scotland. Illus. by Evaline Ness. 1962. Holt [o.p.].

Skillfully woven retellings of tales and legends from Scotland, filled with humor, magic, romance, mystery, and the supernatural. Each is told with the rhythm and lilt of a Scottish song. *Thistle and Thyme* is a Newbery Honor Book.

L'Engle, Madeleine. Meet the Austins. 1961. Farrar, $17 (0-374-34929-0); Dell/ Laurel Leaf, paper, $5.50 (0-440-95777-X).

The doings of a likable family are chronicled with warmth and unusual perception by the 12-year-old daughter.

L'Engle, Madeleine. A Wrinkle in Time. 1962. Farrar, $17 (0-374-38613-7); Dell/ Yearling, paper, $6.50 (0-440-49805-8).

With the help of their new friend, a sister and brother search for their missing father, journeying through space by means of a wrinkle in time. A superb science fantasy with allegorical overtones incorporating concepts of time travel, extrasensory perception, and supernatural beings. A Newbery Medal winner.

Lent, Blair. John Tabor's Ride. 1966. illus. Little, Brown [o.p.].

A shipwrecked whaler's fabulous ride home to Nantucket on the back of a whale, recounted in motion-filled pictures.

Lester, Julius. To Be a Slave. Illus. by Tom Feelings. 1968. Dial [o.p.]; Scholastic, paper, $4.50 (0-590-42460-2).

What it was like to be a slave in America is eloquently revealed through the words of slaves themselves, with commentary by the author. A Newbery Honor Book.

Lifton, Betty J. The Cock and the Ghost Cat. Illus. by Fuku Akino. 1965. Atheneum [o.p.].

An old Japanese tale of a courageous cock who willingly sacrificed his life for his master.

Lindgren, Astrid. The Tomten and the Fox. Illus. by Harald Wilberg. 1965. Coward [o.p.]; Putnam, paper, $6.99 (0-698-11592-9).

Tomten the troll saves the barnyard fowl from a fox on a quiet snowy Christmas Eve. The Swedish winter countryside is evoked in softly colored paintings that illustrate the text, adapted from a poem by Karl-Erik Forsslund.

Lionni, Leo. Inch by Inch. Illus. by Harald Wilberg. 1962. Coward [o.p.]; Harper-Trophy, paper, $4.95 (0-688-13283-9).

A small green inchworm saves himself from hungry birds by proving his usefulness as a measurer, but when a nightingale wants her song measured, he really has to use his wits. An arresting, brilliantly colored view of the grassy world of an inchworm. A Caldecott Honor Book.

Lipsyte, Robert. The Contender. 1967. HarperCollins, $15.89 (0-06-023920-4); paper, $5.99 (0-06-447039-3).

In training at a Harlem boxing center, a 17-year-old dropout finds the courage to grapple with his difficult life.

Livingston, Myra Cohn, ed. A Tune beyond Us: A Collection of Poetry. Illus. by James J. Spanfeller. 1968. Harcourt [o.p.].

An unusual anthology, worldwide in scope and bilingual in presentation, with selections varied in form and subject but uniformly felicitous in expression.

London Bridge Is Falling Down! Illus. by Peter Spier. 1967. Doubleday [o.p.].

Subtle coloring and a wealth of careful detail set the old nursery song against the background of bustling London town.

MacManus, Seumas. Hibernian Nights. Illus. by Paul Kennedy. 1963. Macmillan [o.p.].

Twenty-two Irish folk and fairy tales are included in this superior collection that tell about the little people, kings, queens, cruel stepmothers, and successful youngest sons.

Mayne, William. Earthfasts. 1967. Dutton [o.p.]; Peter Smith $20.25 (0-8446-6430-8).

Two legends—of King Arthur, not dead but sleeping, and a drummer boy long since vanished—come unexpectedly to life for two boys in a quiet English village. A highly original, gripping adventure story.

McClung, Robert M. Lost Wild America: The Story of Our Extinct and Vanishing Wildlife. Illus. by Bob Hines. 1969. Morrow [o.p.].

A thoroughly researched, comprehensive survey.

McKenzie, Ellen K. Taash and the Jesters. 1968. Holt [o.p.].

An intricate but sprightly tale of witchery and high adventure in a mythical kingdom.

McNeill, Janet. The Battle of St. George Without. Illus. by Mary Russon. 1968. Little, Brown [o.p.].
•   Goodbye, Dove Square. 1969. Little, Brown [o.p.].

The "battle" to save their hideout, an abandoned church, from vandals creates new bonds among a gang of city children and their neighbors. The sequel is equally compelling.

Meltzer, Milton. Brother, Can You Spare a Dime? The Great Depression, 1929–1933. 1969. illus. Knopf [o.p.]; Facts On File, $19.95 (0-8160-2372-7).

An effective narrative recreates with immediacy the human side of the Depression years.

Meltzer, Milton, ed. In Their Own Words: A History of the American Negro. 1967. illus. Crowell [o.p.].

The social history of Black Americans from 1619 to 1966 is dramatically told in their own words with selections from letters, diaries, journals, speeches, and other historical documents. Illustrated with many reproductions.

Merrill, Jean. The Pushcart War. Illus. by Ronni Solbert. 1964. Addison-Wesley [o.p.]; Dell/Yearling, paper, $4.99 (0-440-47147-8).

A witty satire set in 1976, in which the pushcart peddlers overthrow a truck monopoly on the streets of New York City.

Miles, Miska. Fox and the Fire. Illus. by John Schoenherr. 1966. Little, Brown [o.p.].

Remarkably telling pictures accent the terror of a young red fox fleeing from a forest fire.

Mizumura, Kazue. If I Were a Mother. 1968. illus. Crowell [o.p.].

A little girl imagines the kind of mother she would be in terms of animal mothers she knows. A tender telling with soft appealing pictures.

Moore, Janet. The Many Ways of Seeing: An Introduction to the Pleasures of Art. 1968. illus. Collins/World [o.p.].

For beginning viewers and artists, a stimulating discussion complemented by a choice selection of reproductions. A Newbery Honor Book.

Morrison, Lillian, ed. Sprints and Distances: Sports in Poetry and the Poetry in Sport. Illus. by Clare Ross and John Ross. 1965. Crowell [o.p.].

Selections from ancient and modern writings, with particular emphasis on sports popular in the U.S.

Mosel, Arlene. Tikki Tikki Tembo. Illus. by Blair Lent. 1968. Holt, $16.95 (0-8050-0662-1); paper, $6.95 (0-8050-1166-8).

A felicitous picture-book version of the Chinese folktale about a young first son honored with a too-long name.

The Mother Goose Treasury. Illus. by Raymond Briggs. 1966. Coward [o.p.].

Robustness and humor characterize the multitude of colorful illustrations in this bountiful collection of nursery rhymes.

Mowat, Farley. Owls in the Family. Illus. by Robert Frankenberg. 1962. Little, Brown [o.p.]; Dell, paper, $4.50 (0-440-41361-3).

A humorous narrative of the author's boyhood experiences with his two pet owls. Each has a distinctive personality; together they upset the household and neighborhood.

Munari, Bruno. Bruno Munari's Zoo. 1963. illus. Collins/World [o.p.].

Brilliant, humorous pictures make this lively and colorful trip to the zoo to meet the birds and beasts a joyous visit for the entire family.

Ness, Evaline. Sam, Bangs & Moonshine. 1966. illus. Holt, $15.95 (0-8050-0314-2); paper, $6.95 (0-8050-0315-0).

Evocative illustrations match the telling of a little girl's flights of fancy spelling trouble.

Neville, Emily. It's Like This, Cat. Illus. by Emil Weiss. 1963. HarperCollins, $15.95 (0-06-024390-2); paper, $5.99 (0-06-440073-5).

The thoughts, feelings, and activities of a 14-year-old New York City boy are engrossing and thought-provoking as related by him to the reader. A Newbery Medal winner.

North, Sterling. Rascal: A Memoir of a Better Era. Illus. by John Schoenherr. 1963. Dutton. $16.99 (0-525-18839-8).

The author's humorous memoir of a rural Wisconsin boyhood year and his mischievous pet raccoon, Rascal. A Newbery Honor Book.

O'Dell, Scott. The Black Pearl. Illus. by Milton Johnson. 1967. Houghton, $17 (0-395-06961-0); Dell/Laurel Leaf, paper, $4.99 (0-440-90803-5).

When Ramon finally steals the stunning black pearl from the cave of the Manta off the coast of Baja California, he is confronted by fear and an enemy he cannot shrug off. A Newbery Honor Book.

O'Dell, Scott. Island of the Blue Dolphins. 1960. Houghton, $16 (0-395-06962-9); Dell/Yearling, paper, $6.50 (0-440-43988-4).

An unforgettable first-person narrative of the experiences of a Native American girl who lived alone on a rocky island off the California coast for 18 years. A Newbery Medal winner.

Ottley, Reginald. Boy Alone. Illus. by Clyde Pearson. 1966. Harcourt [o.p.].

On an isolated cattle station in Australia, a lonely chore boy yearns to own the dog in his care.

Paine, Roberta M. Looking at Sculpture. 1968. illus. Lothrop [o.p.].

A visually exciting introduction to sculpture, accompanied by an inviting, thought-provoking text.

Peyton, K. M. Flambards. Illus. by Victor G. Ambrus. 1968. Collins/World [o.p.].

Fine characterization and narrative style in a romantic English novel of an orphaned heiress living in a household dominated by her egocentric uncle's passion for fox hunting. This is the first of a well-told trilogy.

Piatti, Celestino. Celestino Piatti's Animal ABC. Tr. by Jon Reid. illus 1966. Atheneum [o.p.].
Boldly designed, richly colored pictures animate a striking alphabet book.

Piatti, Celestino. The Happy Owls. 1964. illus. Atheneum [o.p.].
Two owls who live in peace and harmony explain to quarreling barnyard fowl the secret of their happiness—joy and contentment in the changing seasons of the year. Richly colored, striking illustrations with stained glass effects in modernistic style emphasize the thoughtful text.

Pollard, Madeleine. Beorn the Proud. Illus. by William Stobbs. 1962. Holt [o.p.].
Beorn, high-spirited son of a Viking sea king, captures a 12-year-old Irish girl and takes her as his slave and confidant. The arrogant lad loses his throne, learns humility, and finally, with the girl's help, migrates to Ireland.

Ransome, Arthur. The Fool of the World and the Flying Ship: A Russian Tale. Illus. by Uri Shulevitz. 1968. Farrar, $17 (0-374-32442-5); paper, $6.95 (0-374-42438-1).
A lively version of a Russian folktale, with flavorsome, panoramic illustrations in gleaming color. A Caldecott Medal winner.

Raskin, Ellen. Nothing Ever Happens on My Block. 1966. illus. Atheneum [o.p.].
Humorous, stylized illustrations boldly contradict Chester's glum assessment of his boring neighborhood.

Rasmussen, Knud, ed. Beyond the High Hills: A Book of Eskimo Poems. Illus. by Guy Mary-Rousseliere. 1961. Collins/World [o.p.].
A distinctive and beautiful selection of chants and songs celebrating the hunt and other adventures, with complementary full color photographs. The poems, translated by Rasmussen, were collected by a Danish explorer from among the Igluliks of the Hudson Bay region and the Musk Ox people of the Copper Country.

Richard, Adrienne. Pistol. 1969. Little, Brown [o.p.].
The Depression era is vividly depicted in a convincing story of a young Montana horse wrangler.

Robbins, Ruth. Baboushka and the Three Kings. Illus. by Nicolas Sidjakov. 1960. Houghton, $16 (0-395-27673-X); paper, $6.95 (0-395-42647-2).
Striking pictures in rich colors illustrate this skillfully retold Russian folktale. A book distinguished for unity of subject, illustration, and design. A Caldecott Medal winner.

Sachs, Marilyn. Veronica Ganz. Illus. by Louis Glanzman. 1968. Doubleday [o.p.]; Penguin/Puffin, paper, $5.99 (0-14-037078-1).
The belligerent, overgrown bully of Grade 8B meets her match in a taunting pint-size boy in this humorous, sympathetic story.

Saint-Exupéry, Antoine de. The Little Prince. Tr. by Katherine Woods. 1967. illus. Harcourt, $18 (0-15-202398-4); paper, $6 (0-15-652820-7).

The little prince leaves his own tiny planet to discover great wisdom, most of which grownups seem to have missed. An original fantasy.

Sandburg, Carl. The Wedding Procession of the Rag Doll and the Broom Handle and Who Was in It. Illus. by Harriet Pincus. 1967. Harcourt [o.p.]; paper, $6 (0-15-695487-7).

Droll double-spread illustrations capture perfectly the unique humor and imaginativeness of Sandburg's story.

Sawyer, Ruth. Joy to the World: Christmas Legends. Illus. by Trina Schart Hyman. 1966. Little, Brown [o.p.].

Well-told, attractively illustrated stories from Arabia, Serbia, Ireland, and Spain.

Schaefer, Jack. Old Ramon. Illus. by Harold West. 1960. Houghton [o.p.]; Turtleback, $13 (0-606-05959-8).

Ramon, a wise old shepherd, teaches his young charge far more than the ways of tending sheep in this short, beautifully written tale of the Southwest. A Newbery Honor Book.

Schaller, George B. and **Selsam, Millicent E.** The Tiger: Its Life in the Wild. Illus. by Richard Keane. 1969. HarperCollins [o.p.].

Clear text with handsome drawings and photographs taken by S. Schauer tell of Schaller's research in India's Kanha Park.

Schoenherr, John. The Barn. 1968. illus. Little, Brown [o.p.].

Bold drawings dramatize with photographic realism the taut story of a life-and-death struggle between an owl and a skunk.

Scott, Ann. Sam. Illus. by Symeon Shimin. 1967. McGraw-Hill [o.p.].

The feelings of a youngest brother are perfectly captured in the story of a small black boy, always underfoot. Expressive, lifelike illustrations.

Seeger, Elizabeth. The Ramayana. Illus. by Gordon Laite. 1969. Addison-Wesley [o.p.].

Adapted from the English translation of Hari Prasad Shastri, India's great epic poem is retold in graceful prose.

Selden, George. The Cricket in Times Square. Illus. by Garth Williams. 1960. Farrar, $16 (0-374-31650-3); Dell/Yearling, paper, $5.99 (0-440-41563-2).

A captivating tale of a country cricket who is befriended by a mouse, a cat, and a boy in a subway station newsstand. A Newbery Honor Book.

Selsam, Millicent E. Peanut. Illus. by Jerome Wexler. 1969. Morrow [o.p.].

The peanut's life cycle, clearly and simply described, is illustrated with unusual close-up photographs.

Sendak, Maurice. The Nutshell Library. 4 v. 1962. illus. HarperCollins, $16.95 (0-06-025500-5).
A set of four small nonsense books—an alphabet book, *Alligators All Around*; a counting book, *One Was Johnny*; rhymes, *Chicken Soup with Rice*; and a cautionary tale, *Pierre*—with original text and funny drawings.

Sendak, Maurice. Where the Wild Things Are. 1963. illus. HarperCollins, $16.95 (0-06-025492-0); paper, $7.99 (0-06-443178-9).
Sent to his room for wildness, a small boy imagines himself in the land of deliciously grotesque, fanciful monsters where he has a marvelous wild rumpus. Childlike playfulness pervades this original and imaginative picture book. A Caldecott Medal winner.

Shippen, Katherine B. and **Seidlova, Anca.** Heritage of Music. Illus. by Otto van Eersel. 1963. Viking [o.p.].
A vividly written history of the development of Western music from primitive to modern times, which interweaves informal biographical sketches of composers.

Shotwell, Louisa R. Roosevelt Grady. Illus. by Peter Burchard. 1963. Collins/World [o.p.].
After many tribulations and disappointments, a nine-year-old migrant farm boy's dream of a permanent home for his warm, happy, hardworking family is finally achieved.

Shulevitz, Uri. One Monday Morning. 1967. illus. Scribner [o.p.]; Farrar, paper, $6.95 (0-374-45648-8).
One after another, members of a royal household visit a lonely, imaginative little boy in this diverting, cumulative picture-book tale.

Shulevitz, Uri. Rain Rain Rivers. 1969. illus. Farrar [o.p.]; paper, $6.95 (0-374-46195-3).
Soft blue-and-yellow illustrations evoke the varied moods of a rainy day.

Simon, Hilda. Insect Masquerades. 1968. illus. Viking [o.p.].
A detailed description of insect camouflage, complemented by precise drawings in color.

Singer, Isaac B. A Day of Pleasure: Stories of a Boy Growing Up in Warsaw. Illus. by Roman Vishniac. 1969. Farrar [o.p.]; paper, $8.95 (0-374-41696-6).
"Rich in comedy and tragedy, rich in its individuality, wisdom, foolishness, wildness and goodness"; these are a Hasidic Jew's remembrances of his world.

Singer, Isaac B. The Fearsome Inn. Illus. by Nonny Hogrogian. Tr. by Isaac B. Singer and Elizabeth Shub. 1967. Scribner [o.p.].

Evocative illustrations complement a masterful tale of witches, devils, and magic spells. A Newbery Honor Book.

Singer, Isaac B. Mazel and Shlimazel; or, The Milk of a Lioness. Illus. by Margot Zemach. Tr. by Isaac B. Singer and Elizabeth Shub. 1967. Farrar [o.p.]; Turtleback, $13.10 (0-374-44786-1).

Spirited pictures illustrate a Jewish tale about a wager between Mazel (Good Luck) and Schlimazel (Bad Luck) in which each is—and is not—the winner.

Singer, Isaac B. Zlateh the Goat and Other Stories. Illus. by Maurice Sendak. Tr. by Isaac B. Singer and Elizabeth Shub. 1966. HarperCollins. $15.95 (0-06-028477-3); paper, $7.99 (0-06-440147-2).

A choice volume of seven Jewish tales superbly told and illustrated. A Newbery Honor Book.

Snyder, Zilpha K. The Egypt Game. Illus. by Alton Raible. 1967. Simon & Schuster/Atheneum, $17 (0-689-30006-9); Dell/Yearling, paper, $5.99 (0-440-42225-6).

An absorbing, inventive game played by six children in a deserted storage yard has unexpected results. Wonderfully real in every respect. A Newbery Honor Book.

Southall, Ivan. Ash Road. Illus. by Clem Seals. 1966. St. Martin's [o.p.].

This taut story recounts the reactions of a handful of Australian children caught in the path of a raging bush fire.

Speare, Elizabeth George. The Bronze Bow. 1961. Houghton, $16 (0-395-87769-5); paper, $6.95 (0-395-13719-5).

His father's crucifixion, followed by his mother's death and his sister's broken spirit, lead a teen-age boy to strike out in hatred. But he has second thoughts upon seeing and hearing the messages and teachings of Jesus in this dramatic story of biblical times. A Newbery Medal winner.

Steele, Mary Q. Journey Outside. Illus. by Rocco Negri. 1969. Viking [o.p.].

In this provocative allegory, Dilar daringly escapes from the subterranean river tunnels where his people live to search for a "better place." A Newbery Honor Book.

Steig, William. Sylvester and the Magic Pebble. 1969. illus. Simon & Schuster, $16 (0-671-66154-X); Aladdin, paper, $6.99 (0-671-66269-4).

Sylvester's wish backfires, and the wisher is turned to stone until chance and good fortune restore him in this witty modern variation on traditional motifs. A charming, tender telling equaled by its delightful illustrations. A Caldecott Medal winner.

Steptoe, John. Stevie. 1969. illus. HarperCollins, $12.95 (0-06-025763-6); paper, $6.95 (0-06-443122-3).

Strong lines and vibrant colors illuminate the story of a small boy who resents then misses his foster brother.

Sterling, Dorothy. Forever Free: The Story of the Emancipation Proclamation. Illus. by Ernest Crichlow. 1963. Doubleday [o.p.].

Dramatic presentation of the Black slavery issue in the U.S.—the people involved and the events leading to the Emancipation Proclamation.

Stevenson, William. The Bushbabbies. Illus. by Victor Ambrus. 1965. Houghton [o.p.].

The life of a Swahili headman is risked when he accompanies the daughter of a game warden on a journey through the African bush to return her pet bushbaby to its native home in Kenya.

Stockton, Frank R. The Griffin and the Minor Canon. Illus. by Maurice Sendak. 1963. Holt [o.p.]; HarperCollins, $15.95 (0-06-029731-X).

Humorous adventures, illustrated with superb drawings, of the last griffin who wants to see his stone likeness over the church door of a small town. This creates many problems for the townspeople.

Stolz, Mary. Belling the Tiger. Illus. by Beni Montresor. 1961. HarperCollins [o.p.].

Two unimportant, timid, waterfront mice are cast in heroic roles. Assigned the job of belling the cat, they bell a tiger and frighten the elephant! Engaging drawings accompany a story showing marked originality and humor. A Newbery Honor Book.

The Story of Prince Ivan, the Firebird, and the Gray Wolf. Tr. by Thomas P. Whitney. Illus. by Nonny Hogrogian. 1968. Scribner [o.p.].

With the help of a gray wolf, a young prince triumphs over his two older brothers. Charming line and watercolor illustrations lend enchantment to this Russian fairy tale.

Sutcliff, Rosemary. Beowulf. Illus. by Charles Keeping. 1962. Dutton [o.p.]; Peter Smith, $20.75 (0-8446-6165-1).

Stirring poetic retelling of the epic of Beowulf the warrior—his battles with the monster Grendel, Grendel's mother, and the fiery dragon.

Sutcliff, Rosemary. The Hound of Ulster. Illus. by Victor Ambrus. 1963. Dutton [o.p.].

An exciting retelling of the great exploits of Cuchulain, an Irish legendary hero, named the "guard hound of all Ulster" when he kills a ferocious watchdog.

Sutcliff, Rosemary. The Mark of the Horse Lord. 1965. Walck [o.p.].

Set in second-century Britain, this gripping historical novel tells of a young ex-slave and gladiator from the Roman arena disguising himself as the Horse Lord of Dalriadain, overthrowing a usurper queen, and leading the tribe into battle to freedom.

Swift, Hildegarde. From the Eagle's Wing: A Biography of John Muir. Illus. by Lynd Ward. 1962. Morrow [o.p.].
Quotes from Muir's writings help to re-create the life of this great nature conservationist and preserver of American forests, and to convey his enthusiasm and sense of wonder.

Tashjian, Virginia A. Once There Was and Was Not: Armenian Tales Retold. Illus. by Nonny Hogrogian. 1966. Little, Brown [o.p.].
Graceful illustrations and a lively text enhance these seven Armenian tales of princes and peasants, wise men and simpletons, based on stories by H. Toumanian.

Tolstoi, Aleksei. The Great Big Enormous Turnip. Illus. by Helen Oxenbury. 1969. Watts [o.p.].
Whimsical illustrations enliven the simply told, humorous folktale about a gigantic vegetable that is difficult to get out of the ground.

Tom Tit Tot: An Old English Folk Tale. Illus. by Evaline Ness. 1965. Scribner [o.p.].
Lavishly illustrated with bold woodcuts, this retelling of the familiar old English folktale from Joseph Jacob's collection will bring new readers and listeners to enjoy the story for years to come. A Caldecott Honor Book.

Trease, Geoffrey. This Is Your Century. 1965. Harcourt [o.p.].
A stimulating overview of world history in the twentieth century.

Tresselt, Alvin. Hide and Seek Fog. Illus. by Roger Duvoisin. 1965. Lothrop, $16.89 (0-688-51169-4).
Impenetrable fog is discomforting to adults but fun for children in a seacoast village. A mood picture book filled with misty beauty. A Caldecott Honor Book.

Tresselt, Alvin. The Mitten. Illus. by Yaroslava. 1964. HarperCollins, $16.89 (0-688-51053-1); paper, $5.99 (0-688-09238-1).
A humorous Ukrainian folktale about a little boy's lost mitten and some cold animals—large and small—seeking a warm home. Charming pictures with bright and wintry colors illustrate this tale, adapted from the version by E. Rachev.

Tunis, Edwin. Colonial Craftsmen and the Beginnings of American Industry. 1965. illus. Collins/World [o.p.].
This is a treasure trove of eighteenth-century American crafts, with a wealth of detail and a profusion of meticulous drawings.

Turkle, Brinton. Obadiah the Bold. 1965. illus. Viking [o.p.].

Obadiah, a small Quaker boy in old Nantucket, dreams of becoming a pirate until he learns that pirates, if caught, walk the plank. From a tale about his sea captain grandfather, he learns what true bravery is. Likable, atmospheric illustrations in full color.

Uden, Grant. A Dictionary of Chivalry. Illus. by Pauline Baynes. 1969. Crowell [o.p.].
Detailed marginal drawings illuminate the more than 1,000 entries in this treasury of knighthood.

Ungerer, Tomi. The Three Robbers. 1962. illus. Atheneum [o.p.]; Rinehart, paper, $6.95 (1-57098-206-6).
A little orphan girl is delighted to be kidnapped by three robbers, rather than live with a wicked aunt.

Valens, Evans G. The Attractive Universe: Gravity and the Shape of Space. Illus. by Berenice Abbott and others. 1969. Collins/World [o.p.].
Imaginative science writing combined with instructive diagrams and exceptional photographs.

von Juchen, Aurel. The Holy Night: The Story of the First Christmas. Illus. by Celestino Piatti. Tr. by Cornelia Schaeffer. 1968. Atheneum [o.p.].
Striking, reverent paintings accompany a simple retelling.

Walsh, Jill P. Fireweed. 1969. Farrar [o.p.].
Against a background of London during the 1940 blitz, two homeless teens meet and develop a poignant relationship in a haunting story made more powerful by the controlled intensity of the writing.

Wersba, Barbara. The Dream Watcher. 1968. Atheneum [o.p.].
A contemporary story of an unhappy misfit whose companionship with an eccentric actress gives him the courage to be himself.

Wier, Ester. The Loner. Illus. by Christine Price. 1963. McKay [o.p.]; Scholastic/Apple, paper, $4.50 (0-590-44352-6).
Traveling with migrant farm workers, a nameless, orphan boy finds a sense of identity and a permanent home during a winter on an isolated sheep ranch. A Newbery Honor Book.

Wiesner, William. The Tower of Babel. 1968. illus. Viking [o.p.].
A dignified retelling complemented by richly designed, brilliantly colored pictures that extend the text.

Wildsmith, Brian. Brian Wildsmith's ABC. 1963. illus. Watts [o.p.]; Star Bright, $6.95 (1-887-734-02-3).

Radiant paintings of animals and objects introduce readers to the uppercase and lowercase letters in this stunning alphabet board book.

Wilson, Erica. Fun with Crewel Embroidery. 1965. illus. Atheneum [o.p.].

A well-known teacher of needlework gives concise, easy directions for the beginner, combining the techniques with colorful designs.

Withers, Carl, ed. A World of Nonsense: Strange and Humorous Tales from Many Lands. Illus. by John E. Johnson. 1968. Holt [o.p.].

An entertaining anthology of little-known nonsense stories garnered from the folklore of many lands.

Wojciechowska, Maia. Shadow of a Bull. Illus. by Alvin Smith. 1964. Simon & Schuster/Atheneum, $16 (0-689-30042-5); Aladdin, paper, $4.99 (0-689-71567-6).

The son of a great Spanish bullfighter must make an important choice between the bullring and the world of medicine. A sensitive, powerful story of a boy's entrance into the adult world. A Newbery Medal winner.

Wrightson, Patricia. A Racecourse for Andy. Illus. by Margaret Horder. 1968. Harcourt [o.p.].

Andy, a mentally challenged child, "buys" the local racetrack from a ragpicker for three dollars in this poignant, memorable story.

Wyndham, Robert, ed. Chinese Mother Goose Rhymes. Illus. by Ed Young. 1968. Collins/World [o.p.]; Penguin, paper, $7.99 (0-698-11622-4).

Chinese calligraphy and jewel-like paintings illuminate this delightful collection.

Yashima, Taro. Seashore Story. 1967. illus. Viking [o.p.].

Misty paintings in delicate colors help tell the tale of Urashima, whose kindness to a turtle was repaid by the sea people.

Yulya. Bears Are Sleeping. Illus. by Nonny Hogrogian. 1967. Scribner [o.p.].

Soft, snow-colored blues and browns capture perfectly the gentle, minor mood of a Russian lullaby.

Zei, Alki. Wildcat under Glass. Tr. by Edward Fenton. 1968. Holt [o.p.].

The effect of living under fascism on young and old in a Greek household, told with deftness and spontaneity. A Mildred L. Batchelder Medal winner.

Zemach, Harve. The Judge: An Untrue Tale. Illus. by Margot Zemach. 1969. Farrar [o.p.]; paper, $6.95 (0-374-43962-1).

Five accused prisoners try to warn the unseeing judge of an approaching monster in this droll, suspenseful picture book. A Caldecott Honor Book.

Zindel, Paul. The Pigman. 1968. HarperCollins, $17.89 (0-06-026828-X); Bantam/Starfire, paper, $5.99 (0-553-26321-8).

A teenage prank involves John and Lorraine with Mr. Pignati, a sad old man whose brief burst of joy they share before it is tragically extinguished.

Zolotow, Charlotte. Mr. Rabbit and the Lovely Present. Illus. by Maurice Sendak. 1962. HarperCollins, $16.99 (0-06-026945-6); paper, $5.95 (0-06-443020-0).

A distinguished rabbit assists a very serious small girl in securing a colorful basket of fruit for mother's birthday gift. Humorous watercolor pictures and gentle, rhythmic text. A Caldecott Honor Book.

4

Notable Children's Books
of the 1970s

Aardema, Verna. Who's in Rabbit's House? A Masai Tale. Illus. by Leo and Diane Dillon. 1977. Delacorte [o.p.]; Dial, paper, $6.99 (0-14-054724-X). **Y.**

Long One, hiding in Rabbit's house, threatens all that dare approach. This humorous tale is presented graphically in the form of a stylized play.

Aardema, Verna. Why Mosquitoes Buzz in People's Ears: A West African Tale. Illus. by Leo and Diane Dillon. 1975. Delacorte, $16.99 (0-8037-6089-2); Dial, paper, $5.99 (0-14-54905-6). **A.**

This simple cumulative *pourquoi* telling is lavishly illustrated in rich color and bold modern design. A Caldecott Medal winner.

Adoff, Arnold, ed. My Black Me: A Beginning Book of Black Poetry. 1974. Dutton $14.99 (0-525-45216-8); Penguin/Puffin, paper, $5.99 (0-14-037443-4). **M.**

Pride, hope, and beauty speak through this collection of poetry.

Alexander, Lloyd. The Cat Who Wished to Be a Man. 1973. Dutton [o.p.]; Penguin/Puffin, paper, $4.99 (0-14-130704-8). **M.**

Reluctantly given human shape by his wizard master, a cat immerses himself so completely in human emotions that he becomes a real man in this comic fantasy.

Alexander, Lloyd. The First Two Lives of Lukas-Kasha. 1978. Dutton [o.p.]; Penguin/Puffin, paper, $5.99 (0-14-130057-4). **O.**

The adventures of Lukas are magically transferred to a strange place where people call him King of Abadan.

Alexander, Lloyd. The Town Cats and Other Tales. Illus. by Laszlo Kubinyl. 1977. Dutton [o.p.]; Penguin/Puffin, paper, $5.99 (0-14-130122-8). **M.**

Each of these eight original stories features a witty, articulate cat who solves a problem for human friends.

Ancona, George. It's a Baby! 1979. illus. Dutton [o.p.]. **Y.**

Baby's first year is revealed in a delightful photo-essay sharing a family's pride in and love for the child.

Anno, Mitsumasa. Anno's Alphabet: An Adventure in Imagination. 1975. illus. Crowell [o.p.]. **A**.

Solid oak, three-dimensional objects provide a puzzle in perspective for each letter of the alphabet in an elegant visual wordless mind-game.

Anno, Mitsumasa. Anno's Journey. 1978. illus. Putnam/Philomel, $16.99 (0-399-20762-7); Paper Star, paper, $7.99 (0-698-11433-7). **A**.

A traveler approaches, experiences, and then leaves behind a western European medieval festival that is seen to transcend time.

Babbitt, Natalie. The Devil's Storybook. 1974. illus. Farrar, paper, $5.95 (0-374-41708-3). **M**.

Fiendishly clever stories of a Middle Ages devil, often thwarted, but on occasion deservedly and deliciously triumphant.

Babbitt, Natalie. The Eyes of the Amaryllis. 1977. Farrar, paper, $4.95 (0-374-42238-9). **O**.

Four people's lives are profoundly affected by a forceful reminder from the sea in this haunting tale of lost souls and timeless love.

Babbitt, Natalie. Knee-Knock Rise. 1970. illus. Farrar [o.p.]; Turtleback, $11 (0-606-04375-6). **M**.

How people cherish their foolish illusions is depicted in a gently satirical fable, told with freshness and artless clarity.

Babbitt, Natalie. Tuck Everlasting. 1975. Farrar, paper, $5.95 (0-374-48013-3). **M**.

Rich, evocative prose permeates this unique fantasy of the Tucks, an ordinary family who has acquired an unwanted immortality by drinking from a magical spring.

Bang, Molly Garrett. Wiley and the Hairy Man. 1976. illus. Simon & Schuster, $14 (0-689-81141-1); Aladdin, paper, $3.99 (0-689-81142-X). **Y**.

Wiley's mother helps him outwit a terrible swamp creature in this simple effectively illustrated version of a Black conjure tale.

Baskin, Hosea and others. Hosie's Alphabet. Illus. by Leonard Baskin. 1972. Viking [o.p.]. **A**.

The illustrator's three children provided the word combinations—"bumptious baboon . . . furious fly"—that accompany his stunning paintings in this sophisticated alphabet offering. A Caldecott Honor Book.

Bawden, Nina. Carrie's War. 1973. HarperCollins, $14.89 (0-397-31450-7). **O**.

As an adult, Carrie returns to the Welsh mining town to which she and her brother had been evacuated during World War II, confronting painful memories.

Bawden, Nina. The Robbers. 1979. Lothrop [o.p.]. **M.**
When nine-year-old Philip leaves the castle-home to live with Dad in England, a dramatic change occurs and an important new friendship begins.

Baylor, Byrd. The Desert Is Theirs. Illus. by Peter Parnall. 1975. Scribner. Simon & Schuster/Atheneum, $16 (0-684-14266-X); Aladdin, paper, $6.95 (0-689-71105-0). **Y.**
Papago Indians' life and survival are depicted in poetic text and fine line drawings illuminated with crisp color. A Caldecott Honor Book.

Baylor, Byrd. Hawk, I'm Your Brother. Illus. by Peter Parnall. 1976. Simon & Schuster/Atheneum, $16 (0-684-14571-5), Aladdin, paper, $6.99 (0-689-71102-6). **M.**
Hawks and boys can be friends only when hawks fly free. Told in poetic prose and stark simple line drawings. A Caldecott Honor Book.

Baylor, Byrd. The Way to Start a Day. Illus. by Peter Parnall. 1978. Simon & Schuster/Atheneum, $17 (0-684-15651-2); Aladdin, paper, $5.99 (0-689-71054-2). **M.**
The strength and flow of the illustrations dramatize multifaceted ways the dawn is greeted in different parts of the world. A Caldecott Honor Book.

Bealer, Alex W. Only the Names Remain: The Cherokees and the Trail of Tears. Illus. by William Sauts Bock. 1972. Little, Brown, paper, $5.95 (0-316-08519-7). **O.**
Stark black-and-white illustrations effectively depict the tragic history of the dispersal of a great Native American nation after the arrival of the white settlers.

Blos, Joan W. A Gathering of Days: A New England Girl's Journal, 1830-32. 1979. Simon & Schuster/Atheneum, $16 (0-684-16340-3); Aladdin, paper, $4.99 (0-689-71419-X). **O.**
Thirteen-year-old Catherine details in her diary the "gathering of days wherein we lived, we loved, were moved, learned how to accept." A Newbery Medal winner.

Blume, Judy. Are You There God, It's Me, Margaret. 1970. Bradbury [o.p.]; Dell/Yearling, paper, $5.50 (0-440-40419-3). **M.**
All the uncertainties of the awkward age of 11 shared by Margaret and her friends are captured in a witty and sympathetic novel.

Bodecker, N. M. Let's Marry, Said the Cherry; and Other Nonsense Poems. 1974. illus. Simon & Schuster/Margaret K. Margaret K. McElderry [o.p.]. **Y.**
Clever union of melodic verse and humorously expressive line drawings.

Bødker, Cecil. Silas and the Black Mare. Tr. by Sheila La Farge. 1978. Delacorte [o.p.]. **O.**

Runaway Silas is repeatedly robbed and roughed up in a story as wild and vigorous as its hero. Adventures are picaresque in nature in this first of a trilogy.

Bond, Nancy. A String in the Harp. 1976. Simon & Schuster/Atheneum, $19 (0-689-50036-X); Aladdin, paper, $5.50 (0-689-80445-8). **O.**
When a 12-year-old American boy finds an ancient harp-tuning key he is drawn into a sixth-century Welsh Taliesin legend. A Newbery Honor Book.

Bonners, Susan. Panda. 1978. illus. Delacorte [o.p.]. **Y.**
A terse text follows the birth and life of a giant panda, with soft watercolor and gouache paintings enriching the picture-book format.

Bowden, Joan Chase. Why the Tides Ebb and Flow. Illus. by Marc Brown. 1979. Houghton, $16 (0-395-28378-7); paper, $7.95 (0-395-54952-3). **Y.**
An old woman gains possession of the rock that plugs the hole in the sea. Charcoal pencil and ink drawings evoke the ebb and flow of this tale.

Brenner, Barbara. A Snake-Lover's Diary. 1970. Addison-Wesley [o.p.]. **M.**
Young herpetologists will find a wealth of information, humorously presented, in the form of a boy's enthusiastic journal.

Brenner, Barbara. Wagon Wheels. Illus. by Don Bolognese. 1978. HarperCollins, paper, $3.99 (0-06-444052-4). **Y.**
Based on actual happenings, this easy reader follows the trek of a motherless Black family as they seek land in the Kansas territory.

Bridgers, Sue Ellen. Home before Dark. 1976. Knopf [o.p.]; Replica, $29.95 (0-7351-0053-5). **O.**
Fourteen-year-old Stella learns what having roots means when her migrant family settles down in her father's hometown.

Briggs, Raymond. The Snowman. 1978. illus. Random, $17 (0-394-83973-0). **Y.**
A small boy's enchanted night of wordless adventure with his snowman, indoors and out, is revealed in softly colored pictures.

Brown, Marcia. All Butterflies: An ABC. 1974. illus. Scribner [o.p.]. **Y.**
Pairs of words, such as *cat dance* and *elephants fly* are set against bright woodcuts to create an unusual alphabet book.

Bryan, Ashley, ed. Walk Together Children: Black American Spirituals. 1974. illus. Atheneum [o.p.]. **A.**
A heritage of song lovingly interpreted in bold black-and-white woodcuts.

Burningham, John. Come Away from the Water, Shirley. 1977. illus. HarperCollins [o.p.]. **Y.**

Her parents' constant mundane admonitions to be careful alternate with Shirley's fantastic imaginary adventures aboard a pirate ship.

Burningham, John. Mr. Grumpy's Outing. 1971. illus. Holt, $21.95 (0-8050-3854-X). **Y.**
Muted color lends a pastoral quality to the tale of an exuberant summer boating party. Although the high jinks of the guests cause the punt to capsize, spirits remain undampened.

Burton, Hester. Beyond the Weir Bridge. Illus. by Victor G. Ambrus. 1970. Crowell [o.p.]. **O.**
A thought-provoking historical account of unshakable faith and political commitment—as well as of romantic love—involving three children in the strife-ridden period of England's Civil War.

Byars, Betsy. The Pinballs. 1977. HarperCollins, $16.89 (0-06-020918-6); paper, $4.95 (0-06-440198-7). **O.**
Tough, cynically humorous Carlie grudgingly becomes the mainstay of a trio of foster children she dubs the pinballs.

Byars, Betsy. The Summer of the Swans. Illus. by Ted Coconis. 1970. Viking, $15.99 (0-670-68190-3); paper, $4.99 (0-14-031420-2). **M.**
Siblings cope with the problems and pain of adolescence and the challenge of retardation. A Newbery Medal winner.

Cameron, Eleanor. The Court of the Stone Children. 1973. Penguin/Puffin, paper, $4.99 (0-14-034289-3). **O.**
Nina meets a spectral girl of Napoleonic France in a fascinating time-fantasy, mingling the present day problems of her loneliness with mystery and treason in the First Empire.

Cameron, Eleanor. Julia and the Hand of God. Illus. by Gail Owens. 1977. Dutton [o.p.]. **M.**
To 11-year-old Julia, life in San Francisco in the 1920s is full of strangeness and seemingly chance occurrences.

Cameron, Eleanor. A Room Made of Windows. Illus. by Trina Schart Hyman. 1971. Atlantic-Little [o.p.]. **M.**
In this literate novel, rich in characterization and setting, Julia awakens to the dreams and needs of her family and friends as she vigorously tumbles into adolescence.

Carle, Eric. The Very Hungry Caterpillar. 1970. illus. Putnam/Philomel, $19.99 (0-399-20853-4). **Y.**

Emerging at last as a beautiful butterfly, a green caterpillar eats his way through the days of the week in a staggering succession of meals complemented by double-page-spreads of unusually appealing design.

Charlip, Remy and others. Handtalk: An ABC of Finger Spelling and Sign Language. 1974. Parents' [o.p.]. **A.**
Expressive color photographs depict the rudiments of two kinds of sign language in this creative gamelike approach to communication.

Cleary, Beverly. Ramona and Her Father. Illus. by Alan Tiegreen. 1977. Morrow, $15.95 (0-688-22114-9); Camelot, paper, $4.99 (0-380-70916-3). **M.**
Ramona Quimby copes with frequent domestic crises amid tears and laughter in this warm, exuberant family story. A Newbery Honor Book.

Cleary, Beverly. Ramona the Brave. Illus. by Alan Tiegreen. 1975. Morrow, $15.99 (0-688-22015-0); Camelot, paper, $5.99 (0-380-70959-7). **M.**
Ramona, a favorite heroine, discovers with astonishment that the way others see her is not always the way she sees herself.

Cleaver, Vera and **Cleaver, Bill.** Queen of Hearts. 1978. Lippincott [o.p.]. **O.**
Grandmother and grandchild battle the pains of growing up and growing older.

Clifton, Lucille. Amifika. Illus. by Thomas DiGrazia. 1977. Dutton [o.p.]. **Y.**
The fears of a young boy about the homecoming of his long-absent father are vanished in this warm telling appropriately illustrated with soft pencil drawings.

Cobb, Vicki. More Science Experiments You Can Eat. Illus. by Giulio Maestro. 1979. Lippincott [o.p.]; Turtleback, paper, $10.95 (0-606-0704-0). **M.**
Enticing experiments that demonstrate scientific principles with edible results are described.

Coerr, Eleanor. Sadako and the Thousand Paper Cranes. Illus. by Ronald Himler. 1977. Putnam, $16.99 (0-399-23799-2); Penguin/Puffin, paper, $4.99 (0-698-11802-2). **M.**
Sadako, a victim of radiation from the atomic bomb, reveals her valiant effort to make 1,000 paper cranes before she dies in this extremely moving story.

Cole, Joanna. A Chick Hatches. Illus. by Jerome Wexler. 1976. Morrow [o.p.]. **Y.**
Simple text and stunning photographs, greatly magnified, clearly detail the development and growth of a chicken embryo.

Collier, James Lincoln and **Collier, Christopher.** My Brother Sam Is Dead. 1974. Simon & Schuster, $17 (0-02-122980-7); Scholastic, paper, $5.99 (0-590-42792-X). **O.**

Tim, the politically ambivalent son of Tory parents and brother to a patriot soldier, views the American Revolution, its agonies and its injustices. A Newbery Honor Book.

Cooper, Susan. Dawn of Fear. Illus. by Margery Gill. 1970. Harcourt [o.p.]; Aladdin, paper, $4.99 (0-689-71327-4). **O.**

Tragedy and a sudden awareness of adult hatred, violence, and fear in this World War II tale shatter an English schoolboy.

Cooper, Susan. The Dark Is Rising. Illus. by Alan E. Cober. 1973. Simon & Schuster/Margaret K. McElderry, $17 (0-689-30317-3); Aladdin, paper, $3.95 (0-689-71087-9). **O.**

Will Stanton, seventh son of a seventh son, learns on his eleventh birthday that he is one of the Old Ones, possessed of supernatural powers and destined to play a vital, dangerous role in combating the rising forces of evil. A Newbery Honor Book.

Cooper, Susan. The Grey King. Illus. by Michael Heslop. 1975. Simon & Schuster/Margaret K. McElderry, $17 (0-689-50029-7); paper, $4.99 (0-689-71087-9). **O.**

Will Stanton's quest in this selection, using his power to locate the golden harp, will aid him as he continues to fight the forces of dark and evil. A Newbery Medal winner.

Cormier, Robert. I Am the Cheese. 1977. Knopf, $19.95 (0-394-83462-3); Dell/Laurel Leaf, paper, $4.99 (0-440-94060-5). **O.**

In this complex, chilling novel, teenage Adam's reliving of his past is juxtaposed with the interrogation and trauma of his present life.

Cresswell, Helen. Ordinary Jack: Being the First Part of the Bagthorpe Saga. 1977. Macmillan [o.p.]. **O.**

Mayhem and misadventure reign in this laugh-out-loud story about an ordinary boy in an eccentric family of geniuses.

Crews, Donald. Freight Train. 1978. illus. Greenwillow, $15.99 (0-688-80165-X); paper, $5.95 (0-688-11701-5). **Y.**

Clear, bright illustrations show all the cars of a train, from red caboose to black steam engine, bringing the excitement of movement through day and night, country and city. A Caldecott Honor Book.

Curtis, Edward S. The Girl Who Married a Ghost and Other Tales from the North American Indian. Ed. by John Bierhorst. 1978. illus. Macmillan [o.p.]. **Y.**

Nine Native American stories are brought together by a famous writer-photographer of the early 1900s.

Dana, Doris. The Elephant and His Secret/El Elafante y Su Secreto. Illus. by Antonio Frasconi. 1974. Simon & Schuster/Margaret K. McElderry [o.p.]. **Y.**

Elephant knows the secret of the mountain and, as an ark, transports the world's animals on his back to Mt. Ararat. Striking two-color woodcuts illustrate the fable.

d'Aulaire, Ingri and **d'Aulaire, Edgar P.** d'Aulaire's Trolls. 1972. illus. Doubleday [o.p.]. **M.**

Scandinavian troll creatures, their food, fun, and shapes as well as some of their tales, are depicted in this natural history. Color lithographs highlight the text.

Davis, Hubert. A January Fog Will Freeze a Hog and Other Weather Folklore. Illus. by John Wallner. 1977. Crown [o.p.]. **M.**

Unusual collection of pithy American weather rhymes is captured in texturally exciting and provocatively designed black-and-white illustrations. Notes are appended.

Degens, T. Transport 7-41-R. 1974. Viking [o.p.]. **O.**

A powerful story of an independent young girl's wrenching experiences journeying in 1946 from East Germany to Cologne on a train packed with refugees.

dePaola, Tomie. Charlie Needs a Cloak. 1974. illus. Prentice-Hall [o.p.]; Simon & Schuster/Aladdin, paper, $5.99 (0-671-66467-0). **Y.**

From the genesis of the idea of making a new red cloak through shearing sheep to spinning wool and sewing the cloak, this is an understated delightful picture book. Irresistible humor elicits humor as Charlie's naughty sheep's antics are witnessed.

dePaola, Tomie. The Clown of God: An Old Story. 1978. illus. Harcourt [o.p.]. **Y.**

Rich renaissance style illustrations equal the retelling of the legend of a juggler whose offering to the Holy Child surpasses the gifts of the wealthy.

dePaola, Tomie. Strega Nona: An Old Tale. 1975. illus. Simon & Schuster, $16.95 (0-671-66283-X); paper, $6.95 (0-671-66606-1). **Y.**

When grandmother witch Strega Nona leaves to visit a friend, her servant Anthony nearly buries the community in pasta from her magic pot. *Commedia dell'arte*, amiably enacted by a peasant cast before an earthy, clay-toned backdrop. A Caldecott Honor Book.

DePauw, Linda Grant. Founding Mothers: Women in America in the Revolutionary War. Illus. by Michael McCurdy. 1975. Houghton [o.p.]. **O.**

A vigorous portrait of the acumen, strength, dignity, and responsibility of many eighteenth-century American women.

Dennis, Landt. Catch the Wind: A Book of Windmills and Windpower. Illus. by Lisl Dennis. 1976. Four Winds [o.p.]. **M.**

Effectively illustrated presentation of the ways windmills and wind power have been used in the past and could be used in the future.

Dickinson, Peter. The Blue Hawk. 1976. Little, Brown [o.p.]; Peter Smith, $22 (0-844-66478-2). **O.**

A novice priest in a place reminiscent of ancient Egypt steals the Blue Hawk and thus condemns himself to a life of exile and a search for wisdom.

Dickinson, Peter. Tulku. 1979. Dutton [o.p.]. **O.**

Theodore, orphaned by events of the Boxer Rebellion, travels to Tibet with a female botanist and her companion. The three become involved with Buddhist monks in search of a new leader, or Tulku.

Din Dan Don, It's Christmas. Illus. by Janina Domanska. 1975. Greenwillow [o.p.]. **A.**

A traditional Polish carol is stunningly pictured with brilliant stained-glass effects: a procession of animals and people celebrate as they bring gifts to the Christ Child.

Donovan, John. Family. 1976. HarperCollins [o.p.]. **O.**

Sasha, an ape who has spent his life participating in experiments, tells of the discoveries he and his family make about themselves and humanity.

Eckert, Allan. Incident at Hawk's Hill. Illus. by John Schoenherr. 1971. Little, Brown [o.p.]; paper, $6.99 (0-316-20948-1). **O.**

A six-year-old boy is lost in the Canadian prairie and adopted by a female badger in this appealing, ageless tale, based on an actual incident, rich in nature lore. A Newbery Honor Book.

Engdahl, Sylvia Louise. Enchantress from the Stars. Illus. by Rodney Shackell. 1970. Simon & Schuster/Atheneum [o.p.]; Putnam/Firebird, paper, $6.99 (0-14-250037-2). **O.**

Three worlds at different levels of development are represented in a rich work of science fiction that suggests several philosophical questions. A Newbery Honor Book.

Epstein, Sam and **Epstein, Beryl.** Dr. Beaumont and the Man with the Hole in His Stomach. Illus. by Joseph Scrofani. 1978. Coward [o.p.]. **O.**

An ambitious nineteenth-century doctor and his wounded Native American patient together make a tremendous contribution to our knowledge of the digestive system.

Feelings, Muriel. Jambo Means Hello: Swahili Alphabet. Illus. by Tom Feelings. 1974. Delacorte, $18.99 (0-8037-4346-7); paper, $6.99 (0-14-054652-9). **Y.**

Warm, lush black-and-white paintings graphically portray the Swahili letters, accompanied with a word, its pronunciation, and an explanation of the cultural happening. A Caldecott Honor Book.

Feelings, Muriel. Moja Means One: Swahili Counting Book. Illus. by Tom Feelings. 1971. Delacorte [o.p.]; Dial, paper, $6.99 (0-14-054662-6). **Y.**

Spacious, smoky-brown double-spread illustrations evoke the sights and sounds of rural East Africa. A Caldecott Honor Book.

Fleischman, Albert Sidney. Humbug Mountain. Illus. by Eric von Schmidt. 1978. Little, Brown [o.p.]. **M.**

Suspense, tall-tale humor, and a frontier setting enliven young Wiley Flint's account of the adventures that he and his peripatetic family encounter as they search for his missing grandfather and a permanent home.

Fox, Paula. The Slave Dancer. Illus. by Eros Keith. 1973. Simon & Schuster/Atheneum, $16.95 (0-02-735560-8); Dell/Yearling, paper, $5.99 (0-440-40402-9). **O.**

A stunning telling of adventure and horror on the high seas experienced by a teenager shanghaied aboard a slave ship to play his fife for the health-dancing exercise of the slaves. A Newbery Medal winner.

Fritz, Jean. And Then What Happened, Paul Revere? Illus. by Margot Tomes. 1973. HarperCollins [o.p.]; Paper Star, paper, $6.99 (0-698-11351-9). **M.**
* Why Don't You Get a Horse, Sam Adams? Illus. by Trina Schart Hyman. 1974. Coward [o.p.]; Paper Star, paper, $6.99 (0-689-11416-7). **M.**
* Where Was Patrick Henry on the 29th of May? Illus. by Margot Tomes. 1975. HarperCollins [o.p.]; Paper Star, paper, $6.99 (0-698-11439-6). **M.**

In each of these biographies of early American leaders, the man and the times in which he lived are vividly and humorously brought to life.

Frost, Robert. Stopping by Woods on a Snowy Evening. Illus. by Susan Jeffers. 1978. Dutton, $15.99 (0-525-46734-3). **A.**

A highly original, visual interpretation of this well-loved poem.

Gardam, Jane. A Long Way from Verona. 1972. Macmillan [o.p.]. **O.**

England during World War II finds Jessica as the most arbitrary and most honest pupil in the girl's school in this fresh telling with identifiable characters and contagious humor.

George, Jean Craighead. Julie of the Wolves. Illus. by John Schoenherr. 1972. HarperCollins, $15.95 (0-06-021943-2); paper, $5.99 (0-06-440058-1). **O.**

In order to escape an arranged marriage, 13-year-old Julie disappears into the Alaskan tundra and is successfully aided by a wolf pack. A Newbery Medal winner.

Ginsburg, Mirra. How Wilka Went to Sea and Other Tales from West of the Urals. Illus. by Charles Mikolaycak. 1975. Crown [o.p.]. **Y.**

A cluster of witty, buoyant tales from far-flung agricultural or nomadic areas of the USSR. Vivid, skillful drawings against crimson backgrounds accentuate the vitality of the stories.

Ginsburg, Mirra. Mushroom in the Rain. Illus. by Jose Aruego and Ariane Dewey. Adapted from the Russian of V. Suteyev. 1974. Macmillan [o.p.]; Simon & Schuster/Aladdin, paper, $6.99 (0-689-71441-6). **Y.**

Clean, colorful illustrations humorously depict a marvelous mushroom sheltering all comers during a rainstorm.

Gladstone, M. J. A Carrot for a Nose: The Form of Folk Sculpture on America's City Streets and Country Roads. 1974. Scribner [o.p.]. **O.**

Succinct text and carefully selected photographs reveal the variety of folk art around us. Examples range from the city's solid iron manhole covers to more ephemeral country scarecrows.

Goble, Paul. The Girl Who Loved Wild Horses. 1978. illus. Simon & Schuster, $17 (0-02-736570-0); paper, $6.99 (0-689-71696-6). **Y.**

Vivid color illustrations with care for detail, mood, and movement frame the dramatic story of a Plains Indian girl's love for wild, free horses. A Caldecott Medal winner.

Greene, Bette. Summer of My German Soldier. 1973. Dial, $16.99 (0-8037-2869-7); Penguin/Puffin, paper, $6.99 (0-14-130636-X). **O.**

Mistreated and misunderstood, a Jewish girl befriends an escaped German prisoner of war. This poignant, tragic story is set in a small Arkansas town during World War II.

Greene, Constance. Beat the Turtle Drum. Illus. by Donna Diamond. 1976. Viking [o.p.]; Penguin/Puffin, paper, $5.99 (0-14-036850-7). **O.**

The unexpected death of her sister leaves Kate confused and angry as she lives through the "right now that hurts."

Greenfield, Eloise. Honey, I Love, and Other Love Poems. Illus. by Leo and Diane Dillon. 1978. HarperCollins, $14.99 (0-690-01334-5); paper, $5.99 (0-06-443097-9). **M.**

A poetic blend of illustrations and words describes everyday life and lifelong love.

Greenfield, Eloise. She Come Bringing Me That Little Baby Girl. Illus. by John Steptoe. 1974. Lippincott [o.p.]. **Y.**

Rich, vivid illustrations create a unique visual backdrop for this warm, realistic telling of Kevin's slow acceptance of his baby sister.

Greenfield, Eloise and **Little, Lessie Jones.** Child-Times: A Three-Generation Memoir. Illus. by Jerry Pinkney. 1979. Crowell [o.p.]. **O.**
  Reminiscences of three black women—grandmother, mother, and daughter—demonstrate both continuity and change in recalling such experiences of their respective childhoods. Illustrated with stunning drawings and photos.

Grimes, Nikki. Something on My Mind. Illus. by Tom Feelings. 1978. Dial [o.p.]. **M.**
  A series of stunning sketches and portrait studies of black American children are presented in free verse.

Grimm, Jakob and **Grimm, Wilhelm.** Snow White and the Seven Dwarfs: A Tale from the Brothers Grimm. Illus. by Nancy Ekholm Burkert. Tr. by Randall Jarrell. 1972. Farrar [o.p.]; paper, $5.95 (0-374-46868-0). **Y.**
  A smooth new translation of the familiar tale, embellished with full-page, extravagantly detailed paintings illustrative of medieval life. A Caldecott Honor Book.

Grimm, Jakob and **Grimm, Wilhelm.** Tom Thumb. Tr. by Felix Hoffman. 1973. Simon & Schuster/Margaret K. McElderry [o.p.]. **Y.**
  Full-page color contrasted with black-and-white illustrations brings to life, with verve and humor, a classic folktale. The setting, clothing, and characters reflect simplicity and authenticity.

Haley, Gail E. A Story A Story: An African Tale. 1970. illus. Simon & Schuster/Atheneum [o.p.]; Turtleback, $12.14 (0-606-00981-7). **Y.**
  Strong woodcuts in striking colors accompany this retelling of a traditional story of Ananse, the spider man. A Caldecott Medal winner.

Hall, Donald. Ox-Cart Man. Illus. by Barbara Cooney. 1979. Viking, $16.99 (0-670-53328-9); paper, $6.99 (0-14-050441-9). **Y.**
  Earth-tone paintings and sparse prose depict quiet scenes of life and the changing seasons of early-nineteenth-century New England. A Caldecott Medal winner.

Hamilton, Virginia. Justice and Her Brothers. 1978. Greenwillow [o.p.]; Scholastic, paper, $4.99 (0-590-36214-3). **O.**
  Eleven-year-old Justice and her twin brothers discover they have supernatural powers in this first book of a trilogy.

Hamilton, Virginia. M. C. Higgins, the Great. 1974. Simon & Schuster, $17 (0-02-742480-4); Aladdin, paper, $4.99 (0-02-043490-1). **O.**
  A haunting novel about a boy's struggle to know himself, his family, and his way of life on Sarah's Mountain. Elegant, singing prose gives the landscape and people palpable reality. A Newbery Medal winner.

Hamilton, Virginia. The Planet of Junior Brown. 1971. Simon & Schuster, $18 (0-02-742510-X); paper, $4.99 (0-02-043540-1). **O.**

Junior—neurotic, obese, a musical prodigy—and Buddy—homeless, street-wise, protective, and lonely—confront their demons and try to survive together in a gripping surrealistic novel. A Newbery Honor Book.

Hamilton, Virginia. W. E. B. Du Bois: A Biography. 1972. Crowell [o.p.]. **O.**
A well-researched biography dealing with the contributions made by a black leader. It reveals, too, Du Bois's struggles in the U.S., his disillusionment, and his emigration to Ghana.

Harris, Christie. Mouse Woman and the Mischief-Makers. Illus. by Douglas Tait. 1977. Simon & Schuster/Atheneum [o.p.]. **M.**
Tiny Mouse Woman, a supernatural being of Northwest coast Native American legend, uses wiles and trickery to achieve her unique ideas of justice.

Harris, Rosemary. The Moon in the Cloud. 1970. Macmillan [o.p.]; Peter Smith, $20.25 (0-844-66429-4). **M.**
An imaginative, suspenseful novel based on the story of Noah and notable for its memorable characters and sparking blend of comedy and fantasy.

Haviland,Virginia, ed. The Fairy Tale Treasury. Illus. by Raymond Briggs. 1972. Coward [o.p.]. **Y.**
A varied, robustly illustrated collection of both familiar and less well-known folk and fairy tales from around the world. Witty black-and-white drawings contrast the zesty full-color illustrations.

Heide, Florence Parry. The Shrinking of Treehorn. Illus. by Edward Gorey. 1971. Holiday [o.p.]. **M.**
Treehorn is shrinking fast, but nobody in his tidy, conventional suburban world will recognize his extraordinary problem. A comic fantasy with droll, understated pictures.

Highwater, Jamake. Anpao: An American Indian Odyssey. Illus. by Fritz Scholder. 1977. Lippincott [o.p.]. **O.**
In the course of his lengthy dangerous quest, Anpao encounters many people and powers that help him discover the secret of his birth. A Newbery Honor Book.

Hoban, Tana. Count and See. 1972. illus. Simon & Schuster, $17 (0-02-744800-2). **Y.**
Familiar objects in a city child's life are imaginatively photographed in a counting book that encourages observation and concept development.

Hoban, Tana. Look Again! 1971. illus. Macmillan [o.p.]; Simon & Schuster, paper, $15 (0-02-744050-8). **Y.**
Superb photographs and an imaginative format transform a wordless book into an experience in visual aesthetics.

Hodges, C. Walter. The Overland Launch. 1970. illus. Coward [o.p.]. **M.**

A vivid re-creation of one wildly stormy night on the Devonshire coast in 1899 when a lifeboat was hauled 13 miles by land to be launched for a rescue at sea.

Hodges, Margaret. The Fire Bringer: A Paiute Indian Legend Retold. Illus. by Peter Parnall. 1972. Little, Brown [o.p.]. **M.**

Coyote helps a young boy capture fire from the firewatchers of the mountain so he may bring it to his people. Black, white, and scarlet drawings add dramatic simplicity to the tale.

Hoffmann, Felix. The Story of Christmas: A Picture Book. 1975. Simon & Schuster/Margaret K. McElderry [o.p.]. **A.**

The nativity of Christ is interpreted with quiet dignity in both text and full-page, full-color paintings.

Hogrogian, Nonny. The Contest. 1976. illus. Greenwillow, $17.89 (0-688-84042-6). **Y.**

A saucy Armenian folktale focusing on two robbers, betrothed to the same woman, who strive to outwit each other and end by joining forces. A Caldecott Honor Book.

Hogrogian, Nonny. One Fine Day. 1971. illus. Simon & Schuster/Aladdin, paper, $6.99 (0-02-043620-3). **Y.**

A cumulative animal tale from Armenia, with perfect balance between lively text and zestful full-color spreads. A Caldecott Medal winner.

Holman, Felice. The Murderer. 1978. Scribner [o.p.]. **O.**

Sometimes funny, sometimes poignant vignettes portray the life of a Jewish boy growing up in a Polish mining town.

Holman, Felice. Slake's Limbo. 1974. Simon & Schuster/Atheneum, $16 (0-684-13926-X); Aladdin, paper, $4.99 (0-689-71066-6). **O.**

Artemis Slake, a lonely, fearful 13-year-old, flees into the subway, where he discovers a cave alongside the tracks. His life underground and gradual self-awaking are perceptively told.

Hoover, H. M. Rains of Eridan. 1977. Viking [o.p.]. **O.**

Carnivorous, caterpillar-like creatures that are released during the rains threaten the colonists of the planet Eridan.

Hunter, Mollie. A Sound of Chariots. 1972. HarperCollins [o.p.]. **O.**

When Dad's unexpected death leaves nine-year-old Bridie in a state of desolation, she escapes through creative writing. Family relationships and Bridie's maturing attitude are poignantly portrayed.

Hunter, Mollie. A Stranger Came Ashore: A Story of Suspense. 1975. Harper-Collins [o.p.]; paper, $5.99 (0-06-440082-4). **O**.

The Shetland Islands provide the setting for the Selkie legend of a seal king in the guise of a sailor seeking a mortal wife.

Hutchins, Pat. Changes, Changes. 1971. illus. Simon & Schuster [o.p.]. **Y**.

In an original wordless picture book, bold, bright colored drawings demonstrate what wooden building blocks can become in a child's imaginative play.

Hutchins, Pat. Goodnight. Owl! 1972. illus. Simon & Schuster [o.p.]. **Y**.

Illustrations and repetition relate Owl's unsuccessful efforts to fall asleep amidst the cacophony of woodland creatures.

Isadora, Rachel. Ben's Trumpet. 1979. illus. Greenwillow, $17.95 (0-688-80194-3); paper, $6.99 (0-688-10988-8). **Y**.

Dazzling black-and-white art deco paintings set the jazz age scene in which a small boy dreams of becoming a trumpeter. A Caldecott Honor Book.

Jeffers, Susan. Three Jovial Huntsmen. 1973. illus. Bradbury [o.p.]; Simon & Schuster, paper, $3.95 (0-689-71309-6). **Y**.

Understated humor and unusual four-color pen-and-ink drawings distinguish this creative interpretation of the Mother Goose tale of cleverly hidden animals and their outwitted, self-centered huntsmen. A Caldecott Honor Book.

Johnson, James Weldon and **Johnson, J. Rosamond.** Lift Every Voice and Sing: Illus. by Mozelle Thompson. 1970. Hawthorn [o.p.]. **Y**.

Known to many as the black national anthem, the song is accompanied by stark, dignified charcoal drawings.

Jones, Adrienne. The Hawks of Chelney. Illus. by Stephen Gammell. 1978. HarperCollins, $13.95 (0-06-023057-6). **O**.

Mystery and myth combine in this tale of a boy who has a unique relationship with nature.

Jones, Diana Wynne. Dogsbody. 1977. Greenwillow, $16.95 (0-06-029880-4); paper, $6.95 (0-06-441038-1). **O**.

His power circumscribed by the physical limitations of his dog body, the exiled Dog Star Sirius struggles to aid an Irish political prisoner's daughter and complete a perilous quest of his own.

Jones, Hettie, ed. The Trees Stand Shining: Poetry of the North American Indians. Illus. by Robert Andrew Parker. 1971. Dial [o.p.]. **A**.

Poems of Native Americans express great wonder, joy, despair, and determination. Verses are effectively illuminated with full-color paintings.

Jordan, June and **Bush, Terri.** The Voice of the Children. 1970. Holt [o.p.]. **O.**

Strength—of imagery, of language, of emotion—characterizes the poems and prose selected from the writings of black and Puerto Rican children.

Kadesch, Robert R. Math Menagerie. Illus. by Mark A. Binn. 1970. HarperCollins [o.p.]. **Y.**

Twenty-five ingenious mathematical experiments utilizing inexpensive, readily available materials are clearly described and illustrated.

Karl, Jean E. The Turning Places: Stories of a Future Past. 1976. Dutton [o.p.]. **O.**

Like layers of time, these stories meld into and overlap each other as they relate the changing nature of earth's civilization following a holocaust.

Kerr, Judith. When Hitler Stole Pink Rabbit. 1972. Coward [o.p.]; Paper Star, paper, $5.99 (0-698-11589-9). **O.**

The intangible values of human relationships are emphasized in this telling of a Jewish family as they escape Hitler's reign of terror.

Kherdian, David. The Road from Home: The Story of an Armenian Girl. 1979. Greenwillow, $15.89 (0-688-84205-4). **O.**

Veron's struggle to survive the Turkish attempt to exterminate her people in 1916 provides a vivid reminder of the suffering in pre-Hitler Europe. A Newbery Honor Book.

Koehn, Ilse. Mischling, Second Degree. 1977. Greenwillow [o.p.]. **O.**

Autobiographical memoirs are revealed by a girl growing up in Hitler's Germany. She has been protected from the knowledge that her grandmother is Jewish.

Kohl, Judith and **Kohl, Herbert.** The View from the Oak: The Private Worlds of Other Creatures. Illus. by Roger Bayless. 1977. Scribner [o.p.]. **O.**

In a model of scientific discourse, the Kohls have created an absorbing way of seeing nature from the perspective of time, space, senses, and movement.

Konigsburg, E. L. Father's Arcane Daughter. 1976. Simon & Schuster/Atheneum, $15 (0-689-30524-9); paper, $4.99 (0-689-82680-X). **O.**

A gripping account of a mysterious "long lost" sister and her two younger siblings.

Konigsburg, E. L. A Proud Taste for Scarlet and Miniver. 1973. illus. Simon & Schuster/Atheneum, $18 (0-689-30111-1); Dell/Yearling, paper, $4.99 (0-440-47201-6). **O.**

Set in Heaven at the present time, this sparkling, witty tale gives an authentic portrayal of the life and times of Eleanor of Aquiline, revealed through her own conversation and three of her contemporaries, also heavenly residents.

Kraus, Robert. Milton the Early Riser. Illus. by Jose and Ariane Aruego. 1972. Windmill [o.p.]; Simon & Schuster/Aladdin, paper, $6.99 (0-671-66911-7). **Y.**

Wide-awake Milton, a panda, gambols across gaily colored pages filled with sleeping animals.

Kraus, Robert. Whose Mouse Are You? Illus. by Jose Aruego. 1970. Simon & Schuster, $17 (0-689-84052-7); Aladdin, paper, $5.99 (0-689-71142-5). **Y.**

Bright red-and-yellow colors contrast happily with mouse gray in pictures for a terse text that has the satisfying simplicity of a nursery rhyme.

Krementz, Jill. A Very Young Dancer. 1976. illus. Knopf [o.p.]. **M.**

Excellent photographs are paired with an engaging account by a 10-year-old girl about her participation in the preparation for and performance of *The Nutcracker* by the New York City Ballet.

Kurelek, William. Lumberjack. 1974. illus. Houghton [o.p.]; Tundra, paper, $9.95 (0-88776-378-2). **A.**

The warmth and camaraderie of Canadian working men are recreated in vibrant paintings accompanied by a conversational text.

Langstaff , Nancy and **Langstaff, John.** Jim Along Josie: A Collection of Folk Songs and Singing Games for Young Children. Illus. by Jan Pienkowski. 1970. Harcourt [o.p.]. **A.**

A generous gathering that is particularly suitable as an introduction to both music and poetry.

Lasker, Joe. Merry Ever After: The Story of Two Medieval Weddings. 1976. illus. Viking [o.p.]. **Y.**

A panorama of medieval customs and life is shown in the wedding preparations of a noble couple and a peasant couple.

Lauber, Patricia. What's Hatching Out of That Egg? 1979. illus. Crown [o.p.]. **M.**

Sharp, clear photographs offer clues to the ways in which 11 animals are born.

Leen, Nina. The Bat. Photos. 1976. illus. Holt [o.p.]. **M.**

The unusual characteristics of this much-maligned winged mammal are stressed in text and photographs.

Le Guin, Ursula K. The Tombs of Atuan. Illus. by Gail Garraty. 1971. Simon & Schuster/Atheneum, $21 (0-689-31684-4). **O.**

Deeply rooted in mythology, a superb tale of high fantasy in which a young priestess, together with Sparrowhawk, escapes the divinities of death and destruction. A Newbery Honor Book.

Le Guin, Ursula K. Very Far Away from Anywhere Else. 1976. Simon & Schuster/Atheneum [o.p.]. **O.**

An intellectual 17-year-old boy learns a great deal about himself through friendship with a musically gifted girl.

Leodhas, Sorche Nic. Twelve Great Black Cats and Other Eerie Scottish Tales. Illus. by Vera Bock. 1971. Dutton [o.p.]. **O.**

Ghostly tales with eerie, shadowy pictures and enough Scottish dialect to preserve the flavor but not discourage the reader, are presented for those who like to shiver with pleasure.

Le Shan, Eda J. Learning to Say Goodbye: When a Parent Dies. Illus. by Paul Giovanopoulos. 1976. Macmillan [o.p.]. **O.**

A direct, honest approach is taken to children's problems resulting from the death of a parent.

Lester, Julius. The Knee-High Man and Other Tales. Illus. by Ralph Pinto. 1972. Dial [o.p.]. **M.**

Warm, vibrant colors heighten the appeal of six gentle, humorous animal stories from black American folk literature.

Levoy, Myron. Alan and Naomi. 1977. HarperCollins [o.p.]. **O.**

An unusually sensitive tale of a friendship affected by external circumstances as Alan attempts to assist Naomi, a refugee from World War II Gestapo terrorism, overcome her haunting nightmares.

Little Red Hen. Illus. by Janina Domanska. 1973. Macmillan [o.p.]. **Y.**

Brilliant, geometric designs provide a lasting appeal to this classic telling of the hardworking mother hen as she grows the wheat for her family's bread.

Lobel, Arnold. Frog and Toad Are Friends. 1970. illus. HarperCollins, $15.89 (0-06-023957-3); paper, $3.99 (0-06-444020-6). **Y.**
* Frog and Toad Together. 1972. illus. HarperCollins, $15.89 (0-06-023959-X); paper, $3.99 (0-06-444021-4). **Y.**
* Frog and Toad All Year. 1976. illus. HarperCollins, $15.89 (0-06-023951-4); paper, $3.99 (0-06-444059-1). **Y.**
* Days with Frog and Toad. 1979. illus. HarperCollins, $15.89 (0-06-023963-8); paper, $3.99 (0-06-444058-3). **Y.**

Whether they are flying a kite, receiving a birthday hat that doesn't fit, or celebrating the seasons, Frog and Toad's friendship perseveres in this skillful amalgam of words and illustrations for beginning readers. *Frog and Toad Are Friends* is a Caldecott Honor Book; *Frog and Toad Together* is a Newbery Honor Book.

Lobel, Arnold. A Treeful of Pigs. Illus. by Anita Lobel. 1979. Greenwillow, $16.89 (0-688-84177-5). **Y.**

A humorously presented story of a wife's attempt to have her lazy husband help raise the pigs is matched with Eastern European folk textiled, patterned, rib-tickling art.

Lombardy, William and **Marshall, Bette.** Chess for Children, Step by Step: A New, Easy Way to Learn the Game. Illus. by Bette Marshall. 1977. Little, Brown, $18.95 (0-316-53091-3). **O.**
This unique approach for beginners is presented through the use of the pawn in combination, one at a time, with each of the other chess pieces. Chess art by John Schnell.

Lowry, Lois. Anastasia Krupnik. 1979. Houghton, $16 (0-395-28629-8); Dell/ Yearling, paper, $4.99 (0-440-40852-0). **M.**
Humor and warm family relationships add important dimensions to this gentle tale of 10-year-old Anastasia and her ever-changing lists of "things I love" and "things I hate."

Lowry, Lois. A Summer to Die. Illus. by Jenni Oliver. 1977. Houghton, $16 (0-395-25338-1); Bantam, paper, $5.50 (0-440-21917-5). **O.**
Meg's gradual acceptance of her older sister's approaching death develops as she explores relationships with an elderly photographer, a modern young couple, and her own parents.

Lueders, Edward and **St. John, Primus,** eds. Zero Makes Me Hungry: A Collection of Poems for Today. Illus. by John Reuter-Pacyna. 1976. Lothrop [o.p.]. **O.**
Twentieth-century poems, from a wide range of ethnic and cultural traditions, speak directly to today's young people.

Macaulay, David. Castle. 1977. illus. Houghton, $18. (0-395-25784-0); Houghton, paper, $8.95 (0-395-32920-5). **O.**
This architectural and cultural exploration, focusing on a single dimension of thirteenth-century British life is startling in concept and realization and enlightening in its perception. A Caldecott Honor Book.

Macaulay, David. Cathedral: The Story of Its Construction. 1973. illus. Houghton, $18 (0-395-17513-5); paper, $8.95 (0-395-31668-5). **A.**
Again focusing on a single architectural dimension, a cathedral, Macaulay's direct writing and meticulously detailed line drawings celebrate the craftsmen. A Caldecott Honor Book.

Mahy, Margaret. The Boy Who Was Followed Home. Illus. by Steven Kellogg. 1975. Watts [o.p.]. **Y.**
Neither delighted Robert nor his bewildered parents can understand why so many hippopotamuses follow him home. A fantastic, absurd story told in understated text and detailed laughable art.

Mark, Jan. Thunder and Lightning. Illus. by Jim Russell. 1979. Crowell [o.p.]. **O.**
  Two boys learn the truth about their place in the world in a strongly characterized telling about the planes that fly from an English airfield.

Marshall, James. George and Martha. 1972. illus. Houghton, $16 (0-395-16619-5); paper, $6.95 (0-395-19972-7). **Y.**
* George and Martha One Fine Day. 1978. illus. Houghton, $16 (0-395-27154-1); paper, $6.95 (0-395-32921-3). **Y.**
  Brief, blithe chapter stories center around the friendship of two appealing hippopotamuses, adroitly conveyed through endearing drawings.

Mathis, Sharon Bell. The Hundred Penny Box. Illus. by Leo and Diane Dillon. 1975. Viking [o.p.]; Paper Star, paper, $5.99 (0-14-032169-1). **O.**
  Michael enjoys hearing centenarian Aunt Drew talk about her life as, one by one, he counts out the pennies in her cherished box. A Newbery Honor Book.

Mathis, Sharon Bell. Teacup Full of Roses. 1972. Viking [o.p.]. **O.**
  In this strong novel of urban life, Joe's decision to leave home is prompted by despair over his mother's blindness to one sibling's talents and the other's drug addiction.

Mayne, William. Ravensgill. 1970. Dutton [o.p.]. **M.**
  A family feud and an unexplained murder form the core of this tightly woven tale of intrigue.

McCaffrey, Anne. Dragonsong. 1976. Simon & Schuster/Atheneum [o.p.]; paper, $5.99 (0-689-86008-0). **O.**
* Dragonsinger. 1977. Simon & Schuster/Atheneum. $18 (0-689-30570-2); paper, $5.99 (0-689-86007-2). **O.**
* Dragondrums. 1979. Simon & Schuster/Atheneum [o.p.]; paper, $5.99 (0-689-86006-4). **O.**
  With great difficulty, a young girl wins a respected place in her society as a song maker. A position previously held only by males in this intricate, intriguing fantasy trilogy set on the planet of Pern.

McDermott, Beverly Brodsky. The Golem: A Jewish Legend. 1976. illus. Lippincott [o.p.]. **M.**
  Swathes of watercolor project the raw power of the Golem, who became more terrible than the evil he had been summoned to dispel. A Caldecott Honor Book.

McDermott, Gerald. Anansi the Spider: A Tale from the Ashanti. 1972. illus. Holt, $16.95 (0-8050-0310-X); paper, $6.95 (0-8050-0311-8). **Y.**
  All the charm and wisdom of Anansi are revealed through not only terse text but also bold graphic illustrations of Ashanti patterns on colored paper. A Caldecott Honor Book.

McDermott, Gerald. Arrow to the Sun: A Pueblo Indian Tale. 1974. illus. Viking, $16.99 (0-670-13369-8); paper, $6.99 (0-14-050211-4). **Y.**

Symbolic hero quest to the Sun by his earthly son, vividly designed and projected in sharp, brilliant colors. A Caldecott Medal winner.

McKay, David, ed. A Flock of Words: An Anthology of Poetry for Children and Others. Illus. by Margery Gill. 1970. Harcourt [o.p.]. **A.**

Extraordinary unity and impact in a collection—wide-ranging in subject, time and place—uniquely arranged in clusters and linked by themes.

McKillip, Patricia. The Forgotten Beasts of Eld. 1974. Simon & Schuster/ Atheneum [o.p.]; Harcourt, paper, $6 (0-15-200869-1). **O.**

In this powerful fantasy set in two worlds, wondrous beasts and their wizard mistress are caught up in the destructive power of human emotions through a boy-king who is secretly reared by the wizard.

McKinley, Robin. Beauty: A Retelling of the Story of Beauty and the Beast. 1978. HarperCollins, $15.95 (0-06-024149-7); paper, $5.99 (0-06-440477-3). **O.**

This romantic retelling of a classic fairy tale provides in-depth character appreciation of well-loved individuals.

Meltzer, Milton. Never to Forget: The Jews of the Holocaust. 1976. HarperCollins [o.p.]; paper, $7.95 (0-06-446118-1). **O.**

Compelling account of the Holocaust and the spirit of resistance with selections from diaries, letters, poems, and songs.

Meyer, Carolyn. The Bread Book: All about Bread and How to Make It. Illus. by Trina Schart Hyman. 1971. Harcourt [o.p.]. **M.**

Imaginative drawings enrich an unusual presentation of the traditions, folklore, and history of bread and bread making. Recipes are included.

Miles, Miska. Annie and the Old One. Illus. by Peter Parnall. 1971. Little, Brown, $16.95 (0-316-57117-2); paper, $7.95 (0-316-57120-2). **A.**

Text and pictures become an artistic whole in this poignant telling of a young Navajo's attempt to ward off her grandmother's death. A subtle portrayal of Navajo traditions and contemporary life. A Newbery Honor Book.

Mizumura, Kazue. Flower Moon Snow: A Book of Haiku. 1977. illus. Harper-Collins, $12.89 (0-690-01290-X). **M.**

Soft brown-and-black woodcuts attractively portray the seasonal moods of nature captured in evocative haiku.

Monjo, F. N. The Drinking Gourd. Illus. by Fred Brenner. 1970. HarperCollins, $15.99 (0-06-024329-5); paper, $3.99 (0-06-444042-7). **M.**

A mischievous mid-century New England boy helps an African American family to escape on the Underground Railroad in an effectively illustrated "I Can Read" history book.

Monjo, F. N. Letters to Horseface, Being the Story of Wolfgang Amadeus Mozart's Journey to Italy, 1769–1770, When He Was a Boy of Fourteen. Illus. by Don Bolognese and Elaine Raphael. 1975. Viking [o.p.]. **M.**

Imaginary letters to his sister Nanerl reveal a youthful Mozart immersed in his art, ingenuously pleased with the reception his prodigious talent wins from musical leaders.

Monjo, F. N. Poor Richard in France. Illus. by Brinton Turkle. 1973. Holt [o.p.]. **M.**

An engaging portrait of Ben Franklin emerges in an easy-to-read account of a mission to France during the Revolutionary War.

Mosel, Arlene. The Funny Little Woman. Illus. by Blair Lent. 1972. Dutton [o.p.]; Penguin/Putnam, paper, $5.99 (0-14-054753-3). **Y.**

While chasing a dumpling, a Japanese woman is captured by the wicked "Oni," but, outwitting the monsters, she escapes and becomes rich. The Asian setting is richly portrayed in the paintings. A Caldecott Medal winner.

Muller, Jorg. The Changing City. 1977. illus. Simon & Schuster/Atheneum [o.p.]. **M.**

Thought-provoking, visual experience draws the eye to evolving details and moods of a city over a 20-year period. A portfolio of paintings comments on aesthetic, social, and physical urban change.

Muller, Jorg. The Changing Countryside. 1977. illus. Simon & Schuster/ Atheneum [o.p.]. **M.**

Graphic, sequential paintings depict change in the countryside. This portfolio complements and completes the sociological statement of *The Changing City.*

Musgrove, Margaret. Ashanti to Zulu: African Traditions. Illus. by Leo and Diane Dillon. 1976. Dial, $19.99 (0-8037-0357-0); paper, $6.99 (0-14-054604-9). **Y.**

An alphabet of African tribes and customs is stunningly illustrated with representative vignettes of African life. A Caldecott Medal winner.

Myers, Walter Dean. Fast Sam, Cool Clyde, & Stuff. 1975.Viking [o.p.]; Penguin/ Puffin, paper, $5.99 (0-14-032613-8). **O.**

Eighteen-year-old Stuff recalls important, often comic, incidents with friends during the year he was 12-going-on-13 and lived in Harlem.

Nostlinger, Christine. Konrad. Illus. by Carol Nicklaus. Tr. by Anthea Bell. 1977. Watts [o.p.]. **O.**

Factory-programmed to be intelligent, well mannered, and obedient, seven-year-old Konrad is delivered by mistake to an unconventional lady.

O'Brien, Robert C. Mrs. Frisby and the Rats of NIMH. Illus. by Zena Bernstein. 1971. Simon & Schuster/Atheneum, $18 (0-689-20651-8); Aladdin, paper, $5.50 (0-689-71068-2). **M.**

Blending scientific possibility with fantasy, a fascinating talking animal tale with intriguing contemporaneous—if not prophetic—implications. A Newbery Medal winner.

O'Brien, Robert C. Z for Zachariah. 1975. Simon & Schuster/Atheneum [o.p.]; Aladdin, paper, $4.99 (0-02-044650-0). **O.**

Left alone on her father's farm in a protected futuristic valley when a nuclear holocaust strikes, Ann survives with capable assurance until a stranger invades her space.

O'Dell, Scott. Sing Down the Moon. 1970. Houghton, $18 (0-395-10919-1); Dell/Yearling, paper, $5.99 (0-440-40673-0). **O.**

A young Navajo girl tells the proud, dignified story of the tragic degradation of a great people in their forced march to Fort Sumner in 1864. A Newbery Honor Book.

Orgel, Doris. The Devil in Vienna. 1978. Dial [o.p.]; Penguin/Puffin, paper, $5.99 (0-14-032500-X). **O.**

A poignant, suspenseful tale of love and loss between two Viennese girls, one Jewish, one not, as Hitler gains powers, making clear the tragedy of alienation forced by society's norms.

Pace, Mildred Mastin. Wrapped for Eternity: The Story of the Egyptian Mummy. Illus. by Tom Huffman. 1974. McGraw-Hill [o.p.]. **M.**

A detailed, readable account of the mummification process, tomb robbing, modern anthropological investigative techniques, and the many myths surrounding the dead of ancient Egypt.

Paterson, Katherine. Bridge to Terabithia. Illus. by Donna Diamond. 1977. HarperCollins, $15.99 (0-690-01359-0); paper, $5.99 (0-06-440184-7). **M.**

Jess, defeated by Leslie in his effort to be the fifth-grade's fastest runner, becomes her best friend. Together they create their own world of imaginative play. A Newbery Medal winner.

Paterson, Katherine. The Great Gilly Hopkins. 1978. HarperCollins, $16.89 (0-690-03838-0); paper, $5.99 (0-06-440201-0). **O.**

Gilly, bounced from two foster homes, meets a trio that challenges her defenses and leads to an understanding of life and love. A Newbery Honor Book.

Paterson, Katherine. The Master Puppeteer. Illus. by Haru Wells. 1976. Crowell [o.p.]; HarperTrophy, paper, $5.99 (0-06-440281-9). **O.**

Eighteenth-century Japan and a traditional Osakan puppet theater are the backdrop for this rousing adventure.

Paterson, Katherine. Of Nightingales That Weep. Illus. by Haru Wells. 1974. Crowell [o.p.]; HarperTrophy, paper, $5.99 (0-06-440282-7). **O**.

During a civil war in feudal Japan, Takiko is torn between her duty to the emperor and her love for an enemy warrior in this sensitive, stimulating tale.

Peck, Richard. Father Figure. 1978. Viking [o.p.]; Penguin/Puffin, paper, $5.99. (0-14-037969-X). **O**.

After their mother's death, two brothers respond to their complex situation with disagreement, but perception and dignity as an absentee father returns to their lives.

Pinkwater, D. Manus. Lizard Music. 1976. illus. Dodd [o.p.]. **M**.

A strangely logical, zany story in which Victor learns of an invasion from an unknown planet, an eccentric identity-switcher called Chicken Man, and a lizard rock band.

Prelutsky, Jack. Nightmares: Poems to Trouble Your Sleep. Illus. by Arnold Lobel. 1976. Greenwillow [o.p.]. **O**.

Gruesome, grisly, ghoulish creatures of the night are diabolically described in haunting words and chilling pen-and-ink drawings.

Pringle, Laurence. Death Is Natural. 1977. illus. Simon & Schuster, [o.p.]. **M**.

A biologist's viewpoint of the continuity of plant and animal life is succinctly and naturally conveyed through simple, expressive text and photographs.

Pringle, Laurence. Wild Foods: A Beginner's Guide to Identifying, Harvesting, and Cooking Safe and Tasty Plants from the Outdoors. Illus. by Paul Breeden. 1978. Four Winds [o.p.]. **O**.

What closer encounter could one have with the vegetable world than to collect, prepare, and savor some of its more palatable members? A fine field guide to plants.

Provensen, Alice and **Provensen, Martin.** A Peaceable Kingdom: The Shaker Abecedarius. 1978. illus. Viking [o.p.]. **Y**.

A richly illustrated edition of an 1882 Shaker alphabet book in rhyme which is both artistically and historically appealing.

Raskin, Ellen. The Mysterious Disappearance of Leon (I Mean Noel). 1971. illus. Dutton [o.p.]; Putnam, paper, $5.99 (0-14-032945-5). **M**.

Caroline, wed at age five, spends much of her life tracking down her lost bridegroom Leon. This preposterous "puzzle" novel is crammed with trick word clues, zany characters, and mysterious happenings.

Raskin, Ellen. The Westing Game. 1978. Dutton, $15.99 (0-525-42320-6); Penguin/Puffin, paper, $5.99 (0-14-038664-5). **O**.

The game is the thing in this marvelous compilation of events and characters, as several families attempt to solve a puzzle and win a fortune left by an eccentric millionaire. A Newbery Medal winner.

Rayner, Mary. Mr. and Mrs. Pig's Evening Out. 1976. illus. Simon & Schuster/ Atheneum [o.p.]. **Y.**
The sweet, friendly babysitter is none other than Mrs. Wolf! Humor and suspense blend in the story and paintings.

Reiss, Johanna. The Upstairs Room. 1972. HarperCollins, $15.95 (0-690-85127-8); paper, $5.99 (0-06-447043-1). **O.**
An autobiographical novel describing the two-year confinement of Jewish sisters who are hidden by their neighbors during the Nazi occupation of Holland. A Newbery Honor Book.

Reiss, John J. Shapes. 1974. illus. Bradbury [o.p.]. **Y.**
Brilliantly colored squares, triangles, circles, and other shapes are changed into familiar three-dimensional objects with a deftness certain to fascinate.

Richter, Hans. Friedrich. Tr. by Edite Kroll. 1970. Holt [o.p.]; Penguin/Puffin, paper, $4.99 (0-14-032205-1). **O.**
Close friends before Hitler's rise to power, two German boys and their families, one of whom is Jewish, are slowly forced apart by increasing Nazi pressures. A Mildred L. Batchelder Medal winner.

Robinson, Barbara. The Best Christmas Pageant Ever. Illus. by Judith Gwyn Brown. 1972. HarperCollins [o.p.]. **M.**
The humorous, uninhibited Herdman children bring a new meaning to the local church nativity play and prove to be star performers in this realistic slice of small-town life.

Rockwell, Anne. Games (and How to Play Them). 1973. illus. Crowell [o.p.]. **A.**
Clear, simple instructions for 43 outdoor and indoor games, colorfully illustrated with cleverly costumed animals.

Rodgers, Mary. Freaky Friday. 1972. HarperCollins, $16.89 (0-06-025049-6); paper, $4.99 (0-06-440046-8). **M.**
In a funny fantasy with bouncy dialogue, 13-year-old Annabel awakens one morning to find she has become her mother.

Ryan, Cheli Durán. Hildilid's Night. Illus. by Arnold Lobel. 1971. Simon & Schuster [o.p.]. **Y.**
A ridiculous, old woman vainly tries various methods to chase away the night. Eerie black-line drawings provide the perfect accompaniment to the telling. A Caldecott Honor Book.

Ryden, Hope. The Little Deer of the Florida Keys. 1978. illus. Putnam [o.p.]. **M.**
   Miniature deer, and the efforts to save the endangered species are detailed in this photographic essay.

Sachs, Marilyn. The Bear's House. Illus. by Louis Glanzman. 1971. Doubleday [o.p.]. **M.**
   Fran Ellen is the fractious, thumb-sucking heroine of this sensitive novel about a disintegrating family.

St. John, Glory. How to Count Like a Martian. 1975. Walck [o.p.]. **M.**
   A handsomely designed math book, imaginatively dealing with number theory and counting systems, is presented in a conversational cumulative set of puzzles.

Salvadori, Mario George. Building: The Fight against Gravity. Illus. by Saralinda Hooker and Christopher Ragus. 1979. Simon & Schuster/Atheneum [o.p.]. **O.**
   Basic principles of architecture and engineering, including building materials and problems architects and engineers must overcome, are introduced.

Sandler, Martin W. The Story of American Photography: An Illustrated History for Young People. 1979. illus. Little, Brown [o.p.]. **O.**
   This magnificently illustrated book traces the development of photography and its effect on many aspects of life in the U.S.

San Souci, Robert. Legend of Scarface: A Blackfoot Indian Tale. Illus. by Daniel San Souci. 1978. Doubleday [o.p.]. **M.**
   A courageous youth journeys to the sun to overcome obstacles in order to marry the maiden he loves.

Scott, Jack Denton. Discovering the American Stork. Illus. by Ozzie Sweet. 1976. Harcourt [o.p.]. **O.**
   One of the world's most spectacular birds is the stilt-legged, sword-billed stork, which is portrayed vividly in this powerful documentary.

Scott, Jack Denton. Discovering the Mysterious Egret. Illus. by Ozzie Sweet. 1978. Harcourt [o.p.]. **O.**
   A photographic survey discloses the mysteries surrounding the egret's migration and behavior.

Scott, Jack Denton. The Gulls of Smuttynose Island. Illus. by Ozzie Sweet. 1977. Putnam [o.p.]. **O.**
   Lives of herring gulls and great black-headed gulls on New England's Smuttynose Island are described and photographed in black-and-white.

Scott, Jack Denton. Little Dogs of the Prairie. Illus. by Ozzie Sweet. 1977. Putnam [o.p.]. **O.**

Watch, look, and listen is the message in this appealing introduction to a vanishing species of American wildlife.

Sebestyen, Ouida. Words by Heart. 1979. Little, Brown, $15.95 (0-316-77931-8); Dell, paper, $4.99 (0-440-22688-0). **O.**
Triumph over hatred as the first African American family in a pioneer western farm community pays a tragic price for its determination to create a better life.

Segal, Lore. Tell Me a Mitzi. Illus. by Harriet Pincus. 1970. Farrar [o.p.]. **M.**
Flat, comic-strip colors, deliberately homely faces, and earthy humor in the illustrations for three funny, unromanticized stories of urban Jewish family life.

Seixas, Judith S. Living with a Parent Who Drinks Too Much. 1979. Greenwillow [o.p.]. **O.**
Sound, straightforward information provides the potential to help alleviate difficult problems and facilitate improved family relationships.

Selsam, Millicent E. The Harlequin Moth: Its Life Story. Illus. by Jerome Wexler. 1975. Morrow [o.p.]. **A.**
An easy text with bold print blends perfectly with exquisite photographs to detail the life cycle of the moth from egg to caterpillar to adult.

Selsam, Millicent E. Land of the Giant Tortoise. Illus. by Les Line. 1977. Four Winds [o.p.]. **M.**
Two theories of the geological formation of the Galapagos Islands and the evolving of its flora and fauna are discussed.

Selsam, Millicent E. and **Wexler, Jerome E.** The Amazing Dandelion. Illus. by Jerome Wexler. 1977. Morrow [o.p.]. **M.**
Clear, crisp photographs capture the beauty and perseverance of a hardy plant often considered a nuisance.

Selsam, Millicent E. and **Wexler, Jerome E.** Mimosa, the Sensitive Plant. Illus. by Jerome Wexler. 1978. Morrow [o.p.]. **M.**
Sharp photographs, combined with simple text, show the intriguing features of a plant that responds to heat and touch by moving.

Sendak, Maurice. In the Night Kitchen. 1970. illus. HarperCollins, $16.95 (0-06-026668-6); paper, $6.95 (0-06-443436-2). **Y.**
In an extraordinary picture book, a little boy's dream fantasy is set luminously against a transformed, darkened city resembling the flat backdrop of an old vaudeville stage. A Caldecott Honor Book.

Shulevitz, Uri. Dawn. 1974. illus. Farrar, paper, $6.95 (0-374-41689-3). **Y.**

The first appearance of light offers a unique experience as soft watercolors and simple text capture the serenity and magic of daybreak.

Shulevitz, Uri. The Treasure. 1979. illus. Farrar, $16 (0-374-37740-5); paper, $5.95 (0-374-47955-0). **Y.**

Isaac finds treasure in his own eastern European home after traveling far and wide. Spare text is accompanied by gemlike illustrations. A Caldecott Honor Book.

Singer, Isaac Bashevis. Naftali the Storyteller and His Horse, Sus, and Other Stories. Illus. by Margot Zemach. 1976. Farrar [o.p.]. **O.**

A feast of wit and wisdom is served in nine tales by a master storyteller.

Singer, Isaac Bashevis. The Wicked City. Illus. by Leonard Everett Fisher. 1972. Farrar [o.p.]. **M.**

Magnificent scratchboard illustrations in coppery red accentuate a taut retelling of the biblical story of Lot, his wife and family, and the destruction of Sodom.

Skurzynski, Gloria. What Happened in Hamelin. 1979. Four Winds [o.p.]. **O.**

Based on historical records and scientific information about hallucinatory diseases, a plausible explanation for the legend of the Pied Piper is presented from the perspective of an orphan who witnessed the events.

Sleator, William. The Angry Moon. Illus. by Blair Lent. 1970. Little, Brown [o.p.]. **Y.**

Full-color paintings, executed with careful research and creative invention, heighten the dramatic quality of a Tungit Indian legend. A Caldecott Honor Book.

Smith, Doris Buchanan. A Taste of Blackberries. Illus. by Charles Robins. 1973. HarperCollins [o.p.]. **M.**

Jamie, engaged in a lively youngster's usual summertime pursuits, is suddenly, unbelievably dead of bee stings. His best friend must learn to accept both guilt and grief as he adjusts to Jamie's death.

Snow, Richard F. Freelon Starbird. Illus. by Ben F. Stahl. 1976. Houghton [o.p.]. **O.**

Twenty-year-old Freelon offers a unglorified, sometimes earthy view of the war for independence.

Snow, Richard F. The Iron Road: A Portrait of American Railroading. Illus. by David Plowmen. 1978. Four Winds [o.p.]. **O.**

A fascinating tribute to railroads that relates them to the lives of all Americans.

Snyder, Zilpha Keatley. The Witches of Worm. Illus. by Alton Raible. 1972. Simon & Schuster/Atheneum, $17.95 (0-689-30066-2). **M.**

An ugly cat and a lonely disturbed child, seasoned with a hint of witchcraft, equal a fine novel. A Newbery Honor Book.

Spier, Peter. Noah's Ark. 1977. illus. Doubleday, $16.95 (0-085-09473-6); Dell/Yearling, paper, $7.99 (0-440-40693-5). **Y.**

Daily routines of ark life from the familiar dramatic biblical story are wordlessly captured in minutely detailed watercolor drawings. A Caldecott Medal winner.

Steel, Flora Annie. Tattercoats: An Old English Tale. Illus. by Diane Goode. 1976. Bradbury [o.p.]. **M.**

Gentle watercolor illustrations enhance the smooth retelling of an independent princess who takes fortune when it comes in this Cinderella variant.

Steig, William. Abel's Island. 1976. illus. Farrar, $16 (0-374-30010-0); paper, $5.95 (0-374-40016-4). **M.**

During a Robinson Crusoe existence on a river island, Abel, a mouse, reevaluates his easy life. A Newbery Honor Book.

Steig, William. The Amazing Bone. 1976. illus. Farrar, $17 (0-374-30248-0); paper, $5.95 (0-374-40358-9). **Y.**

A talking bone saves a charming piglet from a dastardly fox in this wry, witty telling. A Caldecott Honor Book.

Steig, William. Amos & Boris. 1971. illus. Farrar, $17 (0-374-30278-2); paper, $6.95. (0-374-40360-0). **Y.**

The devoted friendship and mutual admiration between a mouse and a whale are enhanced by attractive wide-page watercolors in this childlike tale

Sutcliff, Rosemary. Sun Horse, Moon Horse. Illus. by Shirley Felts. 1978. Dutton [o.p.]. **O.**

Inspired by the Uffington White Horse, Sutcliff's spare, sensitive narrative focuses on the son of an Iceni chieftain. Through artistry and personal sacrifice, he secures the freedom of his people from the invading Attributes.

Sutcliff, Rosemary. Tristan and Iseult. 1971. Dutton [o.p.]; Sunburst, paper, $5.95. (0-374-47982-8). **O.**

Told in modern English, this retelling of the timeless tragic love story provides historical detail, as well as the insight and understanding of the central characters.

Taylor, Mildred D. Roll of Thunder, Hear My Cry. 1976. Dial [o.p.]; Penguin/Puffin, paper, $6.99 (0-14-038451-0). **O.**

Cassie learns that more than kindness and integrity are needed to grow up black and proud in Mississippi during the Depression. A Newbery Medal winner.

Thrasher, Crystal. The Dark Didn't Catch Me. 1975. Simon & Schuster/Margaret K. McElderry [o.p.]. **O.**

Relocated on an Indiana farm during the Depression, 11-year-old Seeley learns to live with family conflict, and overcome grief and fear. Character, place, and time ring true.

Tompert, Ann. Little Fox Goes to the End of the World. Illus. by John Wallner. 1976. Crown [o.p.]. **Y.**
Little Fox travels safely to the world's end and back home for dinner in this loving story of young adventurers.

Townsend, John R. The Intruder. Illus. by Joseph A. Phelan. 1970. Lippincott [o.p.]. **O.**
A 16-year-old boy and his native environment on England's west coast are inextricably bound together in a compellingly real story of suspense.

Tripp, Wallace, ed. Granfa Grig Had a Pig and Other Rhymes without Reason. 1976. illus. Little, Brown [o.p.]. **Y.**
A rowdy, boisterous Mother Goose is matched with devastatingly hilarious illustrations.

Tunis, Edwin. The Tavern at the Ferry. 1973. illus. Crowell [o.p.]. **M.**
Historical details, enlivened with anecdotes and copious pencil drawings, trace colonial settlement growth and commerce along the Delaware River.

Turkle, Brinton. The Adventures of Obadiah. 1972. illus. Viking [o.p.]. **Y.**
In colorful paintings and dialogue, a Quaker boy's antics are amusingly juxtaposed with his family's straightlaced ways as he is suspected of telling falsehoods.

The Twelve Days of Christmas. Illus. by Brian Wildsmith. 1972. Watts [o.p.]. **A.**
The traditional English Christmas song (without music) is illustrated with trademark festive brilliance.

Van Allsburg, Chris. The Garden of Abdul Gasazi. 1979. illus. Houghton, $17.95 (0-395-27804-X). **A.**
Finely crafted, carbon pencil drawings evoke an atmosphere of bizarre fantasy in this story of a boy who follows a dog into a magician's garden. A Caldecott Honor Book.

Van Iterson, S. R. Pulga. Tr. by Alexander and Alison Gode. 1971. Morrow [o.p.]. **O.**
An impoverished 15-year-old from the Bogota slums meets a succession of violent adventures until he becomes a truck driver's helper. A Mildred L. Batchelder Medal winner.

Van Leeuwen, Jean. Tales of Oliver Pig. Illus. by Arnold Lobel. 1979. Dial [o.p.]; Penguin/Puffin, paper, $3.99 (0-14-036549-4). **Y.**
The love, joy and sorrow experienced by members of a pig family are featured in

many true-to-life situations in this easy-to-read text highlighted with illustrations.

Van Wormer, Joe. Elephants. 1976. illus. Dutton [o.p.]. **M.**
Distinctive close-up photographs show a popular mammal in its natural habitat.

Vasilisa the Beautiful. Illus. by Nonny Hogrogian. Tr. by Thomas P. Whitney. 1970. Macmillan [o.p.]. **Y.**
Colorful pictures on lightly texture paper illustrate this Russian variation on the Cinderella motif.

Viorst, Judith. Alexander and the Terrible, Horrible, No Good, Very Bad Day. 1972. illus. Simon & Schuster/Atheneum, $15 (0-689-30072-7); paper, $5.99 (0-689-71173-5). **Y.**
Alexander wishes he were in Australia on those days when everything goes wrong. Black-and-white illustrations effectively convey the frustration and humor of each episodic catastrophe.

Vipont, Elfrida. The Elephant and the Bad Baby. Illus. by Raymond Briggs. 1970. Coward [o.p.]. **Y.**
Briggs's fine details enhance the rollicking tale of a naughty twosome who helped themselves at every shop in town and went "rumpeta, rumpeta, rumpeta all down the road."

Walsh, Jill Paton. A Chance Child. 1978. Farrar [o.p.]. **O.**
A boy's journey through time into the England of the Industrial Revolution reveals early exploitation of child labor.

Walsh, Jill Paton. Unleaving. 1976. Farrar [o.p.]. **O.**
Stimulated by the intellectual pyrotechnics of some philosophy students, Madge senses that reason devoid of love may fail to penetrate the great mysteries. Sophisticated in structure, this compels attention through depth of characterization.

Watanabe, Shigeo. How Do I Put It On? Illus. by Yasuo Ohtomo. 1979. Collins World [o.p.]. **Y.**
Clear, colored illustrations reinforce the concepts of hats on heads and shoes on feet as the bare bear learns to dress himself, not without some humorous problems.

Watson, Clyde. Father Fox's Pennyrhymes. Illus. by Wendy Watson. 1971. HarperCollins, $15.95 (0-06-029501-5). **Y.**
Original nonsense rhymes singing of American country life and illustrated with watercolor-and-ink pictures depict the high-spirited antics of Father Fox and friends.

Wells, Rosemary. Morris's Disappearing Bag: A Christmas Story. 1975. illus. Dial [o.p.]. **Y.**

Pastel-colored line drawings humorously depict the Christmas Day bickering of rabbit siblings and the triumph of the youngest, whose best present makes him disappear.

Wells, Rosemary. Noisy Nora. 1973. illus. Dial, $15.99 (0-670-88722-6); paper, $6.99 (0-14-056728-3). **Y.**

Her parents just can't give little mouse Nora the attention she wants over her two siblings, so she single-mindedly wreaks a hurricane of household havoc to attract attention.

Westall, Robert. The Machine Gunners. 1976. Greenwillow [o.p.]; paper, $5.95 (0-688-15498-0). **O.**

Confiscating a machine gun from a downed German plane, the children plan to use the gun against Nazi invaders bringing them to the brink of catastrophe.

Westall, Robert. The Wind Eye. 1977. Greenwillow [o.p.]. **O.**

Three English children, on a holiday with their family on the Northumbrian coast, find a boat that takes them back to the time of St. Cuthbert, Norse invaders, and danger.

Willard, Barbara. The Iron Lily. 1974. Dutton [o.p.]. **O.**

Lilias learns to be as hard as the iron she makes in order to survive and leave her rebellious daughter secure in the uncertain world of Tudor England.

Williams, Barbara. Albert's Toothache. Illus. by Kay Chorao. 1974. Dutton [o.p.]. **Y.**

Soft brown pencil drawings enhance this engaging story about a young turtle with a toothache in his toe.

Wolf, Bernard. Anna's Silent World. 1977. illus. HarperCollins, $14.89 (0-397-32503-7). **M.**

Black-and-white photographs sensitively capture the everyday activities of six-year-old Anna, who lives in a world without sound.

Wolf, Bernard. Connie's New Eyes. 1978. illus. HarperCollins, $12.95 (0-397-31697-6). **M.**

A fascinating photo-essay acquainting the reader with a 22-year-old woman and her guide dog.

Wolff, Diane. Chinese Writing: An Introduction. Illus. by Jeanette Chien. 1975. Holt [o.p.]. **M.**

Calligraphy is presented as a high art form, a beautiful expression of the culture it represents. Basic strokes and beginning words for practice are introduced logically. Included are photos from the collection of C. C. Wang.

Wolkstein, Diane. The Magic Orange Tree and Other Haitian Folktales. Illus. by Elsa Henriquez. 1978. Knopf [o.p.]. **M.**

Authentic Haitian stories, with local color and flavorful dialogue, are prefaced by the collector's notes.

Worth, Valerie. More Small Poems. Illus. by Natalie Babbitt. 1976. Farrar [o.p.]. **A.**

Imaginative descriptions in verse of very ordinary objects from safety pins to pumpkins illustrated with precise line drawings.

Worth, Valerie. Still More Small Poems. Illus. by Natalie Babbitt. 1978. Farrar [o.p.]. **A.**

The ordinary becomes astonishing when one experiences these spare poems. Their creator has communicated every nuance of her unique perceptions.

Yarbrough, Camille. Cornrows. Illus. by Carole Byard. 1979. Putnam [o.p.]; paper, $5.99 (0-698-11436-1). **Y.**

Black children learn from their mother and great-grandmother, through conversations and storytelling, about their African heritage.

Yellow Robe, Rosebud. Tonweya and the Eagles and Other Lakota Indian Tales. Illus. by Jerry Pinkney. 1979. Dial [o.p.]. **O.**

A collection of tales, first told by Plains Indians, is interwoven with factual information about the Lakota people.

Yep, Laurence. Dragonwings. 1975. HarperCollins, $16.89 (0-06-026738-0); paper, $6.99 (0-06-440085-9). **O.**

An absorbing historical novel depicting the conflict of a Chinese immigrant caught between two costly dreams—building an aeroplane and bringing his wife to San Francisco in 1903. A Newbery Honor Book.

Zei, Alki. Petros' War. Tr. by Edward Fenton. 1972. Dutton [o.p.]. **O.**

Petros' four-year period of maturing in Greece during World War II affords a gripping picture of war and the involvement of youth, as well as a sense of war's effect on a citizenry. A Mildred L. Batchelder Medal winner.

Zemach, Harve. Duffy and the Devil: A Cornish Tale Retold. Illus. by Margot Zemach. 1973. Farrar, $17 (0-374-31887-5); paper, $6.95 (0-374-41897-7). **A.**

A hint of dialect, lively dialogue, and lusty, droll drawings make this Cornish variant of Rumplestiltskin fun to read, to tell, or to read aloud. A Caldecott Medal winner.

Zemach, Harve. A Penny a Look: An Old Story Retold. Illus. by Margot Zemach. 1971. Farrar [o.p.]. **Y.**

A "red-headed rascal" who tries to use his brother in a wild moneymaking scheme, receives his comeuppance in a spirited, genuinely funny picture book.

Zemach, Margot. Hush, Little Baby. 1976. illus. Dutton [o.p.]. **Y.**
Baby is promised all manner of things for not crying in this old folk lullaby.

Zemach, Margot. It Could Always Be Worse: A Yiddish Folk Tale. 1977. illus. Farrar [o.p.]; Turtleback, $12.10 (0-606-04438-8). **Y.**
Noise and crowding increase in the small home of a villager who follows the advice of a wise Rabbi. Vibrant illustrations explode with action in this familiar, calamitous story. A Caldecott Honor Book.

Zemach, Margot. Self-Portrait: Margot Zemach. 1978. illus. Addison-Wesley [o.p.]. **A.**
A Caldecott-winning artist tells her own story in words and pictures.

Zimnik, Reiner. The Bear and the People. Tr. by Nina Ignatowicz. 1971. illus. HarperCollins [o.p.]. **M.**
Friendship is highlighted in this deceptively simple tale of a dancing bear who walks the roads with his juggler master.

Zolotow, Charlotte. My Grandson Lew. Illus. by William Pené Du Bois. 1974. HarperCollins [o.p.]. **Y.**
A boy and his mother comfort each other with their memories of the boy's dead grandfather in a tender, lovingly rendered story.

Zolotow, Charlotte. William's Doll. Illus. by William Pené Du Bois. 1972. HarperCollins, $15.95 (0-06-027047-0); paper, $5.99 (0-06-443067-7). **Y.**
Despite gifts of a basketball and train and teasing by his older brother, William insists he wants a doll. Grandmother understands and interprets his yearning to his apprehensive father.

5

Notable Children's Books
of the 1980s

Ackerman, Karen. Song and Dance Man. Illus. by Stephen Gammell. 1988. Knopf, $15.95 (0-394-89330-1); paper, $6.99 (0-679-81995-9). **Y.**

Crisp colors and lively images expand Grandpa's stories as he takes his three grandchildren back to his days as a vaudeville entertainer. A Caldecott Medal winner.

Adoff, Arnold. All the Colors of the Race. Illus. by John Steptoe. 1982. Harper-Collins, $15.95 (0-688-00880-1). **M.**

Sensitive poems with a broad emotional range reveal a young girl's attitude toward the significance of her heritage.

Aesop's Fables. Illus. by Heidi Holder. 1981.Viking [o.p.]. **M.**

Sumptuous, intricately detailed, full-color paintings and exceptional design offer rich embellishment to the fables, which are retold in clear but sophisticated language.

Agee, Jon. The Incredible Painting of Felix Clousseau. 1988. illus. Farrar [o.p.]; paper, $4.95 (0-374-43582-0). **Y.**

Witty illustrations show a surprising chain of events when Clousseau's painted duck emerges from a canvas and quacks, involving the king, art critics, and the populace of Paris.

Ahlberg, Janet and **Ahlberg, Allan.** The Baby's Catalogue. 1983. illus. Atlantic Monthly [o.p.]. **Y.**

Far more than a list of things in baby's life, this book provides a humorous depiction of a baby's day from beginning to end.

Alcock, Vivien. The Cuckoo Sister. 1986. Delacorte [o.p.]; Houghton, paper, $4.95 (0-395-81651-3). **O.**

Is tough, vulgar Rosie really the kidnapped child her foster mother claims, or is she falsely usurping Kate's place in a cultured English family?

Alexander, Lloyd. Westmark. 1981. Dutton [o.p.]; Penguin/Putnam, paper, $5.99 (0-14-131068-5). **O.**

Experience high adventure, subtle humor, and a surprising climax in this tale of a printer's apprentice who roams his tyrannized country with a charlatan, his dwarf attendant, and an urchin who possesses ventriloquist powers.

Ancona, George. Turtle Watch. 1987. illus. Macmillan [o.p.]. **M.**
This photo-documentary shows a team of Brazilian scientists working to save endangered sea turtles and the village children who help in the effort.

Anno, Mitsumasa. Anno's Math Games. 1987. illus. Putnam/Philomel [o.p.]. **A.**
Bright, small-scale paintings enliven a creative introduction to mathematical concepts.

Arnold, Caroline. Dinosaur Mountain: Graveyard of the Past. Illus. by Richard Hewett. 1989. Clarion, $16 (0-89919-693-4). **M.**
History blends with science as excellent color photographs and text depict the present excavations at Dinosaur National Monument in Utah.

Arnosky, Jim. Drawing from Nature. 1982. illus. Lothrop [o.p.]. **M.**
A talented artist and naturalist shares his love for nature and his secrets of drawing water, land, plants, and animals.

Arnosky, Jim. Secrets of a Wildlife Watcher. 1983. illus. Lothrop [o.p.]. **M.**
Perfect for the beginner, this informative, practical, and interesting introduction to watching wildlife is illustrated in great detail.

Ashabranner, Brent. Always to Remember: The Story of the Vietnam Veterans Memorial. Illus. by Jennifer Ashabranner. 1988. Dodd [o.p.]. **O.**
Straightforward yet moving description of the building of the Vietnam Memorial, emphasizing the roles of the people behind its creation.

Avi. The Fighting Ground. 1984. HarperCollins, $15.89 (0-397-32073-6); paper, $5.99 (0-06-440185-5). **O.**
This tightly woven tale focuses on the 24 hours of April 3, 1778, during which Jonathan loses his idealized concepts of war.

Azarian, Mary. A Farmer's Alphabet. 1981. illus. Godine, $19.95 (0-87923-394-X); paper, $14.95 (0-87923-397-4). **Y.**
A well-designed ABC featuring 26 handsome woodcuts that reflect the strength and humor of everyday life in rural Vermont of the past.

Baker, Olaf. Where the Buffaloes Begin. Illus. by Stephen Gammell. 1981. Viking, paper, $6.99 (0-14-050560-1). **M.**
As the result of a young Sioux's journey to the fabled lake where buffalo are born, he unexpectedly saves his people from enemy attack. Misty, ethereal black-

and-white illustrations amplify the tale's sense of mystery, drama, and awe. A Caldecott Honor Book.

Bang, Molly. The Grey Lady and the Strawberry Snatcher. 1980. illus. Simon & Schuster, $16 (0-02-708140-0); Aladdin, paper, $5.99 (0-689-80381-8). **Y.**

Surrealistic scenes in this wordless allegorical fantasy depict a mysterious, blue monster chasing an agile, old lady through bright and gloomy scenes. A Caldecott Honor Book.

Bang, Molly. The Paper Crane. 1985. illus. Greenwillow, $16.99 (0-688-04108-6); paper, $5.95 (0-688-07333-6). **Y.**

Striking paper cutouts and a dignified text present a modern variation on this traditional tale of kindness.

Bang, Molly. Ten, Nine, Eight. 1983. illus. Greenwillow, $15.99 (0-688-00906-9); paper, $6.99 (0-688-14901-4). **Y.**

Bright, vibrant paintings and a rhythmic text combine to provide a warm, cozy bedtime countdown for a small African American child and her father. A Caldecott Honor Book.

Barton, Byron. I Want to Be an Astronaut. 1988. illus. HarperCollins, $16.89 (0-694-04744-4); paper, $6.95 (0-06-443280-7). **Y.**

With bold, simply shaped drawings and spare text, Barton follows a crew on a space shuttle mission.

Bauer, Marion Dane. On My Honor. 1986. Clarion, $15 (0-899194-39-7); Dell/Yearling, paper, $4.99 (0-440-46633-4). **M.**

A childhood dare and a sense of personal honor create a nightmare when one boy drowns and his friend must live with his conscience and grief. A Newbery Honor Book.

Bawden, Nina. Kept in the Dark. 1982. Lothrop [o.p.]. **O.**

Suspense builds throughout this gripping tale of two elderly people and three children who feel threatened by a mysteriously sinister young man.

Berry, James. A Thief in the Village and Other Worries. 1988. Watts/Orchard [o.p.]. **O.**

Everyday life in rural Jamaica, reflected both in character and incident, is re-created in several richly textured stories.

Bierhorst, John. The Naked Bear. Illus. by Dirk Zimmer. 1987. Morrow [o.p.]. **M.**

An unexpectedly humorous collection of Iroquois legends, perfect for a wide range of readers.

Bierhorst, John. Spirit Child: A Story of the Nativity. Illus. by Barbara Cooney. Tr. from the Aztec. 1984. Morrow [o.p.]; North-South/SeaStar, $15.95 (1-58717-087-6); paper, $5.95 (0-58717-088-4). **A.**

Faithful to the Aztec language of the mid-1500s, this retelling of the Christmas story is enhanced with imagery from the Aztec culture.

Blumberg, Rhoda. Commodore Perry in the Land of the Shogun. 1985. illus. HarperCollins, $18.95 (0-688-03723-2); paper, $7.99 (0-06-008625-4). **O.**

History comes to life in this richly illustrated book, as the reader follows Perry's efforts to initiate a trade treaty with Japan. A Newbery Honor Book.

Blumberg, Rhoda. The Great American Gold Rush. 1989. illus. Bradbury [o.p.]; Simon & Schuster, $17.95 (0-02-711681-6). **O.**

Well-chosen, contemporary illustrations highlight the exciting history of the search for wealth in California from 1848 to 1852.

Blumberg, Rhoda. The Incredible Journey of Lewis and Clark. 1987. illus. Lothrop [o.p.]; paper, $11.99 (0-688-14421-7). **O.**

A spirited account of the exploration of the Louisiana Purchase with well-chosen maps and photographs.

Bonners, Susan. A Penguin Year. 1981. illus. Delacorte [o.p.]. **Y.**

Adelie penguins, hardy denizens of the South Pole, are the subject of this accessible introduction to lifestyle and habits.

Brittain, Bill. The Wish Giver: Three Tales of Coven Tree. Illus. by Andrew Glass. 1983. HarperCollins, $16.89 (0-06-020687-X); paper, $5.99 (0-06-440168-5). **Y.**

The old adage, "Be careful what you wish, for it might come true," proves true when a mysterious stranger offers wishes to three young people. A Newbery Honor Book.

Brooks, Bruce. The Moves Make the Man. 1984. HarperCollins, $16.89 (0-06-020698-5); paper, $6.99 (0-06-447022-9). **O.**

Sports action provides the background for a moving story of a precarious friendship between an African American basketball player and an emotionally troubled white boy.

Brooks, Polly Schoyer. Queen Eleanor: Independent Spirit of the Medieval World. 1983. HarperCollins [o.p.]; Houghton, paper, $8.95 (0-395-98139-5). **O.**

The story of Eleanor of Aquitaine, a twelfth-century woman who was a queen to two kings and mother of two others, unfolds in an engrossing biography.

Brown, Marc. Dinosaurs Beware! A Safety Guide. 1982. illus. Atlantic Monthly [o.p.]; Little, Brown, paper, $7.99 (0-316-11219-4). **Y.**

Humor in text and pictures carries a safety message in an original way, as dinosaurs are posed in situations applying to people.

Bryan, Ashley. The Cat's Purr. 1985. illus. Simon & Schuster/Atheneum [o.p.]. **Y.**
A lively retelling of a West Indian folktale answers two puzzling questions: why do cats purr, and why do they hate rats?

Bryan, Ashley, ed. I'm Going to Sing: Black American Spirituals, vol. 2. 1982. illus. Simon & Schuster/Atheneum [o.p.]. **A.**
Black American spirituals are illustrated by the selector in moving, majestic woodcuts.

Burch, Robert. Ida Early Comes over the Mountain. 1980. Viking [o.p.]; Penguin/Puffin, paper, $4.99 (0-14-034534-5). **M.**
Ida, a most unusual housekeeper, joins the motherless Sutton family in rural Georgia of the1930s and turns their life around.

Burkert, Nancy Ekholm. Valentine and Orson. 1989. illus. Farrar, $16.95 (0-374-38078-3). **O.**
Itinerant players act out a classic tale of twins separated at birth, told in poetry and illustrated with finely detailed, colorful paintings.

Burleigh, Robert. A Man Named Thoreau. Illus. by Lloyd Bloom. 1985. Simon & Schuster/Atheneum, $15 (0-689-31122-2). **M.**
An insightful profile of the nineteenth-century writer and thinker is enhanced by black-and-white drawings that capture his true essence.

Butler, Beverly. Maggie by My Side. 1987. Dodd [o.p.]. **M.**
The emotional traumas Butler experiences after losing her guide dog, as well as the triumphs, joys, and woes of training a new guide dog, are detailed in this true story.

Cassedy, Sylvia. Behind the Attic Wall. 1983. HarperCollins, $12.95 (0-690-04336-8); Avon, paper, $5.95 (0-380-69843-9). **M.**
Weird whispers draw orphaned, alienated Maggie into a strange world inhabited by dolls that come to life.

Cassedy, Sylvia. M. E. and Morton. 1987. HarperCollins [o.p.]. **M.**
Lonely, imaginative M. E. sees her learning-disabled brother through new eyes when Polly becomes a friend with both of them.

Chaiken, Miriam. A Nightmare in History: The Holocaust, 1933–1945. 1987. Clarion [o.p.]. **O.**
A clear, well-organized, and moving description of the many individuals and governments involved in the Holocaust.

Cleary, Beverly. Dear Mr. Henshaw. 1983. Morrow, $15.95 (0-688-02405-X); HarperTrophy, paper, $5.99 (0-380-70958-9). **M**.

Leigh Botts' letters to his favorite author describe a painful year of growth and changes. A Newbery Medal winner.

Cleary, Beverly. Ramona Quimby, Age 8. Illus. by Alan Tiegreen. 1981. Morrow, $15.89 (0-688-04478-4); paper, $4.95 (0-380-70956-2). **M**.

Ramona shares her inimitable reactions to the ups and downs of being eight. A Newbery Honor Book.

Cleaver, Elizabeth. The Enchanted Caribou. 1985. illus. Simon & Schuster/ Atheneum [o.p.]. **Y**.

Shadow-puppet theater techniques bring life to an Inuit tale of courage and love.

Clifton, Lucille. My Friend Jacob. Illus. by Thomas DiGrazia. 1980. Dutton [o.p.]. **Y**.

A small boy speaks affectionately of his neighbor, older and mentally challenged, in a story of interracial friendship.

Cobb, Vicki. How to Really Fool Yourself: Illusions for All Your Senses. Illus. by Leslie Morrill. 1981. Lippincott [o.p.]. **M**.

Dozens of mind-expanding experiments linking puzzles and scientific fact prove that the senses cannot always be relied upon.

Cohen, Barbara. I Am Joseph. Illus. by Charles Mikolaycak. 1980. Lothrop [o.p.]. **O**.

Earthy, sensual, full-color pencil drawings reinforce the human feelings of a biblical hero. Joseph tells his story in thoughtful, measured tones reflective of his special wisdom.

Cohen, Barbara. Seven Daughters and Seven Sons. 1982. Simon & Schuster/ Atheneum [o.p.]; HarperTrophy, paper, $5.99 (0-688-13563-3). **M**.

In this retelling of a traditional Arabic tale, a resourceful young woman disguises herself as a man and makes her fortune.

Cole, Brock. The Goats. 1987. Farrar [o.p.]; paper, $5.95 (0-374-42575-2). **O**.

Targets of a cruel summer camp joke, a boy and girl escape from an island and struggle for survival.

Cole, Joanna. Cars and How They Go. Illus. by Gail Gibbons. 1983. HarperCollins [o.p.]. **Y**.

All of the important working parts of a car are colorfully diagrammed and clearly explained in a book for the "young mechanic."

Cole, Joanna. A Frog's Body. Illus. by Jerome Wexler. 1980. Morrow [o.p.]. **M**.

Close-up color and black-and-white photographs, diagrams, and informative text clearly and harmoniously depict the anatomy and life cycle of a bullfrog.

Cooper, Susan. The Silver Cow: A Welsh Tale. Illus. by Warwick Hutton. 1983. Simon & Schuster/Margaret K. McElderry [o.p.]; Aladdin, paper, $5.99 (0-689-71512-9). **Y.**
Luminous watercolors enhance a tale of human greed and fairy generosity.

Courlander, Harold. The Crest and the Hide and Other African Stories, Heroes, Chiefs, Bards, Hunters, Sorcerers and Common People. Illus. by Monica Vachula. 1982. Coward [o.p.]. **O.**
Many of the 20 intriguing tales, collected by a well-known authority on African oral literature, appear in print for the first time in this volume.

Cresswell, Helen. The Secret World of Polly Flint. Illus. by Shirley Felts. 1984. Macmillan [o.p.]. **M.**
In a complex fantasy set in England, a wandering boy takes Polly through a net of time.

Crews, Donald. Truck. 1980. illus. Greenwillow, $15.99 (0-688-80244-3); paper, $5.95 (0-688-10481-9). **Y.**
Line drawings, with selective use of bright colors and careful regard for perspective, combine to demand viewer involvement in this wordless depiction of an enormous, red trailer truck rolling across the country. A Caldecott Honor Book.

Cross, Gillian. On the Edge. 1985. Holiday [o.p.]. **O.**
Jinny, hearing a cry from inside an old house, decides to help the boy held prisoner there in this taut psychological tale.

Cumming, Robert. Just Look: A Book about Paintings. 1980. illus. Scribner [o.p.]. **O.**
This introduction to the various elements, such as light, color, and perspective, that make up a painting includes an analysis of over 50 well-known paintings.

Davies, Andrew. Conrad's War. 1980. Crown [o.p.]. **O.**
Conrad discovers that war is not just a game in this well-crafted fantasy that explores the nature of conflict with both wit and bitter reality.

de Regniers, Beatrice Schenk and others, eds. Sing a Song of Popcorn. 1988. illus. Scholastic [o.p.]. **O.**
Nine Caldecott medal winners achieve remarkable diversity that echoes the consistently high quality of the poems collected by Beatrice Schenk de Regniers.

Dickinson, Peter. Eva. 1989. Delacorte [o.p.]; Dell/Laurel Leaf, paper, $5.99 (0-440-20766-5). **O.**

In this highly inventive, futuristic novel, Eva, saved when her brain patterns are transplanted to a chimpanzee, establishes a future for her new self as well as for a troop of endangered apes.

Ehlert, Lois. Color Zoo! 1989. illus. HarperCollins, $16.99 (0-397-32259-3). **Y.**
This innovative introduction to shapes, colors, and geometric variants uses centered die cuts to produce nine animal faces. A Caldecott Honor Book.

Ehrlich, Amy. The Story of Hanukkah. Illus. by Ori Sherman. 1989. Dial [o.p.]. **Y.**
The story of the Jewish Festival of Lights is gracefully told with straightforward dignity and striking illustrations.

Farber, Norma and **Livingston, Myra Cohn,** eds. These Small Stones. 1987. HarperCollins, $12.95 (0-06-024013-X). **M.**
Fifty-seven short poems, taken from a variety of sources, praise the virtues of small things such as marbles, shells, paper clips, and lentils.

Fleischman, Paul. Joyful Noise: Poems for Two Voices. Illus. by Eric Beddows. 1988. HarperCollins/Charlotte Zolotow, $15.99 (0-06-021852-5); paper, $5.99 (0-06-446093-2). **M.**
Vivid language, humor, and the innovative use of two voices make this collection of poems about insects perfect for reading aloud. A Newbery Medal winner.

Fleischman, Sid. The Whipping Boy. Illus. by Peter Sís. 1986. Greenwillow, $16.99 (0-688-06216-4); paper, $4.95 (0-816-71038-4). **M.**
Prince Brat learns about friendship and loyalty when the brave whipping boy. Jemmy, and he run away, are kidnapped, and must find their way back to the palace. A Newbery Medal winner.

Flournoy, Valerie. The Patchwork Quilt. Illus. by Jerry Pinkney. 1985. Dial [o.p.]. **Y.**
A young African American girl and her family create a special quilt of memories.

Fox, Dan, ed. Go In and Out the Window: An Illustrated Songbook for Young People. 1987. illus. Holt [o.p.]. **A.**
In an enchanting collection, 61 familiar American songs, including words, music, and commentary, are cleverly combined with pictures of treasures from the Metropolitan Museum of Art.

Fox, Mem. Wilfred Gordon McDonald Partridge. Illus. by Julie Vivas. 1985. Kane/Miller [o.p.]. **Y.**
In this fresh and endearing story, the exuberance of a small boy who helps an old lady recapture her memories of long ago is portrayed in vivid watercolors.

Fox, Paula. The Moonlight Man. 1986. Simon & Schuster, $14.95 (0-02-735480-6); paper, $4.99 (0-689-85886-8). **O.**

Fifteen-year-old Catherine gets to know her alcoholic father during a summer vacation they spend together in Nova Scotia.

Fox, Paula. One-Eyed Cat. 1984. Simon & Schuster, $16 (0-02-735540-3); paper, $4.99 (0-689-83970-7). **O**.
An 11-year-old boy who believes he has maimed a cat comes to terms with his guilt in this superbly crafted novel. A Newbery Honor Book.

Freedman, Russell. Buffalo Hunt. 1988. illus. Holiday, $21.95 (0-8234-0702-0); paper, $8.95 (0-8234-1159-1). **M**.
Carefully chosen period art illuminates this well-researched account of the buffalo's role in the lives of the Great Plains Indians.

Freedman, Russell. Cowboys of the Wild West. 1985. illus. Clarion [o.p.]; paper, $9.95 (0-395-54800-4). **O**.
An accurate, lively, generously illustrated history portrays real cowboys of the Old West.

Freedman, Russell. Immigrant Kids. 1980. illus. Dutton [o.p.]; Penguin/Puffin, paper, $8.99 (0-14-037594-5). **M**.
Poignant photo-essay depicts the struggles and joys of immigrant children in turn-of-the-century New York.

Freedman, Russell. Indians Chiefs. 1987. illus. Holiday, $19.95 (0-8234-0625-3); paper, $12.95 (0-8234-0971-6). **O**.
In portraying the life histories of six famous chiefs, Freedman provides a different, historical perspective the conflict over land in the West.

Freedman, Russell. Lincoln: A Photobiography. 1987. illus. Clarion, $18 (0-89919-380-3); paper, $7.95 (0-395-51848-2). **O**.
Cogent narrative and well-chosen photographs document and bring to life Abraham Lincoln and his times. A Newbery Medal winner.

Friedman, Ina. How My Parents Learned to Eat. Illus. by Allen Say. 1984. Houghton, $15 (0-395-35379-3); paper, $5.95 (0-395-44235-4). **Y**.
A young Japanese woman and an American sailor learn about cultural differences in this gentle, warm story about lasting customs.

Fritz, Jean. The Double Life of Pocahontas. Illus. by Ed Young. 1983. Putnam, $14.99 (0-399-21016-4). **M**.
The tragic life of this Native American woman is chronicled in a carefully researched biography.

Fritz, Jean. Homesick: My Own Story. Illus. by Margot Tomes. 1982. Putnam, $16.99 (0-399-20933-6); paper, $5.99 (0-689-11782-4). **M**.

Based on the author's childhood memoirs, this fascinating book captures the beauty and turbulence prevalent in China from 1925 to 1927. A Newbery Honor Book.

Fritz, Jean. Make Way for Sam Houston. Illus. by Elise Primavera. 1986. Putnam, $16.99 (0-399-21303-1). **M.**
Flamboyant Sam Houston, effectively portrayed in this involving biography, makes his mark from Virginia to Texas.

Fritz, Jean. Shh! We're Writing the Constitution. Illus. by Tomie dePaola. 1987. Putnam [o.p.]; Turtleback, $12.14 (0-606-16217-8). **M.**
A lively, detailed, and compelling account of the conflicts and compromises in the creation of the U.S. Constitution.

Furlong, Monica. Wise Child. 1987. Knopf, $15.95 (0-294-89105-8). **M.**
This evocative fantasy set on a Celtic island involves the growth of a spoiled girl sent to live with a reputed witch in the early days of Christianity.

Gallaz, Christophe and **Innocenti, Roberto.** Rose Blanche. Tr. by Martha Coventry and Richard Graglia. 1985. illus. Creative Education [o.p.]. **O.**
Through a child's perspective, this unusual picture book for the mature reader approaches with stark realism the horrors of Nazi Germany. A Mildred L. Batchelder Medal winner.

Garfield, Leon. Footsteps. 1980. Farrar, $18 (0-374-32450-6); paper, $6.95 (0-374-42441-1). **O.**
A spine-tingling story set in eighteenth-century London of a young boy's efforts to locate and then appease the man whom his recently deceased father had cheated years before.

Gauch, Patricia Lee. Dance, Tanya. Illus. by Satomi Ichikawa. 1989. Putnam/ Philomel, $16.99 (0-399-21521-2); Paper Star, paper, $6.99 (0-698-11378-0). **Y.**
Endearing text and delicate watercolors combine in a satisfying story about a little girl who earns a chance to have ballet lessons like her big sister.

Giblin, James. From Hand to Mouth; or, How We Invented Knives, Forks, Spoons, and Chopsticks and the Table Manners to Go with Them. 1987. illus. HarperCollins [o.p.]. **O.**
The development of eating utensils and why they are used in both the East and West are presented in this entertaining, informative, historical account.

Giblin, James. Let There Be Light: A Book about Windows. 1988. HarperCollins, $16 (0-690-04693-6). **O.**
This provides an enlightening survey of social history, as the development of windows, from cave to skyscraper, is thoroughly discussed.

Ginsburg, Mirra. Across the Stream. Illus. by Nancy Tafuri. 1982. Greenwillow, $16.89 (0-688-01206-X); paper, $5.95 (0-688-10477-0). **Y.**

Brief verse, complemented by oversize, colorful illustrations, provides focus to the story of a hen and her three chicks, who are rescued by a gracious duck and her ducklings.

Goble, Paul. Buffalo Woman. 1984. illus. Simon & Schuster, $16 (0-02-737720-2); Aladdin, paper, $6.99 (0-689-71109-3). **Y.**

Striking designs and bold colors dramatize the legend of a young hunter, who, when turned away from his own family, joins his wife's people, the Buffalo Nation.

Goble, Paul. Iktomi and the Boulder: A Plains Indian Story. 1988. illus. Watts/ Orchard/Richard Jackson, $16.95 (0-531-05760-7); paper, $6.95 (0-531-07023-9). **Y.**

Iktomi boastfully attempts to outwit a boulder in this amusing, colorfully illustrated and audience-involving trickster tale.

Greenfield, Eloise. Grandpa's Face. Illus. by Floyd Cooper. 1988. Putnam/ Philomel, $16.99 (0-399-21525-5); Paper Star, paper, $6.99 (0-698-11381-0). **Y.**

In a warm family story, Tamika learns that actor Grandpa's angry face could never be meant for her. With rich earth tones and vibrant colors, the illustrator makes an outstanding debut.

Greenfield, Eloise and **Feelings, Tom.** Daydreamers. Illus. by Tom Feelings. 1981. Dial [o.p.]; paper, $6.99 (0-14-054624-3). **A.**

An artist and a poet blend their talents to reveal the spirit of childhood in a sequence of evocative portraits.

Grifalconi, Ann. The Village of Round and Square Houses. 1986. illus. Little, Brown, $16.95 (0-316-32862-6). **Y.**

Through vibrant illustrations, Gran'ma Tika recounts a traditional tale that explains why the women in the Cameroon village of Tos live in round houses while the men live in square ones. A Caldecott Honor Book.

Griffith, Helen. Georgia Music. Illus. by James Stevenson. 1986. Greenwillow [o.p.]; Avon, paper, $4.95 (0-688-09931-9). **Y.**

When a girl's grandfather grows too old to live alone on his Georgia farm, she soothes his homesickness with the musical sounds of home.

Grimm, Jakob and **Grimm, Wilhelm.** The Fisherman and His Wife. Illus. by Margot Zemach. Tr. by Randall Jarrell. 1980. Farrar [o.p.]. **Y.**

When a fisherman is granted three wishes, his greedy wife misuses them. Large, lively, full-color illustrations add zest to this traditional tale.

Grimm, Jakob and **Grimm, Wilhelm.** Hansel and Gretel. Illus. by Lisbeth Zwerger. Tr. by Elizabeth D. Crawford. 1980. Morrow [o.p.]. **Y.**

From Austria, a new version of the familiar tale. With ink-and-wash, the children are depicted in bright colors surrounded with a dark haze suggesting the evil threatening them on all sides.

Grimm, Jakob and **Grimm, Wilhelm.** Little Red Riding Hood. Illus. by Trina Schart Hyman. 1983. Holiday, $16.95 (0-8234-0470-6); paper, $6.95 (0-8234-0653-9). **Y.**
This version of a well-known fairy tale is lavishly illustrated with rich color and an abundance of detail and design. A Caldecott Honor Book.

Gryski, Camilla. Cat's Cradle, Owl's Eyes: A Book of String Games. Illus. by Tom Sankey. 1984. Morrow [o.p.]; Avon, paper, $6.95 (0-688-03941-3). **M.**
Numerous diagrams and line drawings illustrate an easy-to-follow guide to one of childhood's favorite pastimes.

Haldane, Suzanne. Painting Faces. 1988. illus. Dutton [o.p.]. **M.**
Full-color photography enlivens this intriguing glimpse of the many aspects of a worldwide art form.

Hamilton, Virginia. Anthony Burns: The Defeat and Triumph of a Fugitive Slave. 1988. Knopf [o.p.]; paper, $5.50 (0-679-83997-6). **O.**
Carefully reconstructed episodes of a life in slavery highlight this dramatically told story of Burns' historical trial.

Hamilton, Virginia. In the Beginning: Creation Stories from around the World. Illus. by Barry Moser. 1988. Harcourt, $28 (0-15-238740-4); paper, $20 (0-15-238742-0). **O.**
Each of the 25 beautifully retold myths gathered from cultures around the world is illustrated with a stunning Moser painting and accompanied by comments on sources. A Newbery Honor Book.

Hamilton, Virginia. The People Could Fly: American Black Folktales. Illus. by Leo and Diane Dillon. 1985. Knopf [o.p.]. **M.**
Hamilton retells 24 powerful stories, from well-known Brer Rabbit tales to lesser-known slave narratives.

Hamilton, Virginia. Sweet Whispers, Brother Rush. 1982. Putnam/Philomel, $21.99 (0-399-20894-1); HarperCollins, paper, $5.49 (0-380-65193-9). **O.**
A 14-year-old girl's sighting of a ghost changes her life in a rich story that uniquely combines elements of reality and fantasy. A Newbery Honor Book.

Hansen, Joyce. Which Way Freedom? 1986. Walker [o.p.]; Avon/Camelot, paper, $4.99 (0-380-71408-6). **O.**
Three escaped slaves give strength and support to each other as they journey north to join a Union regiment in the Civil War.

Hart, Jane, ed. Singing Bee: A Collection of Favorite Children's Songs. Illus. by Anita Lobel. 1982. HarperCollins, $22.95 (0-688-41975-5). **A.**

This collection of well-known and traditional lullabies, singing games, finger plays, and holiday and everyday songs is appropriately illustrated in the historical style of the eighteenth century.

Hartling, Peter. Crutches. Tr. by Elizabeth D. Crawford. 1988. HarperCollins, $12.95 (0-688-07991-1). **O.**

Searching for his mother in post–World War II Vienna, Thomas finds a compassionate survivor named Crutches, who becomes his mentor and guardian. A Mildred L. Batchelder Medal winner.

Hastings, Selina. Sir Gawain and the Loathy Lady. Illus. by Juan Wijngaard. 1985. Lothrop [o.p.]. **M.**

This distinguished retelling of an Arthurian legend is perfectly complemented by illustrations with jewel-like colors, details, and borders reminiscent of an illuminated manuscript.

Haugaard, Erik Christian. The Samurai's Tale. 1984. Houghton [o.p.]; paper, $6.95 (0-395-54970-1). **O.**

Feudal Japan provides an effective setting for orphaned Taro's efforts to prove himself worthy of his heritage.

Hausherr, Rosmarie. Children and the AIDS Virus: A Book for Children, Parents, and Teachers. 1989. Clarion [o.p.]. **Y.**

In simple terms, Hausherr explains to young children the effects of the HIV virus on the body's immune system. Amplification is provided for older children and adults.

Heide, Florence Parry. Time's Up. Illus. by Marylin Hafner. 1982. Holiday [o.p.]. **M.**

Two families living next door to each other provide contrasts in this hilariously funny story that also provides readers with some lighthearted philosophy.

Hendershot, Judith. In Coal Country. Illus. by Thomas B. Allen. 1987. Knopf [o.p.]. **O.**

The daughter of a coal miner recalls her childhood, which was filled with coal dust and love. Allen enhances this reminiscence with extraordinary pastel and charcoal illustrations.

Hest, Amy. The Purple Coat. Illus. by Amy Schwartz. 1986. Simon & Schuster [o.p.]; Aladdin, paper, $6.99 (0-689-71634-6). **Y.**

Gabrielle longs for a different kind of winter coat, but grandfather is the tailor, and mother believes in a practical navy blue.

Highwater, Jamake. Legend Days: The Ghost Horse Cycle, Part 1. 1984. Harper-Collins [o.p.]. **O.**
A Plains Indian girl's struggle for survival and identity is described in lyrical prose.

Hodges, Margaret. Saint George and the Dragon. Illus. by Trina Schart Hyman. 1984. Little, Brown, $16.95 (0-316-36789-3); paper, $6.99. (0-316-36795-8). **M.**
St. George's battle with the dragon is powerfully depicted in this richly illustrated, dignified retelling. A Caldecott Medal winner.

Hudson, Jan. Sweetgrass. 1989. Putnam/Philomel [o.p.]; paper, $5.99 (0-698-11763-8). **O.**
Fifteen-year-old Sweetgrass hopes to marry her Blackfoot sweetheart, but her intent to prove her maturity is given new direction when smallpox strikes.

Hughes, Shirley. Alfie Gets in First. 1982. illus. Lothrop [o.p.]. **Y.**
Young Alfie beats his mother home, but the door slams shut with the keys inside and the knob out of reach. Humorously detailed pictures show frantic action outside the house, as neighbors gather to help, and inside, as Alfie first cries and then copes.

Hughes, Shirley. The Big Alfie and Annie Rose Storybook. 1989. illus. Harper-Collins, $18 (0-688-07672-6). **Y.**
This ingenious collection of Alfie stories focuses on small events, which often loom large in children's lives.

Hutton, Warwick. Moses in the Bulrushes. 1986. illus. Simon & Schuster/Margaret K. McElderry [o.p.]; paper, $4.95 (0-689-71553-6). **Y.**
Powerful watercolors bring to life the world of baby Moses and his carefully planned rescue by an Egyptian princess.

Jacobs, Joseph. King of Cats. Illus. by Paul Galdone. 1980. Houghton [o.p.]. **M.**
As a gravedigger tells his wife about a strange funeral procession, his cat becomes increasingly agitated. Appropriately scary illustrations add to the tension of this gripping tale.

Jaquith, Priscilla. Bo Rabbit Smart for True: Folktales from the Gullah. Illus. by Ed Young. 1981. Putnam/Philomel [o.p.]. **M.**
Four funny stories about old Bo Rabbit, who doesn't let too much get past him. Expressive black-and-white pencil drawings, arranged in storyboard format, add drama and detail.

Jaspersohn, William. How the Forest Grew. Illus. by Chuck Eckart. 1980. Greenwillow [o.p.]; HarperTrophy, paper, $6.95 (0-688-11508-X). **Y.**
An abandoned farm is gradually transformed into a dense forest. A simple, lucid description of the forest ecosystem is presented with dramatic details masterfully highlighted by pen-and-ink illustrations.

Johnson, Sylvia and **Aamodt, Alice.** Wolf Pack: Tracking Wolves in the Wild. 1985. illus. Lerner, $23.95 (0-8225-1577-6); paper, $6.95 (0-8225-9526-5). **M.**

This well-researched and clearly presented account of life in a wolf pack includes exciting close-up photographs.

Jonas, Ann. Round Trip. 1983. illus. Greenwillow, $15.99 (0-688-01772-X); paper, $5.99 (0-688-09986-6). **Y.**

Illustrated with highly original black-and-white graphics, this inventive picture book may be read forward, backwards, and upside down.

Jonas, Ann. The Trek. 1985. illus. Greenwillow [o.p.]; HarperTrophy, paper, $5.99 (0-688-08742-6). **Y.**

A little girl's walk to school becomes a marvelous fantasy adventure as she sees wild animals in everyday objects.

Jones, Diana Wynne. Howl's Moving Castle. 1986. Greenwillow, $16.95 (0-688-06233-4); paper, $6.99 (0-06-441034-X). **O.**

In a humorous, unpredictable fantasy, an enchanted girl transformed into an old woman tries to force the Wizard Howl into undoing the spell.

Jones, Diana Wynne. The Lives of Christopher Chant. 1988. Greenwillow, $15.95 (0-06-029877-4); paper, $5.95 (0-688-16365-3). **O.**

Christopher explores an array of parallel worlds while discovering his own role in life amid an inventive cascade of comical and satirical words and magic.

Jukes, Mavis. Blackberries in the Dark. Illus. by Thomas B. Allen. 1985. Knopf, $14.95 (0-394-87599-0); paper, $4.50 (0-679-86570-5). **M.**

In a gentle story that binds generation to generation, Austin and his newly widowed grandmother strengthen their relationship.

Jukes, Mavis. Like Jake and Me. Illus. by Lloyd Bloom. 1984. Knopf [o.p.]; paper, $7.99 (0-394-89263-1). **M.**

In a story illustrated with impressionistic pastels, a wolf spider provides an unexpected avenue for bringing Alex and his stepfather closer together in this dramatic story of family relationships. A Newbery Honor Book.

Kasza, Keiko. The Wolf's Chicken Stew. 1987. illus. Putnam, $16.99 (0-399-21400-3); Paper Star, paper, $6.99 (0-698-11374-8). **Y.**

A conniving wolf plots to consume an unsuspecting hen but is outwitted by her charming and numerous chicks.

Kerr, M. E. Little Little. 1981. HarperCollins [o.p.]; paper, $5.99 (0-06-447061-X). **O.**

The unusual romance between a "perfectly formed" 41-inch daughter of wealthy parents and a dwarf who acts in TV commercials comes alive in this witty and compassionate account of people who, though different, have the same feelings and aspirations as those in the mainstream.

Khalsa, Dayal Kaur. I Want a Dog. 1987. illus. Tundra, $16.95 (0-8776-196-8); paper, $7.95 (0-88776-326-X). **Y.**
   Droll paintings illumine this tale of a determined little girl who "trains" a roller skate to prove her readiness to take responsibility for a dog.

Khalsa, Dayal Kaur. Tales of a Gambling Grandma. 1986. illus. Tundra [o.p.]; paper, $7.95 (0-88776-335-9). **M.**
   An offbeat portrait of a young girl's relationship with her zany, Russian-born grandmother.

Kimmel, Eric. Hershel and the Hanukkah Goblins. Illus. by Trina Schart Hyman. 1989. Holiday [o.p.]; paper, $6.95 (0-8234-1131-1). **Y.**
   Eerie, effective artwork illuminates this original tale of a wanderer who outwits the demons who have prevented a village from celebrating Hanukkah. A Caldecott Honor Book.

King-Smith, Dick. Babe: The Gallant Pig. Illus. by Mary Rayner. 1985. Random, $15 (0-517-55556-5); paper, $4.99 (0-679-87393-7). **M.**
   With surprising results, a motherly sheepdog trains an innately courteous pig in the ways of her ancestors.

King-Smith, Dick. Martin's Mice. Illus. by Jez Alborough. 1989. Crown [o.p.]; Knopf, paper, $4.99 (0-679-89098-X). **M.**
   In a beguiling farmyard drama, a kitten learns that, even with the best intentions, it is cruel to keep mice as pets.

King-Smith, Dick. Pigs Might Fly. Illus. by Mary Rayner. 1982. Viking [o.p.]; Penguin/Puffin, paper, $5.99 (0-14-034537-X). **M.**
   Daggie Dogfoot's rise from the runt of the litter to the farm's only swimming pig is told with restrained humor and accompanied by adroit sketches.

Kitchen, Bert. Animal Alphabet. 1984. illus. Dial [o.p.]; Penguin, paper, $7.99 (0-14-054601-4). **Y.**
   Animals humorously interact with letters in this strikingly designed work.

Kitzinger, Sheila. Being Born. Illus. by Lennart Nilsson. 1986. Putnam [o.p.]. **A.**
   Poetic text and astounding in utero photographs combine to record human life from conception to birth.

Krementz, Jill. How It Feels When a Parent Dies. 1981. illus. Knopf [o.p.]; paper, $15 (0-394-75854-4). **M.**

Eighteen young people speak openly and unreservedly of their experiences surrounding a parent's death. Interviews and photographs show that feelings of anguish, guilt, confusion, and anger are normal and even appropriate.

Kuskin, Karla. Dogs and Dragons, Trees and Dreams: A Collection of Poems. 1980. illus. HarperCollins [o.p.]; paper, $7.66 (0-06-023543-8). **Y.**
A retrospective collection brings together the poems of a well-loved children's poet. Subjects range from "Hughbert with the glue" to "a man who was so fat he wore a bathtub for a hat." Includes introductory notes on the writing.

Kuskin, Karla. The Philharmonic Gets Dressed. Illus. by Marc Simont. 1982. HarperCollins, $15.99 (0-06-023622-1); paper, $5.95 (0-06-443124-X). **Y.**
Colored charcoal cartoon drawings allow a lighthearted peek at the members of the orchestra as they don suspenders, stockings, brassieres, and bow ties; pick up their instruments; and go to work to play beautiful music.

Langton, Jane. The Fledgling. Illus. by E. Blegvad. 1980. HarperCollins [o.p.]. **M.**
Georgie, the smallest, soberest member of an eccentric Concord family, finds out she can fly—at least for a while. Fantasy and reality mesh well, with well-carved characters that are warm and believable. A Newbery Honor Book.

Larrick, Nancy, ed. Cats Are Cats. Illus. by Ed Young. 1988. Putnam/Philomel [o.p.]. **M.**
Young's splendid subtlety and artistry complement a fine selection of appealing poems about the endlessly fascinating cat.

Larrick, Nancy, ed. When the Dark Comes Dancing: A Bedtime Poetry Book. Illus. by John Wallner. 1983. Putnam/Philomel, $17.99 (0-399-61288-2). **M.**
This distinctive collection of poetry is a perfect listening and visual treat to share with children before going to bed.

Lasky, Kathryn. Puppeteer. 1985. illus. Macmillan [o.p.]. **M.**
Well-chosen words and sharp photographs introduce readers to a master puppeteer and his art as he carefully prepares and presents a production of "Aladdin and His Wonderful Lamp."

Lasky, Kathryn. Sugaring Time. 1983. illus. Macmillan [o.p.]; Aladdin, paper, $6.99 (0-689-71081-X). **M.**
Photographs of a Vermont family bring the process of maple sugaring vividly to life. A Newbery Honor Book.

Lauber, Patricia. Dinosaurs Walked Here and Other Stories Fossils Tell. 1987. illus. Simon & Schuster [o.p.]; paper, $5.95 (0-689-71603-6). **M.**
Clear, color photographs accompany a lucid description of how fossils reveal information about prehistoric plant and animal life.

Lauber, Patricia. Journey to the Planets. 1982. illus. Crown [o.p.]. **O.**
Stunning photographs and a solid text present the history and physical characteristics of the nine planets and their moons.

Lauber, Patricia. Tales Mummies Tell. 1985. illus. HarperCollins, $17.89
(0-690-04389-9). **O.**
The author describes Egyptian, Incan, and Danish mummies, explaining what
they reveal about ancient civilizations.

Lauber, Patricia. Volcano: The Eruption and Healing of Mount St. Helens. 1986.
illus. Simon & Schuster [o.p.]; Aladdin, paper, $8.99 (0-689-71679-6). **O.**
Insightful text and photographs document the damage and slow rebirth of a
mountain following a volcanic eruption. A Newbery Honor Book.

Lavies, Bianca. It's an Armadillo. 1989. illus. Dutton [o.p.]. **Y.**
Handsome, full-color photographs and brief text present the engaging armadillo.

L'Engle, Madeleine. A Ring of Endless Light. 1980. Farrar, $20 (0-374-36299-8);
Dell/Laurel Leaf, paper, $5.99 (0-440-97232-9). **O.**
Vicky Austin, 15, and her family come to the island to be with their long dying
grandfather in his final months. Life takes on new meaning for Vicky as she
becomes aware of her own ability to cope and communicate with family, friends,
and dolphins. A Newbery Honor Book.

Lerner, Carol. Pitcher Plants—The Elegant Insect Traps. 1983. illus. Morrow
[o.p.]. **O.**
Finely detailed drawings accompany a brief, intelligent look at this family of
insect-eating plants.

Lerner, Carol. Seasons of the Tallgrass Prairie. 1980. illus. Morrow [o.p.]. **O.**
Plant life of an American prairie, season by season, is carefully detailed with attention to ecological interrelationships. Illustrated with meticulous pen drawings.

Levine, Ellen. I Hate English! Illus. by Steve Bjorkman. 1989. Scholastic [o.p.]. **Y.**
Young Mei Mei, newly arrived from Hong Kong, refuses to speak English until
an innovative and sympathetic teacher intervenes.

Levinson, Riki. Watch the Stars Come Out. Illus. by Diane Goode. 1985. Dutton
[o.p.]; Penguin/Puffin, paper, $6.99 (0-14-055506-4). **Y.**
Soft colored paintings enhance the story of the hardships that two immigrant
children experience on their voyage to America and their joy at finally being
reunited with their parents.

Levitin, Sonia. The Return. 1987. Simon & Schuster/Atheneum, $16 (0-689-
31309-8); Fawcett, paper, $5.99 (0-449-70280-4). **O.**

An adolescent Ethiopian Jewish girl escapes to Israel with her older brother and younger sister in a harrowing journey of hardship and hope.

Lindgren, Barbro. Sam's Bath. Illus. by Eva Eriksson. 1983. Morrow [o.p.]; Avon, paper, $6.95 (0-688-02362-2). **Y.**
Sam's bath becomes an adventure portrayed in lively sketches.

Lisle, Janet Taylor. Afternoon of the Elves. 1989. Scholastic, $16 (0-531-08437-X); paper, $4.99 (0-698-1806-5). **M.**
Lisle provides an intriguing portrait of an isolated girl who shares her unique magic world with the girl next door. A Newbery Honor Book.

Little, Jean. Hey World, Here I Am! Illus. by Sue Truesdell. 1989. HarperCollins, $13 (0-06-023989-1); paper, $4.99 (0-06-440384-X). **O.**
Insightful and poignant, these funny poems and vignettes tell about life from a teenage girl's viewpoint.

Little, Jean. Little by Little: A Writer's Education. 1988. Viking [o.p.]; Penguin/ Puffin, paper, $5.99 (0-14-032325-2). **M.**
The author's vivid descriptions of her childhood in Taiwan and Canada reveal the sources of strength and feeling in her work.

Livingston, Myra Cohn. A Circle of Seasons. Illus. by Leonard Everett Fisher. 1982. Holiday [o.p.]; paper, $5.95 (0-8234-0656-3). **M.**
The four seasons are eloquently revealed in a medley of short poems and paintings. Colors blend from one picture to the next until, circle complete, the first is last.

Lobel, Arnold. The Book of Pigericks—Pig Limericks. 1983. illus. HarperCollins, $15 (0-06-023982-4). **M.**
Limericks featuring droll illustrations of pigs are presented in this jolly, hilarious picture book.

Lobel, Arnold. Fables. 1980. illus. HarperCollins, $15.99. (0-06-023973-5); paper, $6.99 (0-06-443046-4). **M.**
Short, original fables with fresh, unexpected morals poke subtle fun at human foibles through the antics of animals. Full-color droll illustrations are complete and humorous stories in themselves. A Caldecott Medal winner.

Lobel, Arnold. Ming Lo Moves the Mountain. 1982. illus. Greenwillow [o.p.]; paper, $5.99 (0-688-10995-0). **Y.**
Soft, luminous illustrations highlight this clever, tongue-in-cheek tale of a man and his wife who love their home—but not the mountain that rises about it.

Lobel, Arnold. On Market Street. Illus. by Anita Lobel. 1981. Greenwillow, $16.95 (0-688-80309-1); HarperTrophy, paper, $6.99 (0-688-08745-0). **Y.**

Detailed, eye-catching, full-color illustrations portray vendors who sell everything from A to Z, ingeniously adorned in their specialty wares. A Caldecott Honor Book.

Lobel, Arnold. The Random House Book of Mother Goose. 1986. illus. Random, $19.95 (0-679-88736-9). **Y.**
An extraordinary, extensive collection of nursery rhymes is vividly illustrated in full color.

Loh, Morag. Tucking Mommy In. Illus. by Donna Rawlins. 1988. Watts/Orchard [o.p.]; Scholastic, paper, $5.95. (0-531-07025-5). **Y.**
When Mommy collapses in exhaustion on the children's bed, Sue and Jenny take charge in this charming and realistic role-reversal story.

Lord, Bette Bao. In the Year of the Boar and Jackie Robinson. Illus. by Marc Simont. 1984. HarperCollins, $16.89 (0-06-024004-0); paper, $5.99 (0-06-440175-8). **M.**
A wonderfully evocative, humorous portrait of a young Chinese girl's introduction to Brooklyn and baseball in the late 1940s.

Louie, Ai-Ling. Yeh-Shen: A Cinderella Story from China. Illus. by Ed Young. 1982. Putnam/Philomel, $16.99 (0-399-20900-X); paper, $6.99 (0-698-11388-8). **Y.**
Translated and retold with graceful simplicity, this ancient tale comes to life in glowing pastels and shimmering watercolors.

Low, Joseph. Mice Twice. 1980. illus. Simon & Schuster/Atheneum [o.p.]; Aladdin, paper, $5.99 (0-689-71060-7). **Y.**
The tale of a humorous battle of wits between a mouse and a cat is told in simple text and bright watercolor drawings. A Caldecott Honor Book.

Lowry, Lois. Anastasia Again! Illus. by Diane deGroat. 1981. Houghton, $16 (0-395-31147-0). **M.**
A move to the suburbs precipitates a host of new and hilarious experiences for Anastasia and her precocious two-year-old brother. The ramifications of being 12 are wittily woven into a tale of learning to deal with unexpected change.

Lowry, Lois. Number the Stars. 1989. Houghton, $16 (0-395-51060-0); Dell/Yearling, paper, $5.99 (0-440-40327-8). **M.**
Lowry powerfully relates the story of 10-year-old Annemarie's crucial role in saving her friend's family from the Nazi roundup of Danish Jews during World War II. A Newbery Medal winner.

Lunn, Janet. The Root Cellar. 1983. Scribner, $17 (0-684-17855-9); Penguin/Puffin, paper, $5.99 (0-14-038036-1). **M.**
Lonely and unhappy in Canada, Rose rushes into an old root cellar and travels back through time to the Civil War period, where she experiences exciting adventures.

Macaulay, David. Mill. 1983. illus. Houghton, $18 (0-395-34830-7); paper, $9.95 (0-395-52019-3). **O.**

Large, detailed drawings and a precise text relate the history of New England's textile industry.

Macaulay, David. The Way Things Work. 1988. illus. Houghton, $35 (0-395-93847-3). **M.**

How and why everything works, from parking meters to pumps and from simple levers to microwave ovens, become wonderfully clear with Macaulay's complete and amusing illustrations.

MacDonald, Suse. Alphabatics. 1986. illus. Simon & Schuster [o.p.]; paper, $6.95 (0-689-71625-7). **Y.**

With the deftness of an acrobat, each brightly colored letter of the alphabet gradually changes its shape until it resembles an object or animal beginning with that letter. A Caldecott Honor Book.

MacLachlan, Patricia. The Facts and Fictions of Minna Pratt. 1988. HarperCollins/ Charlotte Zolotow, $15.89 (0-06-024117-9); paper, $5.99 (0-06-440265-7). **M.**

In a coming-of-age story, Minna achieves her goal as a musician and comes to understand that fact and fiction present different truths.

MacLachlan, Patricia. Sarah, Plain and Tall. 1985. HarperCollins. $14.99 (0-06-024101-2); paper, $4.99 (0-06-440205-3). **M.**

Caleb and Anna hope that their father's mail-order bride, who has come to their prairie home for a trial stay, will love them, decide to stay, and marry their father. A Newbery Medal winner.

Maestro, Betsy and **Maestro, Giulio.** A More Perfect Union: The Story of Our Constitution. 1987. illus. HarperCollins, $15.93 (0-688-06840-5). **M.**

Clear and large watercolor paintings trace the dramatic events surrounding the creation and ratification of the Constitution.

Maestro, Betsy and **Maestro, Giulio.** Traffic: A Book of Opposites. 1981. illus. Crown [o.p.]. **Y.**

On its homeward journey, a rounded little magenta car is the focal point for this exploration of opposites.

Magorian, Michelle. Good Night, Mr. Tom. 1982. HarperCollins, $17.89 (0-06-024079-2); paper, $6.99 (0-06-440174-X). **O.**

In this unflinchingly honest novel set during World War II, a battered child finds love and compassion from a crusty old English villager.

Mahy, Margaret. The Changeover: A Supernatural Romance. 1984. Simon & Schuster/Margaret K. McElderry, $16 (0-689-50303-2). **O.**

Witchery and romance are finely combined as Laura, fighting to save her younger brother from a demon, unleashes the supernatural powers within her.

Marshall, James. Goldilocks and the Three Bears. 1988. illus. Dial, $16.99 (0-8037-0542-5); Penguin/Puffin, paper, $6.99 (0-14-056366-0). **Y.**

A delightfully irreverent retelling of an old favorite is illustrated with delicious humor and contemporary touches. A Caldecott Honor Book.

Martin, Bill and **Archambault, John.** Chicka Chicka Boom Boom. Illus. by Lois Ehlert. 1989. Simon & Schuster, $15 (0-671-67949-X). **Y.**

In rollicking, contagious verse and ingenious visuals, the letters of the alphabet go on an adventure to the top of a coconut tree.

Maruki, Toshi. Hiroshima No Pika. 1982. illus. Lothrop [o.p.]. **O.**

Told from a child's viewpoint, this deeply moving, visual account, translated from the Japanese, describes the devastating effects of the atomic bomb dropped on August 6, 1945. A Mildred L. Batchelder Award winner.

Mazer, Norma Fox. After the Rain. 1987. HarperCollins, $16.95 (0-688-06867-7); Avon, paper, $5.99 (0-380-75025-2). **O.**

Sensitive, journal-writing Rachel and her irascible grandfather develop a special relationship during the last months of his life. A Newbery Honor Book.

Mazer, Norma Fox. Mrs. Fish, Ape, and Me, the Dump Queen. 1980. Dutton [o.p.]; Avon, paper, $3.50 (0-380-69153-1). **M.**

Ostracized by her schoolmates because her uncle manages the town dump, an orphaned adolescent makes friends with Mrs. Fish, an idiosyncratic school custodian—a relationship that eventually welds the three outcasts into a family.

McCully, Emily Arnold. Picnic. 1984. illus. HarperCollins, $16.89 (0-06-024100-4). **Y.**

When he becomes lost on his way to a family outing, a small mouse has his own adventure in this lively, wordless book.

McKinley, Robin. The Blue Sword. 1982. Greenwillow, $16.99 (0-688-00938-7). **O.**

In this romantic fantasy of adventure and swordplay, a young girl, Harry, is transported to the hill country where she becomes a recognized leader and, finally, a queen. A Newbery Honor Book.

McKinley, Robin. The Hero and the Crown. 1984. Greenwillow, $16.99 (0-688-02593-5); Berkley/Ace, paper, $5.99 (0-441-32809-1). **O.**

This exciting story has all one could wish for in high fantasy—dragons, wizards, and a beautiful, competent heroine. A Newbery Medal winner.

McKinley, Robin. The Outlaws of Sherwood. 1988. Greenwillow [o.p.]; Berkley/ Ace, paper, $6.50 (0-441-64451-1). **O.**

A hapless Robin, whose archery is inferior to Maid Marion's, is the semihero of a Sherwood troupe of lively, endearing, and triumphant misfits.

McKissack, Patricia, and **McKissack, Fredrick.** A Long Hard Journey: The Story of the Pullman Porter. 1989. illus. Walker, $21.95 (0-8027-6884-9); paper, $9.95 (0-8027-7437-7). **O.**

The epic struggle of railroad porters to begin the first African American–controlled union is powerfully portrayed.

McKissack, Patricia. Mirandy and Brother Wind. Illus. by Jerry Pinkney. 1988. Knopf, $17 (0-394-88765-4). **Y.**

After capturing Brother Wind, Mirandy uses her newfound power to win first prize in the junior cakewalk with her friend Ezel. A Caldecott Honor Book.

McLaughlin, Molly. Earthworms, Dirt, and Rotten Leaves: An Exploration in Ecology. Illus. by Robert Shetterly. 1986. Simon & Schuster/Atheneum [o.p.]; Avon, paper, $3.50 (0-380-71074-9). **M.**

This simple introduction to ecology explains basic scientific concepts, focusing on the earthworms.

McMillan, Bruce. Counting Wildflowers. 1986. illus. Lothrop [o.p.]; Avon, paper, $4.95 (0-688-14027-0). **Y.**

Complete with an appendix of scientific names and a finding guide, this handsome book of striking color photographs of wildflowers is also a counting book.

McNulty, Faith. Peeping in the Shell. Illus. by Irene Brady. 1986. HarperCollins, $11.95 (0-06-024134-9). **M.**

Inherent drama and suspense enliven the true story of the hatching of a whooping crane chick from an artificially inseminated egg.

Meltzer, Milton. The Black Americans: A History in Their Own Words, 1619–1983. Rev. ed. 1984. illus. HarperCollins [o.p.]; paper, $11.99 (0-06-446055-X). **O.**

Primary sources, effectively used, form a strong statement about the black experience.

Meltzer, Milton. The Jewish Americans: A History in Their Own Words. 1982. illus. HarperCollins [o.p.]. **O.**

Excerpts from diaries, letters, and other sources illuminate the experiences of Jews in America, from colonial times to the resettlement of Holocaust survivors in the 1950s.

Menotti, Gian Carlo. Amahl and the Night Visitors. Illus. by Michele Lemieux. 1986. HarperCollins, $22.95 (0-688-05426-9). **A.**

This faithful adaptation of the much-loved opera tells the story of a child and his mother who are visited by three wise men on their way to Bethlehem. Extraordinary earth-tone watercolors capture the mood of the tale.

Moeri, Louise. Save Queen of Sheba. 1981. Dutton [o.p.]; Penguin/Puffin, paper, $4.99 (0-14-037148-6). **M.**
A compelling survival story of 12-year-old King David, who, regaining consciousness after a wagon-train massacre on a barren plain, realizes he must assume responsibility for his little sister's life.

Moore, Lillian. Something New Begins: New and Selected Poems. Illus. by Mary Kay Dunton. 1982. Simon & Schuster/Atheneum [o.p.]. **Y.**
This handsome volume includes poems, old and new, that make everyday experiences sparkle in a new light.

Myers, Walter Dean. Me, Mop, and the Moondance Kid. Illus. by Rodney Pate. 1988. Delacorte [o.p.]. **M.**
Three kids from Jersey City play baseball and learn to get along with their adoptive parents in this lighthearted but perceptive narrative.

Myers, Walter Dean. Scorpions. 1988. HarperCollins, $16.99 (0-06-024364-3); paper, $5.99 (0-06-447066-0). **O.**
Two vulnerable boys are caught up in overwhelming circumstances involving poverty, drugs, gangs, and guns. A Newbery Honor Book.

Naylor, Phyllis Reynolds. The Agony of Alice. 1985. Simon & Schuster/ Atheneum, $17 (0-689-31143-5); paper, $4.99 (0-689-81672-3). **M.**
Humor and insight spark sixth-grader Alice McKinley's search for a perfect role model.

Nelson, Theresa. And One for All. 1989. Watts/Orchard/Richard Jackson, $16.95 (0-531-05804-2); Dell/Yearling, paper, $4.50 (0-440-40456-8). **O.**
Tensions caused by the Vietnam War dramatically change 12-year-old Geraldine's relationship with her beloved brother, Wing, and his best friend, Sam.

Nilsson, Ulf. If You Didn't Have Me. Illus. by Eva Eriksson. 1987. Simon & Schuster/Margaret K. McElderry [o.p.]. **M.**
Amusing episodes chart the subtle growth of a small Swedish boy as he spends the summer on his grandmother's farm while his parents build a new home. A Mildred L. Batchelder Medal winner.

Noble, Trinka Hakes. The Day Jimmy's Boa Ate the Wash. Illus. by Steven Kellogg. 1980. Dial, $16.99 (0-8037-1723-7); Dutton, paper, $6.99 (0-14-054623-5). **Y.**

A class field trip to a farm turns into an outrageous slapstick romp. Told in low-key, droll, mother-and-child dialogue balanced with action-filled pictures that detail the riotous events.

Norton, Mary. The Borrowers Avenged. Illus. by Beth Krush and Joe Krush. 1982. Harcourt, $17 (0-15-210530-1). **M.**

In this new addition to the Borrowers series, the tiny Clock family, Pod, Homily and Arietty, escape from the wicked Platters, find a new home, and embark on many adventures.

Oakley, Graham. Magical Changes. 1980. illus. Simon & Schuster/Atheneum [o.p.]. **A.**

Split pages enable the reader to create hundreds of combinations of images with Oakley's amazing surrealistic paintings.

Oneal, Zibby. A Formal Feeling. 1982. Viking [o.p.]. **O.**

A family gathering over Christmas vacation serves as the framework for this subtle, poignant study of a girl working through her grief and the memory of a mother she idolized.

Oneal, Zibby. In Summer Light. 1985. Viking [o.p.]. **O.**

The daughter of a famous artist comes to terms with her own talent in a book notable for its verbal imagery.

Opie, Iona and **Opie, Peter.** Tail Feathers from Mother Goose: The Opie Rhyme Book. 1988. illus. Little, Brown [o.p.]. **Y.**

This collection of nursery rhymes includes unusual variations that are as diverse as the illustrations by leading artists from the United Kingdom and the United States.

Orlev, Uri. The Island on Bird Street. Tr. by Hillel Halkin. 1984. Houghton $16 (0-395-33887-5); paper, $6.95 (0-395-61623-9). **O.**

A riveting chronicle of World War II details the survival of Alex, who is kept alive by his wits and the hope of his father's return, as he hides out in an abandoned building in the Warsaw ghetto. A Mildred L. Batchelder Medal winner.

Ormerod, Jan. Sunshine. 1981. Lothrop [o.p.]. **Y.**

Illustrated with warmth and humor, this wordless picture book depicts a family's morning routines as viewed through the eyes and activities of its youngest member.

O'Shea, Pat. Finn MacCool and the Small Men of Deeds. Illus. by Steven Lavis. 1987. Holiday [o.p.]. **Y.**

Finn and a team of remarkably talented small men solve a giant problem in fine, high style.

Otsuka, Yuro. Suho and the White Horse: A Legend of Mongolia. Illus. by Suekichi Akaba. 1981. Viking [o.p.]. **Y.**

A noble's greed is portrayed in spacious paintings that take the reader to the heart of the Mongolian steppes. Adapted from a translation by Ann Herring.

Owens, Mary Beth. A Caribou Alphabet. 1988. illus. Dog Ear Press [o.p.]; Farrar/Sunburst, paper, $4.95 (0-374-41043-7). **Y.**

From *A* for antlers to *Z* for below-zero weather, lighthearted couplets take readers into the natural world of the caribou.

Oxenbury, Helen. The Dancing Class. 1983. illus. Dial [o.p.]. **Y.**

Both children and parents will enjoy this joyful, funny look at a preschool ballet class.

Park, Ruth. Playing Beatie Bow. 1982. Simon & Schuster/Atheneum [o.p.]. **O.**

In this spellbinding novel, set in Sydney, Australia, Abigail follows a strange girl and finds herself living in the previous century.

Parks, Van Dyke and **Jones, Malcolm.** Jump! The Adventures of Brer Rabbit. Illus. by Barry Moser. 1986. Harcourt [o.p.]. **M.**

Small, feisty, and occasionally too sure of himself, Brer Rabbit proves smarter and faster than most of his fellow animals.

Paterson, Katherine. Jacob Have I Loved. 1980. HarperCollins, $15.99 (0-690-04078-4); paper, $6.50 (0-06-440368-8). **O.**

Living in the shadow of her talented twin sister, Louise views herself as inadequate and unloved. Retreating to the Chesapeake Bay waterways where her father plies his boat, she ultimately leaves her family and the island for the Appalachian hills, where she finds a sense of her own worth. A Newbery Medal winner.

Paulsen, Gary. Dogsong. 1985. Simon & Schuster, $16 (0-02-770180-8); Aladdin, paper, $15.50 (0-689-80409-1). **O.**

An Inuit teenager discovers his "dogsong" on a vision quest across the tundra. A Newbery Honor Book.

Paulsen, Gary. Hatchet. 1987. Simon & Schuster [o.p.]; Aladdin, paper, $5.99 (0-689-80882-8). **O.**

Brian's amazing 54-day survival in the Canadian wilderness following a single-engine plane crash is chronicled in fascinating and exciting detail. A Newbery Honor Book.

Paulsen, Gary. The Winter Room. 1989. Watts/Orchard/Richard Jackson, $15.95 (0-531-05839-5); Dell/Yearling, paper, $4.99 (0-440-40454-1). **O.**

Uncle David's powerful stories extend young Eldon's understanding of his heritage and his family in this poetic evocation of life on a Minnesota farm. A Newbery Honor Book.

Peck, Richard. Remembering the Good Times. 1985. Delacorte [o.p.]; Dell/Laurel Leaf, paper, $5.50 (0-440-97339-2). **O.**

A special bond between three teenagers helps two of them survive the loss of their friend.

Peet, Bill. Bill Peet: An Autobiography. 1989. illus. Houghton, $22 (0-395-50932-7); paper, $14 (0-395-68982-1). **M.**

The beloved author/illustrator extends this humorous account of his life with witty pictures. A Caldecott Honor Book.

Pinkwater, Jill. Buffalo Brenda. 1989. Macmillan [o.p.]. **O.**

In these wacky adventures, Brenda Tuna and India Ink Teidlebaum determine to make their freshman year memorable.

Plume, Ilse. The Bremen-Town Musicians. 1980. illus. Doubleday [o.p.]; paper, $6.99 (0-440-41456-3). **Y.**

Four animals, abandoned by their owners, set out to become musicians in Bremen. After outwitting a band of robbers with a unique concert, they decide to stay in the forest instead. Minimal use of line results in an overall stippled effect in the understated, realistic illustrations. A Caldecott Honor Book.

Porte, Barbara Ann. Harry in Trouble. Illus. by Yossi Abolafia. 1989. Greenwillow [o.p.]; HarperTrophy, paper, $3.99 (0-06-001155-6). **Y.**

When Harry loses his library card—for the third time—he finds understanding from family, friends, and his librarian in this delightful easy-to-read title.

Porte, Barbara Ann. Harry's Visit. Illus. by Yossi Abolafia. 1983. Greenwillow [o.p.]. **Y.**

A small boy's anxiety over visiting an unfamiliar household is perfectly captured in this humorous, easy-to-read story.

Powzyk, Joyce. Tasmania: A Wildlife Journey. 1987. Lothrop [o.p.]. **M.**

Distinctive watercolors and a quiet, poetic text bring to life the author's awe and delight in Tasmanian creatures.

Prelutsky, Jack. Poems of A. Nonny Mouse. Illus. by Henrik Drescher. 1989. Knopf [o.p.]. **Y.**

Funny rhymes by the unrecognized author A. Nonny Mouse (Anonymous) are linked by inventive, surrealistic illustrations.

Prelutsky, Jack, ed. The Random House Book of Poetry for Children. Illus. by Arnold Lobel. 1983. Random, $19.95 (0-394-85010-6). **M**.

A cornucopia of verse—funny, scary, moving, and dreamy—accompanied by lively and colorful illustrations proves ideal for reading aloud.

Pringle, Laurence. Lives at Stake: The Science and Politics of Environmental Health. 1980. illus. Macmillan [o.p.]. **O**.

Pringle explores the technological dangers that threaten our environmental health and discusses the problems and potential for finding solutions.

Provensen, Alice and **Martin.** The Glorious Flight: Across the Channel with Louis Bleriot. 1983. illus. Viking, $16.99 (0-670-34259-9); paper, $6.99. (0-14-050729-9). **M**.

Stylized paintings with deadpan humor dramatize Louis Bleriot's historic flight across the English Channel. A Caldecott Medal winner.

Reeder, Carolyn. Shades of Gray. 1989. Simon & Schuster [o.p.]; paper, $4.99 (0-689-82696-6). **O**.

Orphaned by the Civil War, young Will painfully accepts his place in Uncle Jed's family despite the man's pacifistic convictions.

Reuter, Bjarne. Buster's World. Tr. by Anthea Bell. 1989. Dutton [o.p.]. **M**.

With robust humor, a would-be-magician copes with taunting classmates and an alcoholic father. A Mildred L. Batchelder Medal winner.

Rice, Eve. Benny Bakes a Cake. 1981. illus. Greenwillow, $15.95 (0-688-11579-9). **Y**.

Benny helps his mother bake his birthday cake, Ralph the dog eats it, and the family rallies round to resolve the crisis. This tale is warmly illustrated with rounded shapes and bright colors.

Rice, Eve. Goodnight, Goodnight. 1980. illus. Greenwillow [o.p.]. **Y**.

Night comes slowly, and up and down the streets the lights go out as the residents of a town say goodnight. The brief, smooth text is set into full-page night scenes of black-and-white and yellow.

Ride, Sally and **Okie, Susan.** To Space and Back. 1986. illus. HarperCollins, $19.99 (0-688-06159-1); paper, $13.95 (0-688-09112-1). **M**.

A captivating first-person account of the small, intimate details of daily living aboard the space shuttle.

Rogasky, Barbara. Rapunzel: From the Brothers Grimm. Illus. by Trina Schart Hyman. 1982. Holiday, $16.95 (0-8234-0454-4). **Y**.

In this new version of the classic tale romantic illustrations are enclosed in decorative borders.

Rogasky, Barbara. Smoke and Ashes: The Story of the Holocaust. 1988. illus. Holiday, $19.95 (0-8234-0697-0); paper, $12.95 (0-8234-0878-7). **O**.

A powerful and accurate account of the Holocaust from its historical roots to present-day legacy.

Rohmer, Harriet. The Invisible Hunters. Illus. by Joe Sam. 1987. Children's Book Press, $15.95 (0-89239-031-X); paper, $7.95 (0-89239-109-X). **Y**.

This bilingual retelling of a Nicaraguan folktale symbolically recounts the tragic clash of indigenous and Western cultures.

Rosenberg, Maxine. Being Adopted. Illus. by George Ancona. 1984. Harper-Collins, $16 (0-688-02672-9). **Y**.

Based on three families' experiences, this photodocumentary realistically profiles the joys and frustrations of cross-cultural adoption.

Roth-Hano, Renée. Touch Wood: A Girlhood in Occupied France. 1988. Macmillan/Four Winds [o.p.]. **O**.

A harrowing story, based on a true experience, of three Jewish sisters who flee from the Nazis to a Catholic women's residence.

Rylant, Cynthia. A Fine White Dust. 1986. Simon & Schuster [o.p.]; Aladdin, paper, $4.99 (0-689-80462-8). **O**.

When 13-year-old Pete meets young Preacher Man, he finds him so compelling that he is willing to leave his family and best friend to follow the man. A Newbery Honor Book.

Rylant, Cynthia. Henry and Mudge under the Yellow Moon. Illus. by Suçie Stevenson. 1987. Simon & Schuster [o.p.]; Aladdin, paper, $3.99 (0-689-81021-0). **Y**.

Young Henry and his huge, affectionate dog enjoy fall leaves, shiver through Mother's Halloween stories, and learn to appreciate Aunt Sally's annual Thanksgiving visit.

Rylant, Cynthia. The Relatives Came. Illus. by Stephen Gammell. 1985. Simon & Schuster [o.p.]. **Y**.

"It was in the summer of the year when the relatives came." They bring hugs, laughter, and good times in this joyful story enhanced by vivacious drawings painted in sprightly colors. A Caldecott Honor Book.

Rylant, Cynthia. When I Was Young in the Mountains. Illus. by Diane Goode. 1982. Dutton, $15.99 (0-525-42525-X). **M**.

An Appalachian childhood is recalled in scenes reflecting the warmth of family relationships and the serenity of the mountains.

San Souci, Robert. The Talking Eggs: A Folktale from the American South. Illus. by Jerry Pinkney. 1989. Dial [o.p.]. **Y**.

Pinkney uses rich colors in interpreting this Creole variant of a favorite tale about the magical consequences of one girl's kindness and her sister's greed. A Caldecott Honor Book.

Sancha, Sheila. The Lutrell Village: Country Life in the Middle Ages. 1983. illus. HarperCollins [o.p.]. **M.**
Precise, labeled drawings present a fascinating glimpse into the life of a medieval village.

Sandburg, Carl. Rainbows Are Made. Ed. by Lee Bennett Hopkins. Illus. by Fritz Eichenberg. 1982. Harcourt [o.p.]; paper, $13 (0-15-265481-X). **M.**
This collection of Sandburg's poetry is illustrated with wood engravings that dramatically evoke the roughness and strength of the poems.

Sandin, Joan. The Long Way to a New Land. 1981. HarperCollins [o.p.]; paper, $3.99 (0-06-444100-8). **M.**
In 1868-1869, 50,000 Swedes came to America in search of a better life. In an engagingly vivid and direct manner, the story of one family's journey from parched farm to Liverpool to New York is told from their son's viewpoint.

Sanfield, Steve. The Adventures of High John the Conqueror. Illus. by John Ward. 1989. Watts/Orchard/Richard Jackson [o.p.]. **O.**
These stories of a clever, black trickster who outwits white folks dramatically reveal the inhumanity of slavery.

Sargent, Sarah. Weird Henry Berg. 1980. Crown [o.p.]. **M.**
When an antique egg hatches, Henry finds that he is the owner and protector of a dragon.

Sattler, Helen Roney. The Book of Eagles. Illus. by Jean Day Zallinger. 1989. Lothrop [o.p.]. **M.**
Meticulously detailed illustrations accompany a fascinating overview and comprehensive glossary of various species of this regal bird.

Sattler, Helen Roney. Dinosaurs of North America. Illus. by Anthony Rao. 1981. Lothrop [o.p.]. **M.**
Arranged by broad geologic time periods and illustrated with skillfully shaded drawings, this informative and entertaining book features more than 80 different types of dinosaurs and explores the mystery of their extinction.

Say, Allen. The Bicycle Man. 1982. illus. Houghton, $16 (0-395-32254-5); paper, $5.95 (0-395-50652-2). **Y.**
Two American soldiers contribute to the festivities of sports day at a Japanese school. Detailed, realistic illustrations drawn from the author's childhood memory capture the happy mood of this event.

Schroeder, Alan. Ragtime Tumpie. Illus. by Bernie Fuchs. 1989. Little, Brown, [o.p.]. **M.**

This slice of 1900 St. Louis life depicts an incident from the childhood of Josephine Baker.

Schwartz, Alvin. The Cat's Elbow and Other Secret Languages. Illus. by Margot Zemach. 1982. Farrar [o.p.]. **M.**

Instructions for 13 secret languages are clearly described, from the simplest pig latin to Boontling, a language known only to citizens of one California town. Zemach's amusing drawings highlight the text.

Schwartz, Alvin. In a Dark, Dark Room and Other Scary Stories. Illus. by Stephen Gammell. 1984. HarperCollins [o.p.]. **Y.**

Beginning readers will delight in these spine-tingling stories and the single poem, which are accompanied by spooky, eerie illustrations.

Schwartz, Alvin. Unriddling. Illus. by Sue Truesdell. 1983. HarperCollins [o.p.]. **M.**

A variety of riddles taken from the earliest to contemporary American folklore is included in this enjoyable, thought-provoking collection.

Schwartz, Amy. Annabelle Swift, Kindergartner. 1988. illus. Watts/Orchard/Richard Jackson [o.p.]; paper, $6.95 (0-531-07027-1). **Y.**

On the first day of kindergarten, Annabelle discovers that only some of her officious older sister's advice is appropriate.

Schwartz, Amy. Oma and Bobo. 1987. illus. Bradbury [o.p.]; Simon & Schuster/Aladdin, paper, $5.99 (0-689-82115-8). **M.**

Alice's new dog shows little interest in obedience school or blue ribbons until Grandmother Oma takes charge. A smattering of German words and phrases enriches the telling.

Schwartz, David M. How Much Is a Million? Illus. by Steven Kellogg. 1985. HarperCollins, $16.99 (0-688-04049-7); paper, $6.99 (0-688-09933-5). **Y.**

The concept of large numbers is explained in this clear, imaginative, and amusingly illustrated book.

Schwartz, David M. If You Made a Million. Illus. by Steven Kellogg. 1989. HarperCollins, $16.95 (0-688-07017-5); paper, $5.95 (0-688-13634-6). **Y.**

Ebullient pictures extend and clarify concepts of being a millionaire in this humorous introduction to the uses of money.

Scieszka, Jon. The True Story of the Three Little Pigs. Illus. by Lane Smith. 1989. Penguin Putnam, $16.99 (0-670-82759-2); paper, $6.99 (0-14-054451-8). **Y.**

Alexander Wolf gives his side of the famous story in this wickedly illustrated and sophisticated telling.

Sebestyen, Ouida. Far from Home. 1980. Little, Brown, $15.95 (0-316-77932-6). **O.**
A motherless boy of 13 finds the father he had never known, in a subtle and touching novel.

Sendak, Maurice. Outside over There. 1981. illus. HarperCollins, $20 (0-06-025523-4); paper, $9.95 (0-06-443185-1). **Y.**
In an intriguing blend of the real and the fantastic, this story of Ida, who must rescue her kidnapped baby sister from the goblins, is effectively complemented by meticulous, opulent paintings. A Caldecott Honor Book.

Service, Robert. The Cremation of Sam McGee. Illus. by Ted Harrison. 1987. Greenwillow $17.95 (0-688-06903-7). **Y.**
Boldly colored paintings evoke the Yukon setting and the humor of Service's well-known narrative poem.

Siegal, Aranka. Upon the Head of the Goat: A Childhood in Hungary, 1939–1944. 1981. Farrar, $16 (0-374-38059-7); Penguin/Puffin, paper, $5.99 (0-14-36966-X). **O.**
The author vividly depicts her survival from the first moment she hears Hitler's name to the day her family leaves the Beregzasz ghetto on trains headed for Auschwitz. A Newbery Honor Book.

Sills, Leslie. Inspirations: Stories about Women Artists. 1989. illus. Albert Whitman, $17.95 (0-8075-3649-0). **M.**
Excellent color reproductions enhance biographical sketches of four contemporary women artists.

Silverstein, Shel. A Light in the Attic. 1981. illus. HarperCollins, $17.95 (0-06-025673-7). **M.**
From the whimsical to the zany, this hilarious, slapstick collection of verses has appeal for even the most reluctant poetry reader.

Simon, Hilda. The Magic of Color. 1981. Lothrop [o.p.]. **Y.**
A basic, thorough explanation of the elements of color, the way it is perceived, and the technology of reproducing it.

Simon, Seymour. The Moon. 1984. illus. Simon & Schuster, $16 (0-02-782840-9). **Y.**
In a highly accessible book for young readers, large, clear photographs highlight a smooth text that examines the relationship of the moon to earth.

Singer, Isaac Bashevis. Stories for Children. 1984. Farrar [o.p.]. **A.**
A wealth of stories, old and new, vividly reflects the culture of Polish Jewry.

Sleator, William. Interstellar Pig. 1984. Dutton [o.p.]; paper, $5.99 (0-14-037595-3). **O.**

Barney's exotic summer neighbors invite him to play a science-fiction board game that gradually takes on sinister overtones.

Slepian, Jan. The Alfred Summer. 1980. Macmillan [o.p.]; Penguin/Putnam, paper, $5.99 (0-698-11910-X). **O.**
Remarkably perceptive and tender, this story of two boys who are disabled shows how much they share the interests and concerns of all children.

Slepian, Jan. The Broccoli Tapes. 1989. Putnam/Philomel, $15.99 (0-399-21712-6); paper, $5.95 (0-698-11679-8). **O.**
Her father's temporary assignment in Hawaii is a lonely time for Sara, who misses her classmates and her beloved six-grade teacher.

Smith, Doris Buchanan. Return to Bitter Creek. 1986. Viking [o.p.]; paper, $5.99 (0-14-032223-X). **O.**
Lacy must find her own place in changing family relationships in this loving story set in a small Appalachian village.

Sneve, Virginia Driving Hawk, ed. Dancing Teepees. Illus. by Stephen Gammell. 1989. Holiday, $16.95 (0-8234-0724-1); paper, $8.95 (0-8234-0879-5). **M.**
Voices from many Native American traditions are presented in short poems and meditations that are accompanied by distinctive tribal motifs.

Snyder, Dianne. The Boy of the Three-Year Nap. Illus. by Allen Say. 1988. Houghton, $16.95 (0-395-44090-4); paper, $6.95 (0-395-66957-X). **Y.**
Clean, exquisite paintings reflect the wit and humor of this Japanese folktale about a lazy but clever boy who is ultimately outwitted by his mother. A Caldecott Honor Book.

Speare, Elizabeth. Sign of the Beaver. 1983. Houghton, $16 (0-395-33890-5); Dell/Yearling, paper, $5.95 (0-440-47900-2). **O.**
Left alone to guard his family's wilderness cabin in colonial Maine, 13-year-old Matt survives through the friendship and teaching of a Native American. A Newbery Honor Book.

Spier, Peter. Peter Spier's Rain. 1982. illus. Doubleday [o.p.]; Dell/Yearling, paper, $6.99 (0-440-41347-8). **Y.**
In this wordless picture book, a brother and sister share the fun of a summer rainstorm as they play indoors and out-of-doors.

St. George, Judith. The Brooklyn Bridge: They Said It Couldn't Be Built. 1982. illus. Putnam [o.p.]. **M.**
The remarkable story of a world-famous bridge and the family of engineers behind its creation is told with much detail and the effective use of photographs, diagrams, and contemporary illustrations.

St. George, Judith. The Mount Rushmore Story. 1985. illus. Putnam [o.p.]. **M.**
An engrossing account of Gutzon Borglum's 14-year struggle to sculpt Mount Rushmore.

Stanley, Diane. Peter the Great. 1986. illus. Macmillan [o.p.]; HarperCollins, $16.95 (0-688-16708-X). **M.**
This predominately visual historical account documents Peter's role in opening Russia to the Western world.

Staples, Suzanne Fisher. Shabanu: Daughter of the Wind. 1989. Knopf [o.p.]; paper, $5.99 (0-679-81030-7). **O.**
With astonishing immediacy, this splendid first novel takes the reader into the life and mind of a courageous, intelligent, and contemporary girl who lives in the Pakistani desert. A Newbery Honor Book.

Steig, William. Doctor De Soto. 1982. illus. Farrar, $17 (0-374-31803-4); paper, $5.95. (0-374-41810-1). **Y.**
A clever dentist takes a risk in helping a fox with a toothache. These anthropomorphized animals tell a humorous, but dramatic story. A Newbery Honor Book.

Steptoe, John. Mufaro's Beautiful Daughters: An African Tale. 1987. illus. HarperCollins, $16.99 (0-688-04045-4). **Y.**
Lush watercolor paintings and a Zimbabwe setting distinguish this tale of two sisters and a wise king's search for the perfect wife. A Caldecott Honor Book

Steptoe, John. The Story of Jumping Mouse. 1984. illus. HarperCollins, $16.99 (0-688-01902-1); paper, $4.95 (0-688-08740-X). **Y.**
Elegant black-and-white drawings bring to life the Native American story of a small mouse who reaches "the far-off land" through his unselfish acts. A Caldecott Honor Book.

Stevenson, James. Howard. 1980. illus. Greenwillow [o.p.]. **Y.**
Witty, cartoon-style illustrations and text tell the story of Howard the duck who misses the annual migration and spends the winter in New York City.

Stevenson, James. That Terrible Halloween Night. 1980. illus. Greenwillow [o.p.]. **Y.**
Were Halloween celebrations scarier in Grandpa's time? His zesty tale of a deliciously terrible night is backed up with cartoon-style, softly colored drawings and can be enjoyed every night of the year.

Taylor, Mildred D. The Friendship. Illus. by Max Ginsburg. 1987. Dial, $16.99 (0-8037-0417-8). **O.**
The four Logan children witness a cruel, racist attack on the dignified, stubborn Mr. Tom Bee.

Taylor, Mildred D. Let the Circle Be Unbroken. 1981. Dial, $17.99 (0-8037-4748-9); paper, $6.99 (0-14-034892-1). **O.**
The Logans' strength and struggles as an African American family, firmly rooted in a Mississippi farm community in the 1930s, are seen from 13-year-old Cassie's perspective. A gripping sequel to *Roll of Thunder, Hear My Cry.*

Tejima, Keizaburo. Owl Lake. 1987. illus. Putnam/Philomel [o.p.]. **Y.**
Striking woodcuts and poetic text recount an owl family's nocturnal search for food.

Thiele, Colin. Farmer Schultz's Ducks. Illus. by Mary Milton. 1988. HarperCollins [o.p.]. **M.**
In a poignant story about an Australian family, farmer Schulz finally solves the problem of how to get his ducks safely across a busy highway on their daily trip to the river.

Thomas, Dylan. A Child's Christmas in Wales. Illus. by Trina Schart Hyman. 1985. Holiday, $16.95 (0-8234-0565-6). **M.**
The poet's remembrance of Christmas past glows anew in Hyman's visualization.

Thomson, Peggy. Auks, Rocks, and the Odd Dinosaur: Inside Stories from the Smithsonian's Museum of Natural History. 1985. illus. HarperCollins, $13.95 (0-690-04491-7). **M.**
This fascinating introduction to the Smithsonian Museum of Natural History includes an account of the way exhibits are researched, prepared, and maintained.

Tinkelman, Murray. Rodeo: The Great American Sport. 1982. illus. Greenwillow [o.p.]. **M.**
Exciting events and unique features of a rodeo are treated in photographs and clear, concise explanations.

Trezise, Percy and **Roughsey, Dick.** Turramulli the Great Quinkin. 1988. illus. Gareth Stevens [o.p.]. **Y.**
Two young children overcome the largest and fiercest spirit roaming the Australian bush in this authentically illustrated tale from aboriginal mythology.

Turkle, Brinton. Do Not Open. 1981. illus. Dutton [o.p.]. **Y.**
Vibrant illustrations lend great charm to this tale of Miss Moody, who refuses to be frightened by anything she does not believe in. Thus, she is able to outwit an enormous monster.

Turner, Ann. Dakota Dugout. Illus. by Ronald Himler. 1985. Simon & Schuster [o.p.]; paper, $7.60 (0-689-71296-0). **M.**
Elegant prose and evocative black-and-white illustrations unite to recall the hard times and warm moments of life on the high plains.

Van Allsburg, Chris. Jumanji. 1981. illus. Houghton, $17.95 (0-395-30448-2). **Y.**

A mysterious, magical board game unleashes a frightening jungle world in the home of its two young players. Stunning black-and-white, velvet-flat illustrations offer fascinating perspectives. A Caldecott Medal winner.

Van Allsburg, Chris. The Mysteries of Harris Burdick. 1984. illus. Houghton, $17.95 (0-395-35393-9). **A.**

Contrasting shadow and light enhance enigmatic drawings in which readers are challenged to exercise their imaginations to create stories about the illustrations, which have only an accompanying title and caption.

Van Allsburg, Chris. The Polar Express. 1985. illus. Houghton, $18.95 (0-395-38949-6). **Y.**

Multidimensional, full-color paintings illuminate a magical Christmas Eve train ride. A Caldecott Medal winner.

Van Allsburg, Chris. The Z Was Zapped: A Play in Twenty-Six Acts. 1987. illus. Houghton, $17.95 (0-395-44612-0); paper, $8.95 (0-395-93748-5). **M.**

In dramatic black-and-white, sculptured letters meet their unexpected fates on stage.

Van Leeuwen, Jean. Amanda Pig and Her Big Brother Oliver. Illus. by Ann Schweninger. 1982. Dial [o.p.]; Penguin/Puffin, paper, $3.99 (0-14-037008-0). **Y.**

Five warm stories of loving, sibling rivalry featuring Amanda Pig and her family are complemented by soft pencil drawings.

Vincent, Gabrielle. Ernest and Celestine's Picnic. 1982. illus. Greenwillow [o.p.]. **Y.**

A rainy day makes a picnic special for little mouse Celestine and her big bear Ernest, whose happy times are portrayed in whimsical, pastel paintings.

Vivas, Julie. The Nativity. 1988. illus. Harcourt/Gulliver, $13.95 (0-15-200535-8); paper, $6 (0-15-200117-4). **Y.**

To accompany the biblical text, Australian artist Vivas provides engaging watercolors that affectionately, amusingly, and reverently interpret the Nativity.

Voigt, Cynthia. Dicey's Song. 1982. Simon & Schuster/Atheneum, $17 (0-689-30944-9); paper, $5.99 (0-689-85131-6). **O.**

In this sequel to *Homecoming*, Dicey must learn when to hold on and when to let go in her relationships with family and friends. A Newbery Medal winner.

Voigt, Cynthia. A Solitary Blue. 1983. Simon & Schuster/Atheneum, $18 (0-689-31008-0); Scholastic, paper, $5.99 (0-689-86434-5). **O.**

Turning to a father he has always feared, Jeff learns to cope with his mother's constant betrayals in this vividly written companion to *Dicey's Song*. A Newbery Honor Book.

Walsh, Jill Paton. Birdy and the Ghosties. Illus. by Alan Marks. 1989. Farrar [o.p.]. **A.**
A master storyteller describes a small girl's encounter with a trio of shape-changing ghosts who richly reward her for her courage and for sharing her gift of second sight.

Watkins, Yoko Kawashima. So Far from the Bamboo Grove. 1986. HarperCollins [o.p.]; paper, $5.99 (0-688-13115-8). **O.**
Two daughters and their Japanese mother make a difficult journey from North Korea to Japan at the end of World War II.

Weiss, Nicki. Where Does the Brown Bear Go? 1989. illus. Greenwillow, $16.95 (0-688-07862-1). **Y.**
A cavalcade of animals heads toward a cozy homecoming in this lyrical, serenely illustrated bedtime story.

Wells, Rosemary. Max's Breakfast.1985. illus. Dial, 5.99 (0-8037-2273-7). **Y.**
Toddlers will delight in this zesty board book, which shows how young Max avoids eating his egg.

Wells, Rosemary. Max's Chocolate Chicken. 1989. illus. Penguin Putnam, $16.99 (0-670-88713-7); paper, $5.99 (0-14-056672-4). **Y.**
During an Easter egg hunt, Ruby plays by the rules while Max wins the chocolate chicken.

White, Ruth. Sweet Creek Holler. 1988. Farrar [o.p.]; paper, $7.95 (0-374-47375-7). **O.**
Memorable details highlight this poignant story of the six years that Ginny, her mother, and her sister spend in a small Appalachian town in the early 1950s.

Wiesner, David. Free Fall! 1988. illus. HarperCollins, $17.89 (0-688-05584-2); paper, $6.99 (0-688-10990-X). **M.**
An older boy's dream adventures are detailed in a stunning, surrealistic, continuous frieze in this complex, wordless picture book. A Caldecott Honor Book.

Williams, Vera B. A Chair for My Mother. 1982. illus. Greenwillow, $15.99 (0-688-00914-X); paper, $5.95 (0-688-04074-8). **Y.**
Vivid colors illustrate this warm and loving story of a girl, her mother, and her grandmother, who are all saving money for a chair as they begin to recover from a fire.

Williams, Vera B. Stringbean's Trip to the Shining Sea. 1988. illus. Greenwillow, $16.95 (0-688-07161-9); Scholastic, paper, $5.99 (0-590-44851-X). **M.**
Postcards innovatively record the cross-country trek of a young boy and his older brother in a camper.

Wiseman, David. Jeremy Visick. 1981. Houghton [o.p.]; paper, $5.95 (0-618-34514-0). **M.**

Sent by his teacher to explore local gravestones, Matthew is inexorably drawn into an 1852 mine tragedy. A dramatic story in which history becomes reality with commitment extending across time as the binding force.

Wood, Audrey. King Bidgood's in the Bathtub. Illus. by Don Wood. 1985. Harcourt, $16 (0-15-242730-9). **Y.**

In an outrageous tale illustrated with meticulous attention to detail, a self-centered king literally soaks his courtiers, until a clever, young page pulls the plug on his bathtub nonsense. A Caldecott Honor Book.

Wood, Audrey. The Napping House. Illus. by Don Wood. 1984. Harcourt, $16 (0-15-256708-9). **Y.**

Luminous colors, which change from rainy blues to sunshine gold, depict the imaginative events in this rollicking, cumulative tale.

Xiong, Blia. Nine-in-One Grr! Grr! Adapted by Cathy Spagnoli. Illus. by Nancy Hom. 1989. Children's Book Press, $14.95 (0-89239-048-4); paper, $7.95 (0-89239-110-3). **Y.**

Illustrations in the style of folk embroidery enhance this fanciful Hmong tale explaining why there are so few tigers in the world today.

Yagawa, Sumiko. The Crane Wife. Tr. by Katherine Paterson. Illus. by Suekichi Akaba. 1981. Morrow [o.p.]. **M.**

Muted line-and-wash drawings on textured paper bring to life the haunting Japanese folktale of a villager who saves a wounded crane, marries a beautiful stranger, reaps great rewards, and loses all to greed.

Yep, Laurence. The Rainbow People. Illus. by David Wiesner. 1989. HarperCollins, $16 (0-06-026760-7); paper, $5.99 (0-06-440441-2). **O.**

Yep retells twenty Cantonese folktales, collected in Chinatown in Oakland, California, as a WPA project, with loyalty to the style and liveliness of South China's oral tradition.

Yolen, Jane. Owl Moon. Illus. by John Schoenherr. 1987. Putnam/Philomel, $16.99 (0-399-21457-7). **Y.**

Delicate pen-and-ink lines over watercolors capture the wonder and intimacy of a father and child's moonlit winter night search for an owl. A Caldecott Medal winner.

Yorinks, Arthur. Company's Coming. Illus. by David Small. 1988. Crown [o.p.]. **Y.**

A deadpan style permeates this zany story about Moe and Shirley's unexpected visitors from outer space.

Yorinks, Arthur. Hey, Al. Illus. by Richard Egielski. 1986. Farrar, $17 (0-374-33060-3); paper, $6.95 (0-374-42985-5). **Y.**

Al, a modest janitor, and his dog, Eddie, are spirited away to a wonderful new life by a mysterious bird. But they soon learn that paradise has its price and home has its rewards. Energetic, thought-provoking illustrations. A Caldecott Medal winner.

Young, Ed, ed. High on a Hill: A Book of Chinese Riddles. 1980. illus. Penguin Putnam, $9.95 (o-399-20978-6). **M.**

Exquisite soft-pencil drawings complement this brief collection of riddles in Chinese and English. The translations are rendered into free verse.

Young, Ed. Lon Po Po: A Red-Riding Hood Story from China. 1989. illus. Putnam/Philomel, $16.99 (0-399-21619-7); paper, $6.99 (0-698-11382-9). **Y.**

Through dramatic wolf images, Young brings new perspectives to this compelling story of three little girls who outwit a wolf posing as their grandmother. A Caldecott Medal winner.

Yue, David and **Yue, Charlotte.** The Tipi: A Center of Native American Life. 1984. illus. Knopf [o.p.]. **O.**

The tipi's intrinsic role in the life of the Plains Indians is explained in simple, straightforward language and detailed drawings.

Zelinsky, Paul O. Rumplestiltskin. From the Brothers Grimm. 1986. illus. Dutton, $16.99 (0-525-44265-0); Penguin/Puffin, paper, $7.99 (0-14-055864-0). **Y.**

Vivid oil paintings enhance this retelling of the classic story of a strange little man who helps the miller's daughter spin straw into gold. A Caldecott Honor Book.

Ziefert, Harriet. A New Coat for Anna. Illus. by Anita Lobel. 1986. Knopf [o.p.]; paper, $6.99 (0-394-89861-3). **Y.**

Lacking money following World War II, a mother barters with local artisans to secure a badly needed winter coat for her daughter, Anna.

6
Notable Children's Books
of the 1990s

Aardema, Verna. Traveling to Tondo: A Tale of the Nkundo of Zaire. Illus. by Will Hillenbrand. 1991. Knopf [o.p.]. **Y.**

A rhythmic, cautionary tale about an accommodating civet cat whose friends delay him so long that his bride has another husband and children before he arrives for the marriage.

Abelove, Joan. Go and Come Back. 1998. DK Ink [o.p.]; Penguin/Puffin, paper, $5.99 (0-14-13064-7). **O.**

An astute teenage girl, growing up in an Amazon village, tells about two visiting American anthropologists in this candid and comic novel about cultural differences and divergent points of view.

Ada, Alma Flor. Under the Royal Palms: A Childhood in Cuba. 1999. illus. Simon & Schuster, $15 (0-689-80631-0). **M.**

Ada recounts stories of growing up in Cuba in this gentle memoir. A Pura Belpré Author Award winner.

Adler, David. Lou Gehrig: The Luckiest Man. Illus. by Terry Widener. 1997. Harcourt/Gulliver, $16 (0-15-200523-4); paper, $6 (0-15-202483-2). **M.**

According to this picture-book biography, a beloved baseball star stricken with a debilitating illness earns respect and admiration for his on-field stamina and off-field courage.

Aiken, Joan. Cold Shoulder Road. 1996. Delacorte, $15.95 (0-03-853218-2). **O.**

Is Twite supports her cousin Arun on his quest to locate his missing mother in this tongue-in-cheek melodrama heavily populated with villains.

Alarcón, Francisco X. From the Bellybutton of the Moon and Other Summer Poems / del Ombligo de la Luna y otros poemas de verano. Illus. by Maya Christina Gonzalez. 1999. Children's Book Press, $15.95 (0-89239-153-7). **Y.**

Twenty-two short, imagistic bilingual poems, inspired by the author's childhood in Mexico, are illustrated with vivid color and great joy. A 2000 Pura Belpré Author Award Honor Book.

Alexander, Lloyd. The Arkadians. 1995. Dutton, $17.99 (0-525-45415-2); Penguin/Puffin, paper, $5.99 (0-14-038073-6). **O.**

Fleeing the palace to save his life, a likable bean counter is joined along his route by a poet turned jackass and a young priestess. A humorous epic that transforms pre-Homeric Greek myths into a multilayered adventure.

Alexander, Lloyd. The Fortune Tellers. Illus. by Trina Schart Hyman. 1992. Dutton, $15.99 (0-525-44849-7); Penguin/Puffin, paper, $5.99 (0-14-056233-8). **Y.**

The future predicted tongue-in-cheek by the old fortune-teller comes true in an unexpected way for a young carpenter. Splendid details in the illustrations of the characters and the Cameroon setting add lovely wit and sense of wonder to the engaging tale.

Alexander, Lloyd. The Iron Ring. 1997. Dutton, $16.99 (0-525-45597-3); Penguin/Puffin, paper, $5.99 (0-14-130348-4). **O.**

In this novel of high adventure, young Prince Tamar goes on a journey to recover his honor after losing everything in a game of chance.

Almond, David. Skellig. 1999. Delacorte, $15.95 (0-385-32653-X). **O.**

Amidst the turmoil of a new home and a baby sister hovering near death, Michael discovers a mysterious man in the dilapidated garage covered in cobwebs and craving bluebottle flies. A Printz Honor Book.

Applebaum, Diana. Giants in the Land. Illus. by Michael McCurdy. 1993. Houghton, $17 (0-395-64120-7); paper, $6.95 (0-618-03305-X). **M.**

The giants are gone now—the huge pine trees that once covered the New England landscape have all been harvested, but they are richly recalled in lyrical text and scratchboard illustrations.

Armstrong, Jennifer. Chin Yu Min and the Ginger Cat. Illus. by Mary Grandpre. 1993. Crown, paper, $6.99 (0-517-88549-2). **Y.**

When secretary Chin dies, his haughty widow learns humility and self-reliance from a ginger cat. Highly expressive illustrations illuminate the changes in the life and fortune of the widow.

Avi. Nothing but the Truth: A Documentary Novel. 1991. Orchard/Richard Jackson [o.p.]; paper, $16.95 (0-531-05959-6). **O.**

A teacher's objection to a ninth-grader's humming along with "The Star Spangled Banner" leads to a satirical examination of chronic miscommunication and the meaning of civil rights. A Newbery Honor Book.

Avi. Poppy. Illus. by Brian Floca. 1995. Orchard/Richard Jackson [o.p.]; HarperTrophy, paper, $5.99 (0-380-72760-2). **M.**

After seeing her intended gobbled up by the resident bully owl, Poppy conquers her fear and sets out to find a new home for her entire mouse family.

Avi. The True Confessions of Charlotte Doyle. 1990. Orchard/Richard Jackson [o.p.]; Prentice-Hall, paper, $3.99 (0-13-800012-3). **O.**

Murder and intrigue on the high seas, as seen through the eyes of a young girl traveling alone in 1832 equals a gripping novel. A Newbery Honor Book.

Axelrod, Alan. Songs of the Wild West. 1991. illus. Simon & Schuster, paper, $19.95 (0-671-74775-4). **A.**

Forty-five beloved songs are set among handsome reproductions from New York's Metropolitan Museum and the Buffalo Bill Historical Center.

Babbitt, Natalie. Ouch! A Tale from Grimm. Illus. by Fred Marcellino. 1998. Har-perCollins/Michael di Capua, $14.95 (0-06-205067-2). **Y.**

Destiny kicks in as a simple young man outwits the devil and wins himself a princess in this sly and painterly reworking of a Grimm tale.

Bachrach, Susan D. Tell Them We Remember: The Story of the Holocaust. 1994. illus. Little, Brown, $21.25 (0-316-69264-6); paper, $14.95 (0-316-07484-5). **O.**

Powerful images drawn from resources of the U.S. Holocaust Memorial Museum are presented in an informational and readable style.

Baker, Jeannie. The Story of Rosy Dock. 1995. illus. Greenwillow, $14.89 (0-688-11493-8). **Y.**

Stunning collages illustrate this look at Australia's weather cycles and its ecological lessons.

Bang, Molly. When Sophie Gets Angry—Really, Really Angry. 1999. illus. Scholastic/Blue Sky, $15.95 (0-590-18979-4). **Y.**

Bang realistically shows how a young child deals with her emotions when things don't go her way. A 2000 Caldecott Honor Book.

Bannerman, Helen. The Story of Little Babaji. Illus. by Fred Marcellino. 1996. HarperColllins/Michael di Capua, $15.95 (0-06-205064-8); HarperTrophy, paper, $7.95 (0-06-008093-0). **Y.**

Delicately comic art shows how a small boy in India outsmarts four tigers, each more vain than hungry, in this handsomely designed book.

Barber, Antonia. The Mousehole Cat. Illus. by Nicola Bayley. 1990. Macmillion [o.p.]; Simon & Schuster, paper, $5.99 (0-689-80837-2). **M.**

At Christmastime in Cornwall, Old Tom and his cat brave the "Great Storm Cat" to catch fish for their hungry neighbors. Exquisitely precise, imaginative illustrations highlight this gem.

Bartoletti, Susan Campbell. Growing Up in Coal Country. 1996. illus. Houghton, $17 (0-395-77847-6); paper, $7.95 (0-395-97914-5). **M.**

Personal accounts and period photographs help depict the harshness of life for children living in Pennsylvania coal-mining communities 100 years ago.

Bartone, Elisa. Peppe the Lamplighter. Illus. by Ted Lewin. 1993. HarperCollins, $16.95 (0-688-10268-9); Avon, paper, $4.95 (0-688-15469-7). **Y.**

Bustling, scenes lit by lamplight, as well as the hopes and fears expressed by Peppe's family vividly evoke the era of New York's Little Italy. A Caldecott Honor Book.

Bauer, Joan. Rules of the Road. 1998. Putnam, $16.99 (0-399-23140-4). **O.**

A 16-year-old girl and an aging shoe-store chain owner drive from Chicago to Dallas in this fresh and funny novel about recognizing quality in people and products.

Bawden, Nina. Granny the Pag. 1996. Clarion, $15 (0-395-77604-X). **O.**

Twelve-year-old-Catriona comes to appreciate the loving care of an eccentric grandmother after her self-involved parents decide to reclaim her in this coming-of-age novel.

Beake, Lesley. Song of Be. 1993. Holt [o.p.]. **O.**

Namibia's complex, changing landscape; the harsh desert world of the Bushman; and political exigencies of an emerging democracy form the background for a Bushman girl's "song" of life in this strong and compassionate look at modern Africa.

Bedard, Michael. Emily. Illus. by Barbara Cooney. 1992. Doubleday, $16.95 (0-385-30697-0); Random, paper, $6.99 (0-440-41740-6). **Y.**

Reclusive poet Emily Dickinson's life provides the inspiration for this atmospheric tale of music and mystery in nineteenth-century Massachusetts.

Begay, Shonto. Navajo: Visions and Voices across the Mesa. 1995. illus. Scholastic, $17.95 (0-590-46153-2). **O.**

Original poetry, prose, and paintings weave intricate patterns of harmony and balance between two cultures.

Berck, Judith. No Place to Be: Voices of Homeless Children. 1992. Houghton, $17 (0-395-53350-3). **O.**

Thirty homeless young people speak honestly of their lives in shelters, in hotels, and on the streets of New York City.

Berry, James. Ajeemah and His Son. 1992. HarperCollins/Willa Perlman [o.p.]; paper, $4.99 (0-06-440523-0). **O.**

Without warning, two Africans are ripped from their family and shipped to plantations in Jamaica. This searing novel captures the emotional truth of the experience of slavery and the heartless dehumanization of its victims.

Best, Cari. Three Cheers for Catherine the Great! Illus. by Giselle Potter. 1999. DK Ink/Melanie Kroupa, $16.95 (07894-2622-6). **Y.**

Sara struggles to find just the right "no present" for her Russian grandmother's birthday. Teaching her English is the perfect solution in this story of family love.

Bial, Raymond. Amish Home. 1993. illus. Houghton, $17 (0-395-59504-5); paper, $6.95 (0-395-72021-4). **M.**

A beautiful photo-essay poignantly shows the world of the Amish through full-color pictures of their handicrafts and natural environment.

Billingsley, Franny. Folk Keeper. 1999. Simon & Schuster/Atheneum, $16 (0-689-82876-4). **O.**

Shrouded in mystery and adventure, and steeped in ancient Selkie legend, this is the story of a self-taught orphan girl who becomes keeper of the wild and dangerous underground folk.

Blumberg, Rhoda. The Remarkable Voyages of Captain Cook. 1991. illus. Simon & Schuster, $18.95 (0-02-711682-4). **O.**

Historical drawings, charts, and paintings illuminate the explorations of this extraordinary explorer.

Brewster, Hugh. Anastasia's Album. 1996. illus. Hyperion, $17.45 (0-7868-0292-8); paper, $7.99 (0-7868-1395-4). **M.**

Intimate family photographs, keepsakes, and letters bring to life the Romanov girls, focusing on Anastasia, the youngest daughter of the last Russian Czar.

Bridges, Ruby. Through My Eyes. 1999. illus. Scholastic, $16.95 (0-590-18923-9). **A.**

A collage of sepia-toned photographs becomes the backdrop for a moving, personal account of a young girl and her family who cross the lines of segregation in a quest for equality in education.

Brooks, Bruce. Everywhere. 1990. HarperCollins, $13 (0-06-02078-0). **M.**

The lives of two boys briefly connect as they plan a magical ritual to save the life of one's beloved grandfather in this unusually perceptive, compassionate story.

Browne, Anthony. Voices in the Park. 1998. illus. DK Ink [o.p.]; paper, $6.99 (0-7894-8191-X). **A.**

Touching on class issues, this surrealistic picture book convincingly presents dressed-up gorillas as people who see the same event in different ways.

Bruchac, Joseph. A Boy Called Slow. Illus. by Rocco Baviera. 1995. Putnam/Philomel, $16.99 (0-399-22692-3); paper, $6.99 (0-698-11616-X). **Y.**

Deeply shadowed paintings complement the dignified telling of the story of Sitting Bull, the Lakota's greatest leader. As a child he was so deliberate and methodical he was laughingly called Slow.

Buehner, Caralyn. Fanny's Dream. Illus. by Mark Buehner. 1996. Dial, $14.99 (0-8037-1496-3); paper, $6.99 (0-14-250060-7). **Y.**
Fanny, a sturdy farm girl, has Cinderella dreams in this homespun tale humorously exaggerated by oil and acrylic paintings.

Bunting, Eve. Fly Away Home. Illus. by Ronald Himler. 1991. Clarion, $16 (0-395-55962-6); paper, $5.95 (0-395-66415-2). **Y.**
Gentle watercolors reflect the poignantly understated story of a homeless boy's living in the airport with his dad. The boy describes how they manage and tells of their longing for a real home.

Bunting, Eve. Smoky Night. Illus. by David Diaz. 1994. Harcourt, $16 (0-15-269954-6); paper, $6 (0-15-201884-0). **A.**
Richly textured collage illustrations extend the story of an inner-city riot as seen through the eyes of a child. A Caldecott Medal winner.

Bunting, Eve. The Wall. Illus. by Ronald Himler. 1990. Clarion, $16 (0-395-51588-2); paper, $5.95 (0-395-62977-2). **Y.**
Tender illustrations and simple text eloquently detail the visit to the Vietnam War Memorial by a young boy and his father.

Burleigh, Robert. Hoops. Illus. by Stephen T. Johnson. 1997. Harcourt/Silver Whistle, $16 (0-15-201450-0); paper, $6 (0-15-216380-8). **A.**
Action portraits in vibrant pastels portray the poetic rhythms of basketball in this free-verse ode to the sport.

Byars, Betsy. Bingo Brown, Gypsy Lover. 1990. Viking [o.p.]; Penguin/Puffin, paper, $4.99 (0-14-034518-3). **M.**
Bingo deals with shopper's block, a persistent would-be girlfriend, and sibling rivalry in the third book about this thoroughly original preteen.

Byars, Betsy. The Golly Sisters Ride Again. Illus. by Sue Truesdell. 1994. HarperCollins, $15.89 (0-06-021564-X); paper, $3.99 (0-06-444204-1). **Y.**
Energetic, expressive, cartoon-style illustrations humorously convey the joys, fears, and squabbles of two wacky sisters as they sing and dance their way through the Old West.

Byars, Betsy. My Brother Ant. Illus. by Marc Simont. 1996. Viking, $15.99 (0-670-86664-4); Penguin/Puffin, paper, $3.99 (0-14-038345-X). **Y.**
The topsy-turvy logic of a young boy comes through in four easy-to-read chapters, highlighted with gentle watercolors.

Calabro, Marian. The Perilous Journey of the Donner Party. 1999. illus. Clarion, $20 (0-395-86610-3). **O**.

Photographs, diaries, letters, and other primary documents vividly re-create a complex scenario of ultimate survival spurred by the excitement of America's westward expansion.

Carrick, Carol. Whaling Days. Illus. by David Frampton. 1993. Clarion, $15.95 (0-395-50948-3); paper, $6.95 (0-395-76480-7). **O**.

Dramatic, bold woodcut drawings detail the history of the whaling industry and illustrate the necessity of saving the whale species from extinction.

Cassedy, Sylvia. Red Dragonfly on My Shoulder. Illus. by Molly Bang. 1992. HarperCollins [o.p.]. **A**.

Inventive and witty collage illustrations complement thirteen traditional haiku in this book designed to be read vertically.

Chang, Ina. A Separate Battle: Women and the Civil War.1991. illus. Lodestar [o.p.]; Penguin/Puffin, paper, $8.99 (0-14-038106-6). **O**.

Battlefront doctors, spies, the courageous women who managed farms or businesses, and many more are featured in a fascinating presentation handsomely illustrated with archival materials.

Choi, Sook Nyul. Year of Impossible Goodbyes. 1991. Houghton, $16 (0-395-57419-6); Dell/Yearling, paper, $5.50 (0-440-40759-1). **O**.

A Korean girl describes the last months of brutal Japanese rule in Pyongyang and her escape south after the Russian invasion of 1945. Based on the author's experiences.

Cohen, Barbara. David. 1995. Clarion [o.p.]. **O**.

The saga of one of the world's best-known heroes, who was a poet, soldier, politician, lover, father, and religious leader.

Cohn, Amy, ed. From Sea to Shining Sea: A Treasury of American Folklore and Folksongs. 1993. illus. Scholastic, $29.95 (0-590-42868-3). **A**.

A lavish array of stories, songs, poetry, and speeches, with illustrations by 15 award-winning artists, represents various ethnic groups, geographic areas, and historical periods in a well-documented compendium of American folk culture.

Colman, Penny. Rosie the Riveter. 1995. illus. Crown, $20.99 (0-517-59791-8); paper, $10.99 (0-517-88567-0). **O**.

This engrossing chronicle of women in the workforce documents the campaign to get them into industry during World War II and the experiences they had.

Coman, Carolyn. Tell Me Everything. 1993. Farrar [o.p.]. **O**.

A girl is given the personal resources of wisdom, courage, and fierce concentration to face the challenges of the loss of her mother, home, and childhood in this thoughtful first novel.

Coman, Carolyn. What Jamie Saw. 1995. Front Street, $13.95 (1-886910-02-2); Penguin/Puffin, paper, $5.99 (0-14-038335-2). **O.**
Third-grader Jamie, his baby sister, Nin, and mother, Patty, move out the night Jamie's stepfather throws Nin across the room. A Newbery Honor Book.

Conly, Jane Leslie. Crazy Lady! 1993. HarperCollins/Laura Geringer, $16.89 (0-06-021560-4); paper, $4.95 (0-06-440571-0). **O.**
After the sudden death of his mother, 12-year-old Vernon grows in understanding, love, acceptance, and self-esteem with the help of an alcoholic neighbor, her developmentally disabled son, and a retired teacher. A Newbery Honor Book.

Conly, Jane Leslie. Trout Summer. 1995. Holt, $15.95 (0-8050-3933-3); Scholastic, paper, $4.99 (0-590-3975-0). **O.**
An isolated cabin by the Castle River becomes a summer refuge for siblings Cody and Shana, as they struggle to accept the unexpected changes in their lives.

Conrad, Pam. The Rooster's Gift. Illus. by Eric Beddows. 1996. HarperCollins/Laura Geringer [o.p.]; paper, $6.95 (0-06-443496-6). **M.**
Playful text and folksy art team up to tell this humorous, multilayered barnyard tale about a proud rooster who believes he has the gift of calling up the sun.

Cooney, Barbara. Eleanor. 1996. illus. Viking. $15.99 (0-670-86159-6); paper, $6.99 (0-14-055583-8). **M.**
Eleanor Roosevelt's unhappy childhood is sympathetically chronicled in a biography completed by softly hued paintings evoking her solemn mood and unfolding promise.

Cooper, Susan. The Boggart. 1993. Simon & Schuster/Margaret K. McElderry, $15 (0-689-50576-0); Aladdin, paper, $4.99 (0-689-80173-4). **O.**
By mistake, Emily and her brother, Jessup, carry a mischievous old spirit with them from Castle Keep in Scotland to their Canadian home, where it proceeds to disrupt their lives. A believable blend of science and folklore.

Couloumbis, Audrey. Getting Near to Baby. 1999. Putnam, $17.99 (0-399-23389-X). **O.**
With grace, humanity, and humor, two girls deal with the grief of losing their baby sister. A 2000 Newbery Honor Book.

Cowan, Catherine. My Life with the Wave. Based on the Story by Octavio Paz. Illus. by Mark Buehner. 1997. HarperCollins, $16.99 (0-688-12660-X). **Y.**

A boy brings home a wave from the seashore in this highly imaginative picture book that uses magically realistic art to credibly present the incredible.

Cowley, Joy. Red-Eyed Tree Frog. Photos by Nic Bishop. 1999. Scholastic, $16.95 (0-590-87175-7). **Y.**

A playful text and "eye-catching" photographs follow a Central American tree frog on its daily nocturnal adventures and chronicle its survival in the rain forest.

Creech, Sharon. Walk Two Moons. 1994. HarperCollins, $17.89 (0-06-023337-0); paper, $6.50 (0-06-440517-6). **O.**

This funny yet poignant intergenerational story reveals one family's history. The characters' individual journeys of self-discovery provide intricate plot twists. A Newbery Medal winner.

Crews, Donald. Bigmama's. 1991. illus. Greenwillow, $15.99 (0-688-09950-5); paper, $5.95 (0-688-15842-0). **Y.**

Primitive paintings, rich with remembered detail, and a simple text, vividly evoke Crews' memories of happy summers with his grandmother in the South.

Cummings, Pat, ed. Talking with Artists. 1992. illus. Simon & Schuster [o.p.]. **A.**

Contemporary illustrators of children's books share autobiographical accounts in response to questions from the editor in this unique approach to art appreciation.

Curtis, Christopher Paul. Bud, Not Buddy. 1999. Delacorte, $15.95 (0-385-32306-9). **M.**

Ten-year-old Bud finds both danger and kindness on the road as he runs from a mean foster family and searches for his dad. A Newbery Medal winner and a Coretta Scott King Author Award winner.

Curtis, Christopher Paul. The Watsons Go to Birmingham—1963. 1995. Delacorte, $16.95 (0-385-32175-9); Bantam, paper, $5.99 (0-440-41412-1). **M.**

A family story, both comic and moving, focuses on the frightening times of the early civil rights movement. A Newbery Honor Book.

Cushman, Karen. Catherine, Called Birdy. 1994. Clarion, $16 (0-395-68186-3); HarperTrophy, paper, $6.50 (0-06-440584-2). **O.**

Detailed medieval castle life is presented through the eyes of strong-willed Birdy and recorded in her spirited diary. A Newbery Honor Book.

Cushman, Karen. The Midwife's Apprentice. 1995. Clarion, $12 (0-395-69229-6); HarperTrophy, paper, $5.99 (0-06-440630-X). **M.**

An apprenticeship with the local midwife enables a medieval orphan with no name, no past, and no future to get her heart's desire—"a full belly, a contented heart and a place in this world." A Newbery Medal winner.

Dalokoy, Vedat. Sister Shako and Kolo the Goat: Memories of My Childhood in Turkey. Tr. by Guner Ener. 1994. Lothrop [o.p.]. **M.**

The former mayor of Ankara lovingly recalls his childhood in rural Turkey and his special friendship with a widow and her remarkable goat, Kolo. A Mildred L. Batchelder Honor Book.

Daly, Niki. Jamela's Dress. 1999. illus. Farrar, $16 (0-374-33667-9). **Y.**

Accidentally ruining her mother's new dress fabric, Queen Jamela's day is saved when prize money from a winning photograph provides the funds to buy fabric for *two* dresses.

Davol, Marguerite W. The Paper Dragon. Illus. by Robert Sabuda. 1997. Simon & Schuster/Atheneum, $18.95 (0-689-31992-4). **M.**

Cut tissue-paper art elegantly unfolds across triple-page spreads in the dramatic story of a Chinese artist who saves his village from a fearsome dragon.

Deem, James M. Bodies from the Bog. 1998. Houghton, $16 (0-395-85784-8); paper, $5.95 (0-618-35402-6). **M.**

Grisly photos of leatherly mummies fill this absorbing book about the archaeological information mysteriously yielded by the peat bogs of Northern Europe.

De Felice, Cynthia. The Apprenticeship of Lucas Whitaker. 1996. Farrar, $16 (0-374-34669-0); Avon/Camelot, paper, $5.99 (0-380-72920-2). **M.**

A touching novel about a 12-year-old Connecticut farm boy who becomes a doctor's apprentice after his family dies of consumption in 1849.

De Felice, Cynthia. Weasel. 1990. Simon & Schuster, $15 (0-02-726457-2); Avon/Camelot, paper, $4.99 (0-380-71358-6). **O.**

In the frontier wilderness of 1839, a 12-year-old boy confronts an evil Indian fighter and weighs the consequences of revenge.

de Paola, Tomie. 26 Fairmount Avenue. 1999. illus. Putnam, $13.99 (0-399-23246-X). **Y.**

Using a charming colloquial narrative, de Paola recalls the year his family moved from an apartment to their new home on Fairmount Avenue. A 2000 Newbery Honor Book.

Dickinson, Peter. A Bone from a Dry Sea. 1993. Delacorte [o.p.]; Dell/Laurel Leaf, paper, $4.99 (0-440-21928-0). **O.**

Two girls, living on the same piece of land in Africa, four million years apart, yet with their lives connected, are depicted in this multilayered telling, in alternating chapters.

Doherty, Berlie. White Peak Farm. 1990. Watts/Orchard [o.p.]. **O.**

In a series of beautifully written stories set in Britain's Peak District, Jeannie and her family strive toward independence from their authoritarian father.

Dorris, Michael. Guests. 1994. Hyperion, $13.95 (0-7868-0047-X); paper, $4.50 (0-7868-1108-0). **O.**

Unhappy that his father has invited strangers with white faces to the harvest feast, Moss takes his "away time" alone in the forest, beginning his journey into adulthood. A provocative view of Thanksgiving, coming-of-age, and survival.

Dorris, Michael. Sees Behind Trees. 1996. Hyperion, $14.89 (0-7868-2215-5); paper, $4.95 (0-786-81252-4). **M.**

Dorris's pen is finely honed to create so memorable a character as Sees Behind Trees. Clearly defined, multifaceted individuals, humorous and oral telling, yet contemplative with much to ponder upon completing the telling.

Dorros, Arthur. Abuela. Illus. by Elisa Kleven. 1991. Putnam, $16.99 (0-525-44750-4); Penguin/Puffin, paper, $6.99 (0-14-056225-7). **Y.**

Grandmother and child joyfully fly above Manhattan in a magical journey that is recorded in vibrant collage, while the warm text is interlaced with some of Abuela's Spanish words.

Dugan, Barbara. Loop the Loop. Illus. by James Stevenson. 1992. Greenwillow, $16.95 (0-688-09647-6). **M.**

A funny, feisty old woman in a wheelchair and her young neighbor form a friendship that survives the woman's move to a nursing home. Laughs mix with love in this warmhearted story and in the droll and energetic illustrations.

Dyer, Jane. Animal Crackers: A Delectable Collection of Pictures, Poems and Lullabies for the Very Young. 1996. illus. Little, Brown, $19.95 (0-316-19766-1). **Y.**

Soft watercolors provide an added dimension in this eclectic compilation of delightful, delicious rhymes and verses about numbers, seasons, foods, and pastimes.

Ehlert, Lois. Moon Rope: A Peruvian Folktale. Tr. by Amy Prince. 1992. illus. Harcourt, $17 (0-15-255343-6); paper, $7 (0-15-201702-X). **Y.**

Fox and Mole climb a rope of grass in their quest to reach the moon. Bold collages illustrate this retelling in English and in Spanish.

Emberley, Michael. Ruby. 1990. illus. Little, Brown [o.p.]. **Y.**

This delectable parody of "Little Red Riding Hood" stars a feisty mouse and is illustrated with hilarious glimpses of her urban neighborhood.

Enzensberger, Hans Magnus. The Number Devil: A Mathematical Adventure. Tr. by Heim, Michael Henry. Illus. by Rotraut Susanne Berner. 1998. Holt, $27.50 (0-8050-5770-6). **M.**

A 12-year-old math-phobe is visited in his dreams by a strange fellow who devilishly reveals the pleasures of mathematical thinking.

Erdrich, Louise. The Birchbark House. 1999. illus. Hyperion; dist. by Little, Brown, $14.99 (0-7868-03000-2). **M.**
Eight-year-old Omakayas, an Ojibwa girl living in 1847, survives smallpox, but loses a beloved family member in this richly detailed, sensitive historical novel, illustrated by the author's pencil sketches.

Esbensen, Barbara Juster. Tiger with Wings: The Great Horned Owl. Illus. by Mary Barrett Brown. 1991. Orchard, $16.95 (0-531-05940-5); paper, $5.95 (0-531-07071-9). **Y.**
Exquisite watercolors and a flowing text detail the characteristics and habits of this magnificent species.

Facklam, Margery. The Big Bug Book. Illus. by Paul Facklam. 1994. Little, Brown [o.p.]; paper, $6.70 (0-316-25521-1). **M.**
Giant insects—depicted life size—crawl, flutter, or swim across common household items in this lively portrait gallery.

Farmer, Nancy. The Ear, the Eye, and the Arm. 1994. Orchard/Richard Jackson, $18.95 (0-531-06829-3); Penguin/Puffin, paper, $5.99 (0-14-037641-0). **O.**
When the overprotected children from a future police state in Africa are kidnapped, mutant detectives Ear, Eye, and Arm are never far behind in pursuit of the villains. This well-balanced, suspenseful world is steeped in myth, technology, and tension. A Newbery Honor Book.

Farmer, Nancy. A Girl Named Disaster. 1996. Orchard/Richard Jackson, $19.95 (0-531-09539-8); Penguin/Puffin, paper, $5.99 (0-14-038635-1). **O.**
In order to escape a forced betrothal, 11-year-old Nhamo flees through the isolated terrain of Mozambique and Zimbabwe, supported only by her own intelligence and mystical beliefs.

Feelings, Tom. The Middle Passage: White Ships/Black Cargo. 1995. illus. Putnam, $50 (0-8037-1804-7). **O.**
A stunning graphic telling of the heart-wrenching journey of an enslaved people. This is a tribute to their survival.

Feiffer, Jules. Bark, George. 1999. illus. HarperCollins/Michael di Capua, $14.95 (0-06-205185-7). **Y.**
George, the puppy, says only "meow," "moo," or "quack" until a visit to the veterinarian solves his problem . . . or does it? Expressive line drawings heighten the hilarity.

Feiffer, Jules. I Lost My Bear. 1998. HarperCollins, $16 (0-688-15147-7). **Y.**

Crackling cartoon art humorously expresses the anguish of a small girl with a big problem in this comic look at family life.

Fenner, Carol. Yolonda's Genius. 1995. Simon & Schuster/Margaret K. McElderry, $17 (0-689-80001-0); Simon & Schuster/Aladdin, paper, $5.99 (0-689-81327-9). **O.**

Yolonda, an exceptionally bright fifth-grader, proves that her shy younger brother is not a slow learner but, rather, a musical genius. A Newbery Honor Book.

Fine, Anne. Flour Babies. 1994. Little, Brown [o.p.]; Dell/Laurel Leaf, paper, $4.99 (0-440-21941-8). **O.**

Parenting a six-pound flour baby forces Simon to come to grips with his own life and the absence of his father. Lively characters combine with humorous situations.

Fine, Anne. The Tulip Touch. 1997. Little, Brown [o.p.]; Random, paper, $4.99 |(0-440-22785-2). **O.**

The rise and fall of a destructive friendship between girls makes this a gripping novel.

Fleischman, Paul. The Borning Room. 1991. HarperCollins [o.p.]; paper, $4.99 (0-06-447099-7). **O.**

Georgina Lott tells her life story through the births and deaths that took place in one little room.

Fleischman, Paul. Bull Run. 1993. HarperCollins/Laura Geringer, $14.95 (0-06-021446-5); paper, $4.99 (0-06-440588-5). **O.**

The first major battle of the Civil War is powerfully recalled by the voices of 16 participants. A thoughtfully constructed novel.

Fleischman, Paul. Saturnalia. 1990. HarperCollins/Charlotte Zolotow [o.p.]; paper, $4.95 (0-06-447089-X). **O.**

Set in the seventeenth century, this rich story regales readers with a kaleidoscope of masters and servants, their pranks and passions.

Fleischman, Paul. Weslandia. Illus. by Kevin Hawkes. 1999. Candlewick, $15.99 (0-7636-0006-7). **M.**

A strange backyard plant becomes the center of Wesley's newly created civilization. Lush, detailed illustrations zero in on this freethinker's magical and enviable world.

Fleischman, Sid. The Abracadabra Kid: A Writer's Life. 1996. Greenwillow, $16 (0-688-14859-X); paper, $4.95 (0-688-15855-2). **O.**

A rollicking autobiographical journey follows Fleischman from budding magician to award-winning author.

Fleischman, Sid. Jim Ugly. Illus. by Jos. A. Smith. 1992. Greenwillow, $16 (0-688-10886-5); Dell/Yearling, paper, $4.99 (0-440-40803-2). **M.**

Jake and his half-wolf half-dog, Jim Ugly, attempt to solve the mystery of his missing father in this fast-paced spoof of a western melodrama.

Fleming, Denise. Barnyard Banter. 1994. illus. Holt, $16.95 (0-8050-1957-X); paper, $6.95 (0-8050-5581-9). **Y.**

Exuberant, rhyming text and vibrant illustrations add delight to the activity of the barnyard, in this hide-and-seek game.

Fleming, Denise. In the Small, Small Pond. 1993. illus. Holt, $16.95 (0-8050-2264-3); paper, $6.95 (0-8050-5983-0). **Y.**

Lushly colored, textured, double-page spreads combine with a short, jaunty, rhyming text to depict a frog's seasonal journey through a pond. A Caldecott Honor Book.

Fleming, Denise. In the Tall, Tall Grass. 1991. illus. Holt, $16.95 (0-8050-1635-X); paper, $6.95 (0-8050-3941-4). **Y.**

Deftly rhymed words describe a caterpillar's movement through sumptuous collages of textured, handmade paper as it meets other creatures along the way.

Fletcher, Ralph. Fig Pudding. 1995. Clarion, $15 (0-395-71125-8); Dell/Yearling, paper, $4.99 (0-440-41203-X). **M.**

A year in the life of a big family, its joys and its sorrows, is told through the words of 12-year-old Cliff.

Fletcher, Susan. Shadow Spinner. 1998. Simon & Schuster/Atheneum, $17 (0-689-81852-1); Aladdin, paper, $4.79 (0-689-83051-3). **O.**

A serving girl becomes intricately entangled with Shahrazad and her stories in order to spare young women from death in ancient Persia.

Florian, Douglas. Beast Feast. 1994. illus. Harcourt, $16 (0-15-295178-4); paper, $7 (0-15-201737-2). **M.**

Droll, colorful illustrations and wildly inventive poetry combine for a hilarious visit to the animal world.

Florian, Douglas. Insectiopedia. 1998. Harcourt [o.p.]. **A.**

An Io moth and a daddy longlegs are among the bugs highlighted in this playful collection of 21 clever poems with companion paintings.

Foreman, Michael. War Game. 1994. illus. Arcade [o.p.]. **O.**

Christmas Day, 1914, finds four young British soldiers playing a rousing game of soccer with the Germans in the opposite trenches. A powerful explanation of the paradoxical nature of war.

Fox, Mem. Tough Boris. Illus. by Kathryn Brown. 1994. Harcourt, $16 (0-15-289612-0); paper, $6 (0-15-201891-3). **Y.**

No pirate is tougher than Boris, "but when his parrot dies, he cried and cried."

Fox, Paula. Eagle Kite. 1995. Orchard/Richard Jackson, $15.95 (0-531-06892-7). **O.**

Liam must learn to accept his father's homosexuality as well as his impending AIDS-related death.

Fox, Paula. Monkey Island. 1991. Orchard/Richard Jackson, $15.95 (0-531-05962-6); Dell/Yearling, paper, $15.50 (0-440-40770-2). **O.**

A suddenly homeless 11-year-old boy works out a precarious survival on the streets of New York City.

Freedman, Russell. Babe Didrikson Zaharias: The Making of a Champion. 1999. illus. Clarion, $18 (0-395-63367-2). **O.**

Sleek and graceful like the Babe herself, this well-researched biography gives insight into the fierce determination and drive of the greatest female athlete of all time.

Freedman, Russell. Eleanor Roosevelt: A Life of Discovery. 1993. illus. Clarion, $17.95 (0-89919-862-7); paper, $10.95 (0-395-84520-3). **O.**

The marvelously rich and full life of this legendary First Lady is profiled in an outstanding photobiography; a well-documented view of a life of service. A Newbery Honor Book.

Freedman, Russell. Kids at Work: Lewis Hine and the Crusade Against Child Labor. 1994. illus. Clarion, $20 (0-395-58703-4); paper, $9.95 (0-395-79726-8). **O.**

Hine's investigative reporting of early-twentieth-century child labor is presented in black-and-white photographs combined with succinct text.

Freedman, Russell. The Life and Death of Crazy Horse. Illus. by Amos Bad Heart Bull. 1996. Holiday, $21.95 (0-8234-1219-9). **O.**

A moving biography of the Oglala Sioux leader who passionately resisted incursions into his people's lands. Incredible pictographs by a tribal historian heighten the drama.

Freedman, Russell. The Wright Brothers: How They Invented the Airplane. 1991. illus. Holiday, $22.95 (0-8234-1082-X); paper, $12.95 (0-8234-0875-2). **O.**

In a spirited account of the accomplishments of these two pioneers of flight, lively quotations from their correspondence and the brothers' own photographs provide a fascinating portrait of the beginning of a new age. A Newbery Honor Book.

Fritz, Jean. You Want Women to Vote, Lizzie Stanton? Illus. by DyAnne DiSalvo-Ryan. 1995. Putnam, $17.95 (0-399-22786-5); Paper Star, paper, $6.99 (0-698-11764-6). **M.**

This engaging biography of Elizabeth Cady Stanton presents a lively look at the impatient, outspoken personality as she fought for women's suffrage.

Froehlich, Margaret Walden. That Kookoory! Illus. by Marla Frazee. 1995. Harcourt/Browndeer, $15 (0-15-277650-8). **Y.**

Kookoory, a rooster, sets off for the fair, waking all his friends along the way and attracting the notice of a weasel.

Fry, Virginia Lynn. Part of Me Died, Too: Stories of Creative Survival among Bereaved Children and Teenagers. 1995. illus. Dutton [o.p.]. **A.**

Children and families who must cope with the death of a pet, relative, or friend are given the means to grieve.

Gantos, Jack. Joey Pigza Swallowed the Key. 1998. Farrar, $16 (0-374-33664-4); HarperCollins, paper, $5.99 (0-06-440833-7). **M.**

Simultaneously poignant, funny, and horrifying, this staccato novel about a good kid with ADHD brillantly replicates in style the feel of being "wired."

Garland, Sherry. Lotus Seed. Illus. by Tatsuro Kiuchi. 1993. Harcourt, $16 (0-15-249465-0); paper, $7 (0-15-201483-7). **M.**

A young Vietnamese woman is forced to leave her homeland, taking only a lotus seed to serve as a constant reminder of her past life. A terse emotional tale that spans 50 years.

Garza, Carmen Lomas. Magic Windows (Ventanas màgicas). 1999. illus. Children's Book Press, $15.95 (0-89239-157-X). **Y.**

Artist Garza uses her intricate cut-paper art to portray family, community, and ancestors in this bilingual volume. The 2000 Pura Belpré Illustrator Award winner.

George, Kristine O'Connell. Little Dog Poems. Illus. by June Otani. 1999. Clarion, $12 (0-395-82266-1). **Y.**

From morning until night, "puppy-sized" poems follow Little Dog and his loving owner through the day, revealing their happy friendship with humor and insight.

Giblin, James Cross. Charles A. Lindbergh: A Human Hero. 1997. illus. Clarion, $21 (0-395-63389-3). **O.**

This multidimensional portrait explores the achievements of the famous American aviator, as well as the controversies and tragedies that surround him.

Giblin, James Cross. The Riddle of the Rosetta Stone: Key to Ancient Egypt. 1990. illus. HarperCollins/Crowell [o.p.]; paper, $7.99 (0-06-446137-8). **O.**

Giblin offers a clearly written history of the ancient stone with its trilingual inscription that enabled scientists to decode hieroglyphs after more than 1,500 years.

Giblin, James Cross. The Truth about Unicorns. Illus. by Michael McDermott. 1991. HarperCollins [o.p.]. **O.**

A popular subject is linked with its beguiling social history through engaging narrative and thoughtfully chosen reproductions and soft-pencil drawings.

Giblin, James Cross. When Plague Strikes: The Black Death, Smallpox, AIDS. Illus. by David Frampton. 1995. HarperCollins [o.p.]; paper, $7.95 (0-06-446195-5). **O.**

Three plagues are examined in the context of history and society, comparing and contrasting their impact on humans of their time.

Giff, Patricia Reilly. Lily's Crossing. 1997. Delacorte, $15.95 (0-385-32142-2); Dell/Yearling, paper, $5.50 (0-440-41453-9). **M.**

Two children spend the summer of 1944 in quiet Rockaway Beach, New York, where they share their secrets, lies, and worries about the war. A Newbery Honor Book.

Goldin, Barbara Diamond. Journeys with Elijah: Eight Tales of the Prophet. Illus. by Jerry Pinkney. 1999. Harcourt/Gulliver, $20 (0-15-200445-9). **O.**

Eight vibrant tales of the prophet Elijah, lavishly complemented by richly detailed watercolors, travel the world capturing the spirit of history and Jewish folklore.

Goldin, Barbara Diamond. The Passover Journey: A Seder Companion. Illus. by Neil Waldman. 1994. Viking [o.p.]; Penguin/Puffin, paper, $7.99 (0-14-056131-5). **A.**

A meticulous melding of the Israelites' journey from Egyptian bondage to freedom combine with a lucid explanation of the symbolism and origin of the Passover seder, matched with brilliant pastels with geometric borders.

Gollub, Matthew. Cool Melons—Turn to Frogs: The Life and Poems of Issa. Illus. by Kazuko G. Stone. 1998. Lew & Low, $16.95 (1-880000-71-7). **Y.**

This slim and serene volume introduces an eighteenth-century poet with 33 of his haiku, presented in both English and Japanese.

Goor, Ron and **Goor, Nancy.** Insect Metamorphosis: From Egg to Adult. 1990. illus. Simon & Schuster/Atheneum, $14.95 (0-689-31445-0); Simon & Schuster/Aladdin, paper, $5.99 (0-689-82196-4). **M.**

Spectacular color photographs illustrate the lucidly explained concepts of complete and incomplete metamorphosis.

Gray, Libba Moore. My Mama Had a Dancing Heart. Illus. by Raul Colon. 1995. Orchard/Melanie Kroupa, $15.95 (0-531-09470-7). **Y.**

A ballet dancer's memories of how she and her mother welcomed each season with a joyful dance are illustrated with grace and exuberance.

Gray, Luli. Falcon's Egg. 1995. Houghton, $16 (0-395-71128-2). **M**.
Keeping a dragon in a New York City apartment tests young Falcon's ingenuity and resources to the utmost in this beguiling story.

Green, Kate. Number of Animals. Illus. by Christopher Wormell. 1993. Creative Education, $19.95 (0-15-200926-4). **Y**.
Looking for his mother, a tiny chick fearlessly confronts a series of majestic farm animals in boldly rendered pictures. A simple counting book with strong visual impact.

Greenberg, Jan and **Jordan, Sandra.** The Painter's Eye: Learning to Look at Contemporary American Art. 1991. illus. Delacorte [o.p.]. **O**.
A mind-expanding book suggesting that modern painters are saying, "This is what I see," and asking, "What do you see?"

Greenberg, Jan and **Jordan, Sandra.** The Sculptor's Eye: Looking at Contemporary American Art. 1993. illus. Delacorte [o.p.]. **O**.
A series of interviews, plus penetrating analysis of several dozen works of art enhanced by expert color photography, illuminates the free play of imagination and technique that has formed modern sculpture.

Griffin, Adele. The Other Shepards. 1998. Hyperion, $14.95 (0-7868-0423-8); paper, $5.99 (0-7868-1333-4). **O**.
In this haunting novel permeated with sadness, two troubled sisters move beyond family tragedy with the help of a mysterious young artist.

Griffith, Helen V. Grandaddy and Janetta. Illus. by James Stevenson. 1993. Greenwillow, $16 (0-688-11226-9); Avon, paper, $4.95 (0-688-17114-1). **M**.
Another comfortable tale with Grandaddy and Janetta in Georgia is conveyed with gentle humor and tender spirit. Pen-and-wash illustrations enhance this musical text.

Griffith, Helen V. Grandaddy's Stars. Illus. by James Stevenson. 1995. Greenwillow, $15 (0-688-13654-0). **M**.
When Grandaddy travels from his Georgia farm for his first visit to Baltimore, Janetta is concerned he will be bored by the things she wants to share with him.

Grimes, Nikki. Come Sunday. Illus. by Michael Bryant. 1996. Eerdmans, $15 (0-8028-5108-8); paper, $7.50 (0-8028-5134-7). **A**.
An exuberant collection of poems and watercolor illustrations celebrates a day at church as seen through the eyes of a young African American girl.

Grimes, Nikki. Meet Danitra Brown. Illus. by Floyd Cooper. 1994. HarperCollins, $15.89 (0-688-12074-1); paper, $6.99 (0-688-15471-9). **M**.
Meet "the most splendiferous girl in town" in this celebration of friendship in poetry and warmly colored art.

Hahn, Mary Downing. Stepping on the Cracks. 1991. Clarion, $16 (0-395-58707-4); Avon, paper, $4.99 (0-380-71900-2). **O**.

Two close friends discover that the local bully has two terrible secrets: his father is viciously abusive and his brother—a World War II deserter—is hiding out nearby.

Hamanaka, Sheila and **Ohmi, Ayano.** In Search of the Spirit: The Living National Treasures of Japan. 1999. illus. Morrow, $16 (0-688-14607-4). **M**.

Honored for perpetuating the rich culture and traditions of the Japanese culture, six men and their crafts are strikingly depicted in an illuminating presentation.

Hamilton, Virginia. Her Stories: African American Folktales, Fairy Tales, and True Tales. Illus. by Leo and Diane Dillon. 1995. Scholastic/Blue Sky, $19.95 (0-590-47370-0). **O**.

In this beautiful book, a master storyteller presents ordinary slave women, heroines, she-vampires, and witches in African-American folktales, oral histories, and elaborate fairy tales.

Hamilton, Virginia. Many Thousand Gone: African Americans from Slavery to Freedom. Illus. by Leo and Diane Dillon. 1993. Knopf [o.p.]; paper, $12.95 (0-679-87936-6). **O**.

This companion book to *The People Could Fly* traces the history of slavery through short accounts and narratives of those who lived it.

Hamilton, Virginia. When Birds Could Talk & Bats Could Sing: The Adventures of Bruh Sparrow, Sis Wren, and Their Friends. Illus. by Barry Moser. 1996. Scholastic/Blue Sky, $17.95 (0-590-47372-7). **A**.

African American folktales about "feathered folks" are retold in a humorous voice and are further enlivened by lively watercolor illustrations.

Han, Suzanne Crowder. The Rabbit's Escape. Illus. by Yumi Heo. 1995. Holt, $15.95 (0-8050-2675-4). **Y**.

Clever Rabbit, tricked into visiting the underwater kingdom of the Dragon King of the East Sea, manages to escape, in this bilingual Korean tale.

Harris, Robie H. It's Perfectly Normal: A Book about Changing Bodies, Growing Up, Sex and Sexual Health. Illus. by Michael Emberley. 1994. Candlewick, $19.99 (1-56402-199-8); paper, $10.99 (1-56402-159-9). **O**.

A well-organized and straightforward text provides the young adolescent with honest and accurate information. Cartoon drawings provide the right amount of humor to defuse the reader's embarrassment.

Harris, Robie H. It's So Amazing: A Book about Eggs, Sperm, Birth, Babies, and Families. Illus. by Michael Emberley. 1999. Candlewick, $21.99 (0-7636-0051-2). **M**.

Bird and bee cartoon characters help deliver straightforward answers to children's questions in this friendly and sensitive guide to sex and reproduction.

Hartling, Peter. Old John. Tr. by Elizabeth D. Crawford. 1990. Lothrop [o.p.]. **M.**
Comic yet poignant portrait of a family coping with the idiosyncrasies of the grandfather who comes to live with them.

Haugaard, Erik Christian. The Revenge of the Forty-Seven Samurai. 1995. Houghton, $16 (0-395-70809-5). **O.**
A servant boy tells the story of the famous Japanese hero, Oishi Kuvanosuke, a loyal samurai, who, in feudal Japan, avenged his master's dishonorable death by ritualistic suicide.

Heide, Florence Parry and **Gilliland, Judith Heide.** The Day of Ahmed's Secret. Illus. by Ted Lewin. 1990. Lothrop, $16 (0-688-08894-5). **Y.**
As young Ahmed's work day carries him through Cairo's bustle, he looks forward to sharing his new accomplishment with his family—he has learned to write his name. Lewin's tumultuous watercolors capture life in the crowded Egyptian city.

Hendry, Frances Mary. Quest for a Maid. 1990. Farrar [o.p.]. **O.**
In the grand tradition, a novel about a thirteenth-century Scottish girl caught up in the adventures surrounding a voyage to fetch a little princess from the Norwegian court.

Henkes, Kevin. Chrysanthemum. 1991. illus. Greenwillow, $15.95 (0-688-09699-9); paper, $5.99 (0-688-14732-1). **Y.**
Chrysanthemum discovers that the other children don't share her doting parents' enthusiasm for her long, musical name. Her ups and downs are neatly summed up in a witty text and cozily perceptive illustrations.

Henkes, Kevin. Julius: The Baby of the World. 1990. illus. Greenwillow, $15.99 (0-688-08943-7); Mulberry, paper, $5.95 (0-688-14388-1). **Y.**
Despite her happy anticipation, Lilly is not amused by the actual presence of a baby brother, resulting in her spending more than the usual time in the "uncooperative chair."

Henkes, Kevin. Lilly's Purple Plastic Purse. 1996. illus. Greenwillow, $15.99 (0-688-12897-1). **Y.**
When overeager Lilly flaunts her new purse in class, devastating results are exuberantly depicted in this seamless blend of art and text.

Henkes, Kevin. Owen. 1993. illus. Greenwillow, $15.99 (0-688-11449-0). **Y.**
An endearing mouse, Owen, thwarts every attempt to force him to give up his blanket. Mom's solution to recycle his beloved "fuzzy" pleases all. A Caldecott Honor Book.

Henkes, Kevin. Sun & Spoon. 1997. Greenwillow, $15.99 (0-688-15232-5); Penguin/Puffin, paper, $4.99 (0-14-130095-7). **M.**

Spoon and his grandfather work through their grief after Gram's death in this realistic and respectful story.

Herrera, Juan Felipe. Laughing Out Loud, I Fly / A Caracajadas yo vuelo. Illus. by Karen Barbour. 1999. HarperCollins, $15.95 (0-06-027604-5). **Y.**

Sound and rhythm pulse through Herrera's 22 poems, which appear in facing English and Spanish versions. The text is printed over illustrator Barbour's figures, adapted from Mexican folk art. A 2000 Pura Belpré Author Award Honor Book.

Hesse, Karen. Letters from Rifka. 1992. Holt, $16.95 (0-8050-1964-2); Penguin/Puffin, paper, $5.99 (0-14-036391-2). **O.**

Rifka, a 12-year-old Jewish girl leaving Russia in 1919, shares her heartaches, her loneliness, and her hopes for life in America through letters to her cousin Tovah.

Hesse, Karen. Out of the Dust. 1997. Scholastic, $15.95 (0-590-36080-9); paper, $4.99 (0-590-37125-8). **O.**

Through a spare poetic narrative, 14-year-old Billie Jo recalls the hard times and the tragedies her family endures in Oklahoma during the 1930s.

Hesse, Karen. Phoenix Rising. 1994. Holt, $16.95 (0-8050-3108-1); Putnam, paper, $5.99 (0-14-037628-3). **O.**

Thirteen-year-old Nyle and her grandmother try to go on with their lives on a Vermont sheep farm, despite the disastrous radiation leak at a nearby nuclear power plant.

Ho, Minfong. Hush! A Thai Lullaby. Illus. by Holly Meade. 1996. Orchard/Melanie Kroupa, $15.95 (0-531-09500-2). **Y.**

A mother asks nocturnal animals of the Thai countryside to "hush" so baby can sleep. Cut-paper collage art humorously and beautifully complements the text. A Caldecott Honor Book.

Hoestlandt, Jo. Star of Fear, Star of Hope. Tr. by Mark Polizzotti. Illus. by Johanna Kang. 1995. Walker, $16.95 (0-8027-8373-2); paper, $8.95 (0-8027-7588-8). **M.**

Stark paintings reflect Helen's feelings of abandonment after her best friend, a Jewish girl, disappears after they have quarreled during the German occupation of Paris. A Mildred L. Batchelder Honor Book.

Hoffman, Mary. Amazing Grace. Illus. by Caroline Binch. 1991. Dial, $16.99 (0-8037-1040-2). **Y.**

She may be a girl, but Grace learns that she can be anything she wants to be when her classmates agree to give her the coveted role of Peter Pan. Glowing watercolors capture every nuance of a vibrant young personality.

Holm, Jennifer L. Our Only May Amelia. 1999. HarperCollins, $15.95 (0-06-027822-6). **M.**
The life of spunky May Amelia, living in Washington state in the 1880s, is chronicled with robust characterizations and lilting language. A Newbery Honor Book.

Holub, Josef. The Robber and Me. Tr. by Elizabeth D. Crawford. 1997. Holt, $16.95 (0-8050-5599-1). **O.**
Here begins the story of Boniface, who lands in a remote corner of the forest, in the godforsaken village of Graab, where he makes the acquaintance of Robber Knapp. A Mildred L. Batchelder Medal winner.

Hopkinson, Deborah. A Band of Angels: A Story Inspired by the Jubilee Singers. Illus. by Raúl Colón. 1999. Simon & Schuster/Anne Schwartz, $16 (0-689-81062-8). **M.**
A grandchild tells the powerful story of former slave Ella Sheppard and the Jubilee Singers, who are determined to save Fisk College. The text is complemented by Colón's inspiring scratchboard art.

Horvath, Polly. The Trolls. 1999. Farrar, $16 (0-374-37787-1). **M.**
Eccentric Aunt Sally's daily installments of the family's history, full of colorful people and guarded secrets, mesmerize the three Anderson children.

Houston, Gloria. My Great-Aunt Arizona. Illus. by Susan Condie Lamb. 1992. HarperCollins, $15.99 (0-06-022606-4); paper, $5.99 (0-06-443374-9). **Y.**
A beautiful tribute to the author's spirited great-aunt, who taught for 57 years in a one-room "blab" school in the Blue Ridge Mountains.

Howard, Ellen. Sister. 1990. Simon & Schuster/Atheneum [o.p.]. **O.**
Alena yearns for an education but is trapped by the realities of family responsibilities in rural America in the late 1800s.

Hughes, Langston. Sweet and Sour Animal Book. 1994. illus. Oxford [o.p.]; paper, $9.95 (0-19-512030-2). **M.**
Twenty-seven previously unpublished poems chronicle this animal alphabet. The brief verse is decorated with paper, board, and clay sculptures created by children.

Hughes, Ted. Tales of the Early World. Illus. by Andrew Davidson. 1991. Farrar [o.p.]. **M.**
With a playful spirit and a sparkling style, England's poet laureate tells 10 imaginatively witty and original tales about the Creation.

In Daddy's Arms I Am Tall: African Americans Celebrating Fathers. Illus. by Javaka Steptoe. 1997. Lee & Low, $15.95 (0-880000-31-8); paper, $6.95 (1-58430-016-7). **A.**

Strong collage illustrations and 10 emotional poems express the depth and range of the father-child relationship.

Isaacs, Anne. Swamp Angel. Illus. by Paul O. Zelinsky. 1994. Dutton, $15.99 (0-525-45271-0); paper, $6.99 (0-14-055908-6). **A.**

Primitive-style illustrations painted on wood panels provide the perfect visual accompaniment to the spirited tall tale of Anglica Longrider. A Caldecott Honor Book.

Isaacson, Philip M. Short Walk around the Pyramids and Through the World of Art. 1993. illus. Knopf [o.p.]. **A.**

A gifted observer explores the nature and common features of art through all times and places, from the oldest pyramid to the most modern cityscape and from experimental photography to traditional African sculpture.

Isadora, Rachel. At the Crossroads. 1991. illus. Greenwillow [o.p.]; Avon, paper, $15.95 (0-688-13103-4). **Y.**

This quietly moving story with brilliant impressionistic watercolors depicts a group of South African children joyfully awaiting their father's return after 10 months in the mines.

Jackson, Donna M. The Bone Detectives: How Forensic Anthropologists Solve Crimes and Uncover Mysteries of the Dead. Illus. by Charlie Fellenbaum. 1996. Little, Brown, $17.95 (0-316-82935-8); paper, $6.95 (0-316-82961-7). **M.**

An intriguing look at how forensic anthropologists uncover clues to solve crimes and determine the identities of people whose only remains are bits of skeleton.

Janisch, Heinz. Noah's Ark. Tr. by Rosemary Lanning. Illus. by Lisbeth Zwerger. 1997. North-South, $16.95 (1-55858-784-5); paper, $7.95 (0-1358-1419-8). **O.**

Stylish and fanciful illustrations provide a sophisticated interpretation of the story of the Great Flood.

Jenkins, Steve. Top of the World: Climbing Mount Everest. 1999. illus. Houghton, $16 (0-395-94218-7). **M.**

An informative introduction, remarkably illustrated in cut-paper collage, investigates the history, geography, climate, and dangers of the world's tallest mountain.

Jiang, Ji-Li. Red Scarf Girl: A Memoir of the Cultural Revolution. 1997. Harper-Collins [o.p.]. **O.**

Political terror and personal turmoil shape the lives of a girl and her family in this riveting memoir about growing up in China during the Cultural Revolution.

Johnson, Angela. Julius. Illus. by Dav Pilkey. 1993. Orchard/Richard Jackson, $16.95 (0-531-05465-9). **Y.**

A wonderful, wacky tale about sharing, friendship, and an unforgettable pig named Julius who loves to party. The zany tone is matched by vivid and inventive illustrations.

Johnson, Angela. Toning the Sweep. 1993. Orchard/Richard Jackson, $15.89 (0-531-05476-4); Scholastic/Point, paper, $5.99 (0-590-48142-8). **O.**

The terminal illness of Emmie's beloved Grandmama Ola turns the 14-year-old's annual summer visit into discovery of a past family tragedy and an experience of reconciliation.

Johnson, James Weldon. The Creation. Illus. by James E. Ransome. 1994. Holiday, $16.95 (0-8234-1069-2); paper, $6.95 (0-8234-1207-5). **A.**

An African American storyteller shares the poetic version of this biblical story with a circle of entranced young listeners.

Johnson, Stephen T. Alphabet City. 1995. illus. Putnam, $16.99 (0-670-85631-2); paper, $6.99 (0-14-055904-3). **A.**

Letters of the alphabet are seen in the sidewalk cracks, street equipment, building details, and urban scenes depicted by handsomely crafted paintings. A Caldecott Honor Book.

Johnston, Julie. Hero of Lesser Causes. 1993. Little, Brown/Joy Street [o.p.]; Tundra, paper, $9.95 (0-88776-649-8). **O.**

Keely faces the greatest challenge of her life when her brother gets polio and seems to lose his will to live. Compelling conversations and well-developed characters bring to life this realistic story of family and feelings.

Jonas, Ann. Aardvarks, Disembark! 1990. illus. Greenwillow, $17.39 (0-688-07207-2). **Y.**

From zebus and zerens to okapis, ibex, and aoudads, a multitude of little-known creatures—many now endangered or extinct—jauntily emerge from the ark to follow Noah down Mount Ararat.

Jones, Diana Wynne. Castle in the Air. 1991. Greenwillow, $15.95 (0-688-09686-7); paper, $6.95 (0-06-447345-7). **O.**

Nothing is what it seems in this exuberant fantasy of a poor merchant mixed up with a recalcitrant flying carpet, a sulky genie, and hundreds of kidnapped princesses.

Joyce, William. Bently and Egg. 1992. illus. HarperCollins/Laura Geringer, $17.95 (0-06-020385-4); paper, $6.95 (0-06-443352-8). **Y.**

Dashing frog poet Bently Hopperton proves that he, too, can be faithful 100% when the duck egg he's watching is eggnapped. A stylish and hilarious story of friendship and one frog's valor.

Joyce, William. Santa Calls. 1993. illus. HarperCollins/Laura Geringer, $16.95 (0-06-021133-4). **Y.**

Santa Claus himself mysteriously summons Art Aimesworth and his sister, Esther, to the North Pole, where they find not only the joys of toyland but also a life-changing adventure.

Kehret, Peg. Small Steps: The Year I Got Polio. 1996. Albert Whitman [o.p.]; Turtleback, $12 (0-606-17887-2). **M.**

A heartening autobiography that chronicles the sudden illness and excruciating recovery of a young girl stricken with polio.

Kellogg, Steven. Jack and the Beanstalk. 1991. illus. Morrow, $16.95 (0-688-10250-6); Avon, paper, $6.95 (0-688-15281-3). **Y.**

Jack's traditional adventure is delightfully expanded in ebullient illustrations crammed with imaginative details.

Kendall, Russ. Russian Girl: Life in an Old Russian Town. 1994. illus. Scholastic [o.p.]. **M.**

Strikingly clear color photographs follow the life of nine-year-old Olga and her family in an old Russian town—from home and school, through town, chores, and play.

Kennedy, X. J. and **Kennedy, Dorothy M.** Talking Like the Rain: A First Book of Poems. Illus. by Jane Dyer. 1992. Little, Brown, $19.95 (0-316-48889-5); paper, $9.95 (0-316-38491-7). **Y.**

This beautifully illustrated collection of more than 100 poems, classic and modern, provides a memorable introduction for the youngest readers to the art and delight of poetry.

Kimmel, Eric A. The Three Princes: A Tale from the Middle East. Illus. by Leonard Everett Fisher. 1994. Holiday [o.p.]. **M.**

Luminous acrylic paintings illustrate this story of a princess who sends three cousins on a year-long quest to win her hand.

Kindersley, Barnabas and **Kindersley, Anabel.** Children Just Like Me. 1995. illus. DK, $19.95 (0-7894-0201-7); paper, $6.99 (0-789-43626-4). **A.**

In this unique celebration of children all over the world, colorful photographs bring their homelands, families, school, and play to life.

Kindl, Patrice. Owl in Love. 1993. Houghton, $16 (0-395-66162-5); Penguin, paper, $5.99 (0-14-037129-X). **O.**

Owl Tycho, a 14-year-old were-owl, clearly has some adjusting to do to make it in a modern American high school. To make things worse, she has a crush on a teacher who is wrapped up in concern for his disturbed son. Humor and anguish mix in this extraordinary modern fantasy.

King, Elizabeth. Chile Fever: A Celebration of Peppers. 1995. illus. Dutton [o.p.]. **A.**
History, anthropology, botany, and cooking are combined in this handsome celebration of the chile pepper.

King-Smith, Dick. Three Terrible Trins. Illus. by Mark Teague. 1994. Crown [o.p.]; Knopf, paper, $4.99 (0-679-88552-8). **M.**
Three young mice brothers take charge of a farmhouse ruled too long by cats. Read-aloud, laugh-aloud fun!

Klause, Annette Curtis. Alien Secrets. 1993. Delacorte [o.p.]; Random, paper, $4.99 (0-440-91023-4). **M.**
Expelled from a girls' boarding school, 12-year-old Puck finds her journey home to the planet Shoon to be an outer-space adventure filled with danger and intrigue.

Koertge, Ron. Tiger, Tiger, Burning Right. 1994. Orchard [o.p.]. **O.**
This special relationship between Jesse and his unpredictable grandfather, who is becoming old and forgetful, is explored with compassion and humor.

Konigsburg, E. L. The View from Saturday. 1996. Simon & Schuster/Atheneum, $16 (0-689-80993-X); Simon & Schuster/Aladdin, paper, $4.99 (0-689-81721-5). **O.**
While preparing for the Academic Bowl, four students and their teacher learn as much from each other as they do from their books. A Newbery Medal winner.

Krull, Kathleen, ed. Gonna Sing My Head Off! American Folk Songs for Children. Illus. by Allen Garns. 1992. Knopf/Borzoi [o.p.]; Turtleback, paper, $20.10 (0-606-07585-2). **A.**
This collection of 62 all-time favorite songs is accompanied by joyous pastel illustrations and informative musical and historical notes, including geographical locations. Includes simple piano and guitar arrangements.

Krull, Kathleen. Lives of the Musicians: Good Times, Bad Times (And What the Neighbors Thought). Illus. by Kathryn Hewitt. 1993. Harcourt, $20 (0-15-248010-2); paper, $12 (0-15-216436-7). **A.**
Hilarious and fascinating details about the lives of 20 musicians, ranging from Vivaldi to Woodie Guthrie, are presented and accompanied by outrageously funny caricatures.

Krull, Kathleen. Wilma Unlimited: How Wilma Rudolph Became the World's Fastest Woman. Illus. by David Diaz. 1996. Harcourt, $16 (0-15-201267-2); paper, $6 (0-15-202098-5). **M.**
Strong, gritty illustrations support the inspirational story of a three-time Olympic gold medalist who overcame seemingly insurmountable odds.

Kuskin, Karla. Soap Soup and Other Verses. 1992. illus. HarperCollins/Charlotte Zolotow [o.p.]; paper, $4.95 (0-06-444174-1). **Y.**

Kuskin's wonderfully inventive, humorous poems capture the feelings of familiar childhood experiences in an easy-to-read format.

Kvasnosky, Laura McGee. Zelda and Ivy. 1998. Candlewick, $15.99 (0-7636-
0469-0). **Y.**
Three chapters, each short and sweet, follow the dynamic relationship between
two fox sisters, who are at once caring and competitive.

Larrick, Nancy, ed. Mice Are Nice. Illus. by Ed Young. 1990. Putnam/Philomel
[o.p.]. **M.**
Mice are the focus of this captivating collection in which verse from well-known
poets is illustrated with delicacy and humor.

Lasky, Kathryn. The Librarian Who Measured the Earth. Illus. by Kevin Hawkes.
1994. Little, Brown, $17.95 (0-316-52526-4). **M.**
Colorful acrylic paintings enhance this picture biography of the Greek geogra-
pher/librarian Eratosthenes, who accurately calculated the circumference of the
earth 2,000 years ago.

Lasky, Kathryn. Marven of the Great North Woods. Illus. by Kevin Hawkes.
1997. Harcourt, $16 (0-15-200104-2); paper, $7 (0-15-46826-5). **M.**
In 1918, a Jewish boy from Duluth, Minnesota, is sent to live at a frozen logging
camp staffed by French Canadians. A big-hearted, true story about family love and
friendship.

Lasky, Kathryn. Surtsey: The Newest Place on Earth. Illus. by Christopher G.
Knight. 1992. Hyperion, $15.89 (1-56282-300-0). **M.**
A dramatic, multilayered story of a brand-new place, where "once upon a time
was just twenty-nine years ago."

Lauber, Patricia. Seeing Earth from Space. 1990. illus. Watts/Orchard [o.p.];
Scholastic, paper, $9.95 (0-531-07057-3). **M.**
Awesome photos and a precise text dramatize the scientific value of space explo-
ration and provide an inspiring chance to share the astronauts' experiences.

Lauber, Patricia. Summer of Fire: Yellowstone, 1988. 1991. illus. Orchard, $19.95
(0-531-05943-X). **M.**
The effects of the awe-inspiring fires that altered the park's web of life but did
not destroy it are enhanced with outstanding color photographs.

Lavies, Bianca. A Gathering of Garter Snakes. 1993. illus. Dutton [o.p.]. **M.**
A fascinating look at one of the wonders of nature: mass hibernation of red-sided
garter snakes in Manitoba. Dramatic color photos of writhing, wriggling knots of
snakes—eating, shedding skins, and giving birth.

Lawrence, Jacob. The Great Migration: An American Story. 1993. illus. Harper-Collins [o.p.]; paper, $8.95 (0-06-443428-1). **M.**
Lawrence's bold paintings illuminate the migration of African Americans from the rural south to the industrial north around the time of World War I.

Lear, Edward. The Owl and the Pussycat. Illus. by Jan Brett. 1991. Putnam, $15.95 (0-399-21925-0); paper, $6.99 (0-698-11367-5). **Y.**
Lovers, Owl and Pussycat, sail to the Caribbean, where exotic sea creatures and tropical plants provide a lush setting for their marriage celebration.

Lee, Milly. Nim and the War Effort. Illus. by Yangsook Choi. 1997. Farrar/Frances Foster, $16 (0-374-35523-1); paper, $5.95 (0-374-45506-6). **M.**
Patriotism, prejudice, and tradition collide in this thought-provoking story about an earnest girl living in San Francisco's Chinatown in 1943.

Lelooska. Echoes of the Elders: The Stories and Paintings of Chief Lelooska. 1997. illus. DK Ink, $24.95 (0-7894-2455-X). **A.**
Powerful tales of the human and spirit worlds, drawn from ancient legends of the Northwest Coast's Kwakiutl people, are illustrated with paintings that recall traditional woodcuts. CD included.

Lester, Julius. Further Tales of Uncle Remus. Illus. by Jerry Pinkney. 1990. Dial [o.p.]. **M.**
The misadventures of Brer Rabbit, Brer Fox, Brer Wolf, and other creatures continue in a grand retelling highlighted by ebullient artwork.

Lester, Julius. John Henry. Illus. by Jerry Pinkney. 1994. Dial, $18.99 (0-8037-1606-0); paper, $7.99 (0-14-056622-8). **M.**
Never with greater power have the strength, dignity, and courage of this African American hero been expressed. An outstanding match of art and text. A Caldecott Honor Book.

Lester, Julius. Sam and the Tigers: A New Telling of Little Black Sambo. Illus. by Jerry Pinkney. 1996. Dial, $17.99 (0-8037-2028-9); paper, $5.99 (0-8037-2216-8). **Y.**
Sassy Sam outwits five conceited tigers in this grandly embellished tale, humorously retold in a "southern Black storytelling voice." Witty pencil and watercolor art completes the package.

Levine, Gail Carson. Ella Enchanted. 1997. HarperCollins, $16.95 (0-06-027510-3); paper, $6.50 (0-06-440705-5). **M.**
The classic Cinderella story is a springboard for this humorous fantasy about a young girl afflicted with a curse that forces her to obey every command.

Lewin, Ted. I Was a Teenage Professional Wrestler. 1993. illus. Orchard/Richard Jackson, $18.95 (0-531-05477-2); Hyperion, paper, $6.95 (0-7868-1009-2). **O.**

Photos and paintings illustrate the funny, tender account of an unconventional youth. As an insider, Lewin draws us into a strange world with seeming casualness, neither romanticizing nor sensationalizing it.

The Little Dog Laughed. Illus. by Lucy Cousins. 1990. Dutton [o.p.]. **Y.**
Here are 64 traditional rhymes featuring characters, drawn in spiffy black line and bold primary colors, who almost leap from the page.

Livingston, Myra Cohn. Poem-Making: Ways to Begin Writing Poetry. 1991. HarperCollins/Charlotte Zolotow [o.p.]. **O.**
Beginning with Ciardi's seminal question, "How does a poem mean?" Livingston simply and clearly introduces the myriad possibilities of writing poetry.

Llorente, Pilar Molina. The Apprentice. Tr. by Robin Longshaw. Illus. by Juan Ramón Alonso. 1993. Farrar [o.p.]; paper, $4.95 (0-374-40432-1). **O.**
Arduino has his mind set on being an artist, though he comes from a proud family of tailors. He gets his wish but must face an ethical problem that challenges his dream. This powerful story of personal courage is set in the vivid world of Renaissance Florence. A Mildred L. Batchelder Medal winner.

Lobel, Anita. No Pretty Pictures: A Child of War. 1998. Greenwillow, $15.95 (0-688-15935-4); Avon, paper, $4.99 (0-330-73285-8). **O.**
A beloved author-illustrator recounts her childhood experiences as a Polish Jew in hiding, in transit, and in concentration camps before finding refuge in Sweden.

Lomas Garza, Carmen. Family Pictures/Cuadros de Familia. 1990. illus. Children's Book Press, $15.95 (0-89239-050-6); paper, $7.95 (0-89239-108-1). **A.**
Bilingual text and colorful primitive-style paintings describe the author's family life growing up in a Hispanic community in Texas.

Lowry, Lois. The Giver. 1993. Houghton, $16 (0-395-64566-2); Dell/Laurel Leaf, paper, $6.50 (0-440-21907-8). **O.**
In a futuristic dystopia, order and security have prevailed over feeling and beauty. A boy is given a choice between the two. Gradually the hidden secrets are peeled, layer by layer, until the horrible truth is revealed. A Newbery Medal winner.

Lyon, George Ella. Come a Tide. Illus. by Stephen Gammell. 1990. Watts/ Orchard/Richard Jackson [o.p.]; paper, $6.95 (0-531-07036-0). **Y.**
The frenzy of a flood is captured in a lively, poetic text and in art filled with vibrant colors and amusing visual details.

Macaulay, David. Black and White. 1990. illus. Houghton, $17 (0-395-52151-3). **A.**
A brilliantly conceived puzzle that at first appears to be four separate stories about a family, a train station, a bank robber, and some cows but is actually much much more. A Caldecott Medal winner.

Macy, Sue. Winning Ways: A Photohistory of American Women in Sports. 1996. illus. Holt, $16.95 (0-8050-4147-8); Scholastic, paper, $5.99 (0-590-76336-9). **O**.
An eye-opening history of the struggle of American women to compete fully in sports.

Maguire, Gregory. Seven Spiders Spinning. 1994. Clarion, $16 (0-395-68965-1); HarperTrophy, paper, $4.95 (0-06-440595-8). **M**.
High heroic humor pervades this farcical tale of seven gruesome snow spiders closing in on a small Vermont town.

Mahy, Margaret. The Seven Chinese Brothers. Illus. by Jean Tseng. 1990. Scholastic [o.p.]; paper, $7.60 (0-590-42057-7). **Y**.
A traditional Chinese tale retold in witty prose and enhanced by dramatic watercolor illustrations.

Maples in the Mist: Children's Poems from the Tang Dynasty. Tr. by Minfong Ho. Illus. by Jean Tseng and Mou-Sien Tseng. 1996. Lothrop, $16 (0-688-12044-X). **A**.
Sixteen traditional children's poems from the Tang Dynasty appear in both English and Chinese in this slim anthology featuring ethereal jewel-toned watercolors.

Marcellino, Fred. I, Crocodile. 1999. illus. HarperCollins/Michael di Capua, $15.95 (0-06-205168-7). **Y**.
A sly googly-eyed Nile crocodile becomes the toast of Napoleonic Paris in a witty and sophisticated tale enhanced by grand and sumptuously detailed illustrations.

Markle, Sandra. Outside and Inside Birds. 1994. illus. Simon & Schuster, $18 (0-02-762312-2); Simon & Schuster/Aladdin, paper, $6.99 (0-689-85086-7). **M**.
Fascinating details of bird anatomy, from internal organs to feathers and flight, are shared in this inviting photo-essay.

Marshall, James, ed. Old Mother Hubbard and Her Wonderful Dog. 1991. illus. Farrar [o.p.]; paper, $6.95 (0-374-45611-9). **Y**.
The old lady and her indulged pet appear in one outrageously comical setting after another.

Marshall, James. Rats on the Roof and Other Stories. 1991. illus. Dial [o.p.]. **M**.
Seven tongue-in-cheek stories about quirky characters in ridiculous situations: a frog who's vain about his legs, sheep whose foolish chatter puts even a wolf to sleep, and more.

Martin, Jacqueline Briggs. Snowflake Bentley. Illus. by Mary Azarian. 1998. Houghton, $16 (0-395-86162-4). **M**.
Handsome woodcuts recall the impassioned life of a self-taught Vermont scientist, who early in the twentieth century was the first to record snowflakes on film. A Caldecott Medal winner.

Martin, Rafe. Mysterious Tales of Japan. Illus. by Tatsuro Kiuchi. 1996. Putnam [o.p.]. **M.**

Buddhist and Shinto traditions permeate this elegantly haunting collection of 10 traditional Japanese tales, each accompanied by a classic haiku and an eerie color painting.

Mazer, Anne. The Oxboy. 1993. Knopf [o.p.]; Persea, paper, $6.95 (0-89255-240-9). **O.**

A haunting and richly imagined allegory about a boy who must hide the truth of his parentage or be persecuted for his mixed blood.

McBratney, Sam. Guess How Much I Love You. Illus. by Anita Jeram. 1995. Candlewick, $15.99 (1-56402-473-3). **Y.**

Big Nutbrown Hare tenderly "bests" each of Little Nutbrown Hare's declarations of love in this simple bedtime game between father and son.

McCaughrean, Geraldine. The Pirate's Son. 1998. Scholastic [o.p.]; paper, $4.99 (0-590-20348-7). **O.**

Three teenage misfits discover eighteenth-century-style danger and adventure in this swashbuckling novel set on the high seas and in Madagascar and England.

McCully, Emily Arnold. Beautiful Warrior: The Legend of the Nun's Kung Fu. 1998. Scholastic/Arthur A. Levine, $16.95 (0-590-37487-7). **M.**

Martial arts help two young women empower themselves with inner strength in this sweeping original tale set in seventeenth-century China.

McCully, Emily Arnold. Mirette on the High Wire. 1992. illus. Putnam, $16.99 (0-399-22130-1); paper, $6.99 (0-698-11443-4). **Y.**

A famous tightrope walker teaches his art to a young girl, and she, in turn, helps him lose his fear. Impressionistic paintings evoke nineteenth-century Paris, while capturing Mirette's splendid spirit and courage. A Caldecott Medal winner.

McDermott, Gerald. Coyote: A Trickster Tale from the American Southwest. 1994. illus. Harcourt, $16 (0-15-220724-4); paper, $6 (0-15-201958-8). **M.**

Finely detailed graphic designs and brilliant colors reflect the settings and rich telling of the misfortune that befalls Coyote when vanity intrudes.

McGill, Alice. Molly Bannaky. Illus. by Chris K. Soentpiet. 1999. Houghton, $16 (0-395-72287-X). **M.**

Aglow in the richness of watercolors, the story of Benjamin Banneker's grandmother is infused with determination, as a dairymaid exiled to America is indentured and eventually stakes her claim in a new land.

McKay, Hilary. Dog Friday. 1995. Simon & Schuster/Margaret K. McElderry [o.p.]. **M.**

A boy, living quietly with his widowed mother who runs a bed and breakfast, finds himself in a series of often hilarious—occasionally dangerous—scrapes when a wild and eccentric family moves next door.

McKissack, Patricia. The Dark-Thirty: Southern Tales of the Supernatural. Illus. by Brian Pinkney. 1992. Knopf/Borzoi [o.p.]; Random, paper, $5.50 (0-679-89006-8). **M.**
Based on African American history and culture, this collection of 10 original tales of the supernatural tingles the spine and says "boo" to the imagination. A Newbery Honor Book.

McMillan, Bruce. Eating Fractions. 1991. illus. Scholastic, $19.95 (0-590-72732-X). **Y.**
Bright color photographs show two winsome kids sharing some luscious food. Easy-to-swallow math; recipes included.

McMillan, Bruce. Nights of the Pufflings. 1995. illus. Houghton, $16 (0-395-70810-9); paper, $6.95 (0-395-85693-0). **Y.**
For an exciting two weeks a year, children on a tiny Icelandic island rescue newly hatched pufflings and deliver them to the sea. Photographs extend the telling.

McMillan, Bruce. One Sun: A Book of Terse Verse. 1990. illus. Holiday [o.p.]. **Y.**
A little boy's joyful day at the beach is presented in crisp color photographs and ingeniously paired monosyllables.

Meddaugh, Susan. Martha Speaks. 1992. illus. Houghton, $16 (0-395-63313-3); paper, $5.95 (0-395-72952-1). **Y.**
Martha, the family dog, can talk, but can she shut up? Heroism and a quiet compromise provide the happy and satisfying answer in this hilarious tale of a memorable mutt.

Meltzer, Milton. Thomas Jefferson: The Revolutionary Aristocrat. 1991. illus. Scholastic, $18.95 (0-531-11069-9). **O.**
An appealing new portrait that sets Jefferson's extraordinary accomplishments in the context of his time.

Micucci, Charles. The Life and Times of the Apple. 1992. illus. Orchard [o.p.]; Scholastic, paper, $6.95 (0-531-07067-0). **Y.**
Everything you always wanted to know about your teacher's favorite fruit is conveyed in lively drawings, easy-to-understand diagrams, and a witty, informative text.

Mitchell, Margaree King. Uncle Jed's Barbershop. Illus. by James Ransome. 1993. Simon & Schuster, $17 (0-671-76969-3); paper, $6.99 (0-689-81913-7). **Y.**
When young Sarah Jean falls ill, her favorite uncle faces the decision of whether to defer his lifelong dream of owning the first black barbershop in the community.

Color-drenched paintings depict a special bond between a girl and her loving family.

Mochizuki, Ken. Passage to Freedom: The Sugihara Story. Illus. by Dom Lee. 1997. Lee & Low, $15.95 (1-880000-49-0). **M.**

Sepia-toned art sets a somber mood for this personal history of a Japanese diplomat who, in 1940, defied his government to save thousands of Lithuanian Jews.

Mollel, Tololwa M. My Rows and Piles of Coins. Illus. by E. B. Lewis. 1999. Clarion, $15 (0-395-75186-1). **Y.**

Aaruni, a Tanzanian boy, wants a bicycle to help carry his mother's daily load to market. Only by saving coin after coin does he come to realize his dream. A 2000 Coretta Scott King Illustrator Award Honor Book.

Monceaux, Morgan. Jazz: My Music, My People. 1994. Knopf [o.p.]. **O.**

The many talented people who contributed to the creation and development of jazz are profiled in extraordinary mixed-media paintings accompanied by the artists' personal recollections.

Morgenstern, Susie Hoch. Secret Letters from 0 to 10. Tr. by Gill Rosner. 1998. Viking, $16.99 (0-670-88007-8); paper, $4.99 (0-14-130819-2). **M.**

Young Ernest's dull and regimented life is turned upside down by a romantic new classmate in this quirky novel translated from French. A Mildred L. Batchelder Honor Book.

Moss, Lloyd. Zin! Zin! Zin! A Violin. Illus. by Marjorie Priceman. 1995. Simon & Schuster, $16 (0-671-88239-2); paper, $6.99 (0-689-83524-8). **Y.**

Poetry, music, and brilliant colors glide, dance, and sway their way across the pages as Moss introduces 10 musical instruments and their sound. All the while another unspoken drama is taking place! A Caldecott Honor Book.

Murphy, Jim. The Great Fire. 1995. illus. Scholastic, $17.95 (0-590-47267-4). **O.**

Eyewitness reports and contemporary photographs enhance this vivid account of the devastating Chicago fire of 1871 and its aftermath. A Newbery Honor Book.

Myers, Christopher. Black Cat. 1999. illus. Scholastic, $16.99 (0-590-03375-1). **M.**

Striking collages and rhymed text journey through city streets following a lean and independent cat on his nightly rambles. A 2000 Coretta Scott King Illustrator Award Honor Book.

Myers, Walter Dean. Harlem. Illus. by Christopher Myers. 1997. Scholastic, $16.95 (0-590-54341-7). **A.**

Syncopated verses and powerfully evocative collages bring to life the street rhythms and people of Harlem.

Myers, Walter Dean. Toussaint L'Ouverture: The Fight for Haiti's Freedom. Illus. by Jacob Lawrence. 1996. Simon & Schuster, $16 (0-689-80126-2). **M.**

Forty-one grandly ominous paintings, first exhibited in 1940, give backbone to this gripping picture biography of the heroic Haitian freedom fighter who led his country to its independence in 1804.

Napoli, Donna Jo. Stones in Water. 1997. Dutton. [o.p]; Penguin, paper, $5.99 (0-14-130600-9). **O.**

Kidnapped from a movie theater in Venice, Roberto and Samuele must support and protect each other when forced to labor in Nazi work camps.

Naylor, Phyllis Reynolds. All but Alice. 1992. Simon & Schuster/Atheneum, $15.95 (0-689-31773-5); Aladdin, paper, $4.99 (0-689-85044-1). **M.**

Seventh-grader Alice survives cliques, fads, and sex education classes with her usual humor and common sense. The fourth in the series.

Naylor, Phyllis Reynolds. Shiloh. 1991. Simon & Schuster/Atheneum, $16 (0-689-31614-3); Aladdin, paper, $5.99 (0-689-83582-5). **M.**

This haunting story about a boy who befriends a dog explores the universal themes of honesty and commitment. A Newbery Medal winner.

Nelson, Theresa. Earthshine. 1994. Orchard/Richard Jackson, $15.95 (0-531-08717-4); Random, paper, $5.99 (0-440-91082-X). **O.**

Twelve-year-old Slim stays with her father during his last battle with AIDS in this funny, poignant, tragic story.

Nix, Garth. Sabriel. 1996. HarperCollins, $17.99 (0-06-027322-4); paper, $6.99 (0-06-447183-7). **O.**

In this intricate fantasy, Sabriel leaves her sheltered boarding school and enters the Old Kingdom to rescue her necromancer father, whose spirit is trapped by death.

Nolen, Jerdine. Harvey Potter's Balloon Farm. Illus. by Mark Buehner. 1994. Lothrop [o.p.]. **Y.**

A child finds Harvey growing balloons in the middle of the night in this magical fantasy. Bold and bright illustrations seem to glow with a life of their own.

Nye, Naomi Shihab. Habibi. 1997. Simon & Schuster, $16 (0-689-80149-1); paper, $5.99 (0-688-82525-4). **O.**

In this sensitive story, Liyana and her family leave their familiar American surroundings for the cultural richness and political conflict of her Palestinian father's homeland on the West Bank.

O'Connor, Barbara. Me and Rupert Goody. 1999. Farrar/Frances Foster, $15 (0-374-34904-5). **M.**

With heart and humor, Jennalee describes the evolving relationship between herself, beloved Uncle Beau, and his newly discovered son, Rupert.

Onyefulu, Ifeoma. Ogbo: Sharing Life in an African Village. 1996. illus. Harcourt/ Gulliver, $15 (0-15-200498-X). **M.**
A young Nigerian girl explains the responsibilities village members have by virtue of belonging to ogbos (or age groups). Exceptionally clear photographs and textile design motifs add an extra dimension.

Opie, Iona, ed. Here Comes Mother Goose. Illus. by Rosemary Wells. 1999. Candlewick, $21.99 (0-7636-0683-9). **Y.**
A companion volume to *My Very First Mother Goose* (1996) offers 60 more favorite rhymes, whimsically illustrated in bright colors; just perfect for babies and toddlers.

Opie, Iona and **Peter Opie,** eds. I Saw Esau: The Schoolchild's Pocket Book. Illus. by Maurice Sendak. 1992. Candlewick [o.p.]. **A.**
A revised edition of the Opies' first collection of schoolyard rhymes, riddles, insults, tongue twisters, and lore. Sendak's memorable illustrations provide a rollicking accompaniment to the Opies' "feast of laughter."

Oppenheim, Shulamith Levey. Iblis. Illus. by Ed Young. 1994. Harcourt [o.p.]. **Y.**
Haunting illustrations suggest the power of evil in this Muslim version of the story of Adam and Eve.

Orlev, Uri. The Lady with the Hat. Tr. by Hillel Halkin. 1995. Houghton, $14.95 (0-395-69957-6). **O.**
Following World War II survivors as they search for a homeland, for relatives, and for their lives, this eloquent translation from the Hebrew gives voice to various sides of the conflict and its aftermath. A Mildred L. Batchelder Medal winner.

Orlev, Uri. The Man from the Other Side. Tr. by Hillel Halkin. 1991. Houghton, $16 (0-395-53808-4); Penguin/Puffin, paper, $5.99 (0-14-037088-9). **O.**
A gripping story based on a true account of a 14-year-old boy's growing involvement in the struggle to save Jews living in the Warsaw Ghetto. A Mildred L. Batchelder Medal winner.

Orozco, José-Luis. De Colores and Other Latin-American Folk Songs for Children. Illus. by Elisa Kleven. 1994. Dutton, $19.99 (0-525-45260-5). **A.**
Piano and guitar chords accompany this joyful collection of singing games, finger rhymes, lullabies, and songs for special occasions. Spirited illustrations enliven the Spanish and English texts.

Panzer, Nora, ed. Celebrate America in Poetry and Art. 1994. illus. Hyperion, $18.95 (1-56282-664-6). **O.**

The creative energies comprising the kaleidoscope of the American Spirit are celebrated in this eclectic collection of art and poetry.

Partridge, Elizabeth. Restless Spirit: The Life and Work of Dorothea Lange. 1998. Viking, $22.99 (0-670-87888-X); paper, $10.99 (0-14-230024-1). **O.**

A famed photographer blended artistry and activism better than career and family according to this intimate biography featuring more than 60 examples of Lange's stirring documentary-style work.

Paterson, Katherine. Flip-Flop Girl. 1994. Dutton/Lodestar [o.p.]; Penguin/ Puffin, paper, $4.99 (0-14-037679-8). **O.**

Nine-year-old Vinnie's grief and loneliness build to a crescendo of emotion in this tightly written, multilayered story.

Paterson, Katherine. Jip: His Story. 1996. Dutton/Lodestar [o.p.]; Penguin/Puffin, paper, $5.99 (0-14-038674-2). **M.**

Raised on a poor farm during the mid-1800s, a kindhearted orphan cares for the local "lunatic" as he comes to terms with his own destiny.

Paterson, Katherine. Lyddie. 1991. Putnam, $17.99 (0-525-67338-5); paper, $5.99 (0-14-034981-2). **O.**

In the 1890s, a plucky Vermont girl battles to save her family's farm, surviving the harsh conditions of a mill in Lowell, Massachusetts, and her own self-isolation.

Paterson, Katherine. The Tale of the Mandarin Ducks. Illus. by Leo and Diane Dillon. 1990. Putnam, $16.99 (0-525-67283-4); paper, $6.99 (0-14-055739-3). **M.**

Elegant, Japanese-style paintings complement a gracefully told tale of two servants who set free a mandarin duck and are rewarded with a long, happy life.

Paulsen, Gary. Woodsong. 1990. Simon & Schuster, $17 (0-02-770221-9); paper, $5.99 (0-689-85250-9). **O.**

A compelling memoir of Paulsen's intimate relationship with Minnesota's North Woods and the dog team he trained for the Iditarod.

Peck, Richard. A Long Way from Chicago: A Novel in Stories. 1998. Dial, $15.99 (0-8037-2290-7); paper, $5.99 (0-14-130352-2). **O.**

An old man looks back on rollicking summers spent with his larger-than-life grandmother in this colorful Depression-era novel made up of seven masterfully interwoven tales. A Newbery Honor Book.

Pelletier, David. The Graphic Alphabet. 1996. illus. Orchard, $17.95 (0-531-36001-6). **A.**

The traditional alphabet book is reinvented using computer imagery laced with wit and humor. Clever design suggests how each letter can function as a word, image, or concept. A Caldecott Honor Book.

Perkins, Lynne Rae. All Alone in the Universe. 1999. Greenwillow, $16 (0-688-16881-7). **O.**

Noting that three is a lousy number, Debbie is devastated when she is dumped by her best friend in this sharp and funny exploration of loss and growth.

Perrault, Charles. Puss in Boots. Illus. by Fred Marcellino. 1990. Farrar, $17 (0-374-36160-6); paper, $8.95 (0-374-46034-5). **Y.**

The heroic-size paintings for this favorite French tale emphasize the clever rapscallion's central role. A Caldecott Honor Book.

Philip, Neil. Earth Always Endures: Native American Poems. Illus. by Edward S. Curtis. 1996. Viking [o.p.]. **A.**

Historic duotone photographs are paired with timeless songs, prayers, chants, and poetry from diverse Native American traditions in this dignified anthology.

Pinkney, Andrea D. Bill Pickett: Rodeo-Ridin' Cowboy. Illus. by Brian Pinkney. 1996. Harcourt/Gulliver [o.p.]. **M.**

Robust scratchboard art sets the tone for this biography of a famed Africa American cowboy.

Pinkney, Gloria Jean. Back Home. Illus. by Jerry Pinkney. 1992. Dial [o.p.]; Penguin, paper, $6.99 (0-14-056547-7). **Y.**

The visit of a young African American girl to her family's farm in North Carolina is filled with memorable encounters and loving relatives. Sun-drenched watercolors illuminate the setting.

Pinkney, Jerry. The Ugly Duckling. 1999. illus. Morrow, $16 (0-688-15932-X). **M.**

Handsome, oversize artwork brings new life and intense detail to Hans Christian Andersen's familiar classic. A Caldecott Honor Book.

Polacco, Patricia. Chicken Sunday. 1992. illus. Putnam/Philomel, $16.99 (0-399-22133-6). **Y.**

The determination of three children to buy Miss Eula an Easter hat overcomes obstacles of cultural misunderstanding. A lively tribute to neighbors who become loving friends despite differences in age, race, and religion.

Polacco, Patricia. Pink and Say. 1994. illus. Putnam/Philomel, $16.99 (0-399-22671-0). **M.**

A former slave saves the life of a young white soldier and pays for it with his life in this poignant Civil War episode of friendship and caring.

Price, Leontyne. Aida. Illus. by Leo and Diane Dillon. 1990. Harcourt, $20 (0-15-200405-X); paper, $8 (0-15-201546-9). **M.**

This sumptuously illustrated edition of a heroic story is retold by a star long associated with the well-known opera.

Priceman, Marjorie. Emeline at the Circus. 1999. illus. Knopf, $15 (0-679-87685-5). **Y.**

Delicious irony abounds as Emeline takes part in thrilling and "death-defying" circus acts, as her teacher, oblivious to it all, recites circus facts.

Priceman, Marjorie. How to Make an Apple Pie and See the World. 1994. illus. Knopf, $16 (0-679-83705-1); paper, $6.99 (0-679-88083-6). **Y.**

Baking an apple pie is easy unless the grocery store is closed. In that case, you only need to travel around the world to collect ingredients. A lighthearted proof that food doesn't grow on shelves.

Pringle, Laurence. An Extraordinary Life: The Story of a Monarch Butterfly. Illus. by Bob Marstall. 1997. Orchard/Melanie Kroupa, $18.95 (0-531-30002-1). **M.**

The life journey of a monarch butterfly is mapped out in a scientifically sound story accompanied by meticulous paintings.

Pullman, Philip. The Golden Compass. 1996. Knopf [o.p.]; Dell, paper, $6.99 (0-345-41335-0). **O.**

Eleven-year-old Lyra and her daemon, Pantlaimon, journey to the far north to rescue kidnapped children in this complex, provocative tale.

Quintana, Anton. The Baboon King. Tr. by John Nieuwenhuizen. 1999. Walker, $16.95 (0-8027-8711-8). **O.**

In this powerful story, a young hunter, cast out on the African plains, becomes the leader of a group of baboons when he kills their king. A Mildred L. Batchelder Award winner.

Rabinovici, Schoschana. Thanks to My Mother. Tr. by James Skofield. 1998. Dial [o.p.]. **O.**

This haunting memoir, originally written in Hebrew and translated first into German and then English, is as much about maternal love as the horrors of the Holocaust. A Mildred L. Batchelder Award winner.

Raschka, Chris. Charlie Parker Played Be Bop. 1992. illus. Orchard/Richard Jackson, $15.95 (0-531-05999-5); paper, $5.95 (0-531-07095-6). **A.**

A jazzy, happy celebration of the saxophone player who turned music on its ear. As innovative a book as its subject.

Raschka, Chris. Mysterious Thelonious. 1997. illus. Orchard, $13.95 (0-531-33057-9). **A.**

Inspired by a Thelonious Monk composition, this small, hip book teams the tones of the color wheel and the chromatic musical scale to provide a jazzy experience.

Raschka, Chris. Yo! Yes? 1993. illus. Orchard, $15.95 (0-531-05469-1); paper, $6.95 (0-531-07108-1). **Y.**

Two young boys from different cultures meet and communicate with body language and voice—and form bonds of friendship. The bold illustrations and the rhythmic text invite participation. A Caldecott Honor Book.

Rathmann, Peggy. Good Night, Gorilla. 1994. illus. Putnam, $14.99 (0-399-22445-9); paper, $5.99 (0-698-11649-6). **Y.**
Mr. Zookeeper tucks all the animals in, but kids will find they are much sleepier than the animals are! A hilarious bedtime read-aloud.

Rathmann, Peggy. Officer Buckle and Gloria. 1995. illus. Putnam, $16.99 (0-399-22616-8). **Y.**
Officer Buckle is hilariously upstaged by his canine partner, Gloria, when they team up to give safety tips to children. A Caldecott Medal winner.

Reiser, Lynn. The Surprise Family. 1994. illus. Greenwillow [o.p.]. **Y.**
Chicks and ducks wander among and beyond the vibrant illustrations in this sensitive telling of a baby chick's acceptance of a loving surrogate mother.

Reuter, Bjarne. The Boys from St. Petri. Tr. by Anthea Bell. 1994. Dutton [o.p.]; Puffin, paper, $5.99 (0-14-037994-0). **O.**
A group of Danish teenage boys' resistance to the Nazis in 1942 evolves from childish pranks to deadly sabotage in a tension-laden tale that examines the complexities of human relationships and conflicts. A Mildred L. Batchelder Award winner.

Ringgold, Faith. Tar Beach. 1991. illus. Crown, $18 (0-517-58030-6); paper, $6.99 (0-517-88544-1). **Y.**
Basing the telling on one of her distinctive "quilt paintings," a well-known artist depicts a child who imagines flying free from her Harlem rooftop. A Caldecott Honor Book.

Rohmann, Eric. Time Flies. 1994. illus. Crown, $17 (0-517-59598-2). **A.**
In this wordless picture book, a bird flies on a startling journey through a time-shifting dinosaur museum. A Caldecott Honor Book.

Ross, Ramona Royal. Harper and Moon. 1993. Simon & Schuster/Atheneum [o.p.]. **O.**
A unique friendship binds two boys from very different backgrounds in this vivid tale of death, child neglect, courage, and loyalty set in Washington State's Blue Mountains.

Rowling, J. K. Harry Potter and the Chamber of Secrets. Illus. by Mary Granpre. 1999. Scholastic/Arthur A. Levine, $17.95 (0-439-06486-4). **A.**
After a miserable summer with his relatives, Harry returns for a second year of school, where whispers of murder and death emanate from the halls of Hogwarts.

Rowling, J. K. Harry Potter and the Prisoner of Azkaban. Illus. by Mary Granpre. 1999. Scholastic/Arthur A. Levine, $19.95 (0-439-13635-0). **A.**

As he makes his way through the third year of Hogwarts, Harry has to cope with feuding friends, old enemies, and the mysterious Sirius Black.

Rowling, J. K. Harry Potter and the Sorcerer's Stone. Illus. by Mary Grandpre. 1998. Scholastic/Arthur A. Levine, $19.95 (0-590-35340-3); paper, $6.99 (0-590-35342-X). **A.**

Upon turning 11, an orphan boy is summoned to Hogwarts School of Witchcraft and Wizardry in this rousing and richly rendered British fantasy about true identity and destiny.

Ryan, Pam Muñoz. Amelia and Eleanor Go for a Ride. Illus. by Brian Selznick. 1999. Scholastic, $16.95 (0-590-96075-X). **M.**

From a footnote in history, this imaginative picture book chronicles the midnight flight over Washington, D.C., of Eleanor Roosevelt and Amelia Earhart, friends and two of the truly great women of the twentieth century. The book soars to great heights of authenticity and detail.

Rylant, Cynthia. Henry and Mudge and the Happy Cat. Illus. by Suçie Stevenson. 1990. Simon & Schuster, $15 (0-689-81012-1); Aladdin, paper, $3.99 (0-689-81013-X). **Y.**

In a comical story with a bittersweet ending, Henry's huge dog, Mudge, and a stray cat that "looks like mashed prunes" enjoy an affectionate friendship.

Rylant, Cynthia. Mr. Putter and Tabby Pick the Pears. Illus. by Arthur Howard. 1995. Harcourt, $12 (0-15-200245-6); paper, $6 (0-15-200246-4). **Y.**

Mr. Putter and his cat Tabby are too old and creaky to climb ladders but still find a way to enjoy pear jelly!

Sabuda, Robert. The Christmas Alphabet. 1994. illus. Orchard, $21.95 (0-531-06857-9). **A.**

Elegant and inventive paper sculpture makes this an extraordinary alphabet book.

Sachar, Louis. Holes. 1998. Farrar/Frances Foster, $17 (0-374-33265-7); Random, paper, $5.99 (0-440-41480-6). **O.**

Stanley Yelnats finds himself digging holes at a Texas detention camp for wayward boys in this stunningly circular novel about bad luck, justice, friendship, and fate. A Newbery Medal winner.

Salisbury, Graham. Under the Blood Red Sun. 1994. Delacorte, $20.95 (0-385-30985-6); paper, $5.50 (0-440-41139-4). **O.**

A Japanese American and his "haole" best friend find their carefree routine of school, baseball, and fishing trips disrupted by the bombing of their neighborhood, Pearl Harbor.

San Souci, Robert D. The Faithful Friend. Illus. by Brian Pinkney. 1995. Simon & Schuster, $16 (0-02-786131-7); paper, $5.99 (0-689-82458-0). **M.**

This West Indian traditional tale features friends who encounter love, danger, and wizardry. Dramatically illustrated with rich scratchboard and oil art. A Caldecott Honor Book.

San Souci, Robert D. Sukey and the Mermaid. Illus. by Brian Pinkney. 1992. Simon & Schuster, $16 (0-02-778141-0); paper, $6.99 (0-689-80718-X). **M.**

When a young girl encounters a brown-skinned mermaid, her life is suddenly filled with romance. Scratchboard illustrations complement the lyricism of this tale based on an African American folktale.

Sandburg, Carl. Huckabuck Family and How They Raised Popcorn in Nebraska and Quit and Came Back. Illus. by David Small. 1999. Farrar, $16 (0-374-33511-7). **A.**

Delicate and humorous illustrations expressively reintroduce a timeless story to a new generation, who will revel in the language and sheer nonsense of Sandburg's creation.

Sandburg, Carl. More Rootabagas. Illus. by Paul O. Zelinsky. 1993. Knopf [o.p.]. **M.**

Virtuoso wordplay comes as a gift from the past in 10 hitherto unpublished tales from this beloved Midwest poet.

Santiago, Chiori. Home to Medicine Mountain. Illus. by Judith Lowry. 1998. Children's Book Press, $15.95 (0-8923-155-3); paper, $7.95 (0-89239-176-6). **M.**

Homesickness plagues two Maidu brothers forced to attend a government boarding school for Indians in this poignant and powerful picture book set in California in the 1930s.

Sattler, Helen Roney. Giraffes, the Sentinels of the Savannas. Illus. by Christopher Santoro. 1990. Lothrop [o.p.]. **M.**

This lucid, thoroughly detailed portrait of these appealing giants features affectionate, beautifully composed soft-pencil illustrations.

Say, Allen. Grandfather's Journey. 1993. illus. Houghton, $16.95 (0-395-57035-2). **A.**

A powerful evocation of the feelings of someone from two countries, and how "the moment I am in one country, I am homesick for the other." The journey unfolds in pictures, like photographs from an album. A Caldecott Medal winner.

Say, Allen. Tea with Milk. 1999. illus. Houghton/Walter Lorraine, $17 (0-395-90495-1). **M.**

Carefully restrained paintings illuminate the story of Masako, an outsider in her own country, who learns that home is a place she will have to make for herself.

Schami, Rafik. A Hand Full of Stars. Tr. by Rika Lesser. 1990. Dutton [o.p.]; Penguin/Puffin, paper, $4.99 (0-14-036073-5). **O.**

A Syrian boy reveals through his journal entries the difficulties of coming-of-age in a totalitarian state. A Mildred L. Batchelder Medal winner.

Schertle, Alice. Advice for a Frog. Illus. by Norman Green. 1995. HarperCollins, $16 (0-688-13486-6). **A.**

Fourteen animal poems, glowingly illustrated with larger-than-life paintings, are by turns humorous and dramatic, and frequently provoke thoughtful reflection.

Schertle, Alice. Down the Road. Illus. by E. B. Lewis. 1995. Harcourt/Browndeer, $16 (0-15-276622-7); paper, $6 (0-15-202471-9). **Y.**

Hetty finds walking to town for eggs and returning home with them intact is harder than anticipated.

Schroeder, Alan. Minty: A Story of Young Harriet Tubman. Illus. by Jerry Pinkney. 1996. Dial, $16.99 (0-8037-1888-8). **M.**

An eight-year-old slave dreams of freedom in this fictionalized biography intensified by emotion-packed watercolor-and-pencil illustrations depicting plantation life in the 1820s.

Schwartz, David. G Is for Googol: A Math Alphabet Book. Illus. by Marissa Moss. 1998. Tricycle, $15.95 (1-883672-58-9). **M.**

From *abacus* to *zillion*, math is clarified through humor in this highly original introduction to terms, thinkers, and concepts.

Scieszka, Jon. The Frog Prince Continued. Illus. by Steve Johnson. 1991. Viking, $15.95 (0-670-83421-1); Penguin/Puffin, paper, $6.99 (0-14-054285-X). **M.**

So the prince and princess lived happily ever after? Is there a witch willing to leave her fairy tale long enough to save the marriage? A satirical continuation.

Scieszka, Jon. The Stinky Cheese Man and Other Fairly Stupid Tales. Illus. by Lane Smith. 1992. Viking, $16.99 (0-670-03569-6); paper, $5.99 (0-14-055878-0). **A.**

This topsy-turvy book is a feast of fractured fairy tales with wonderfully wacky art and design. A Caldecott Honor Book.

Scieszka, Jon. Math Curse. Illus. by Lane Smith. 1995. Viking, $16.99 (0-670-86194-4). **A.**

Bold, innovative, child-centered design details a student's intense math frustration and the triumphant joy of achieving acceptance.

Scott, Ann Herbert. Hi! Illus. by Gio Coalson. 1994. Putnam/Philomel [o.p.]. **Y.**

Glowing watercolors capture the toddler's perspective, as Margarita persistently attempts to greet every one standing in line at the post office.

Seidler, Tor. The Wainscott Weasel. Illus. by Fred Marcellino. 1993. HarperCollins/Michael di Capua [o.p.]; paper, $11.95 (0-06-205911-4). **O.**

This well-crafted fantasy about a community of ingenious weasels engages the reader with humor, action, suspense, adventure, and romance.

Sendak, Maurice. We Are All in the Dumps with Jack and Guy. 1993. illus. HarperCollins/Michael di Capua, $20 (0-06-205014-1). **A.**

A powerful, dreamlike, disturbing tale of children heroically rescuing other children and making the best of what life gives them. At once harrowing and joyful, this work engenders complex reactions.

Seymour, Tres. Hunting the White Cow. Illus. by Wendy Anderson Halperin. 1993. Orchard/Richard Jackson, $16.95 (0-531-05496-9); paper, $6.95 (0-531-07085-9). **Y.**

Roaming the peaceful countryside at will, a cow with an independent streak eludes the menfolk but lets a young girl rope her—briefly. A tongue-in-cheek tale with illustrations to match.

Shannon, David. No, David! 1998. illus. Scholastic/Blue Sky, $15.95 (0-590-93002-8). **Y.**

This manic picture book records the desparate admonitions of a mom who cannot stop her son from playing with his food or picking his nose. A Caldecott Honor Book.

Shulevitz, Uri. Snow. 1998. Farrar, $16 (0-374-37092-3). **Y.**

Perfectly balanced, this droll picture book captures the joy of a young boy and his dog as snow magically blankets their gray city. A Caldecott Honor Book.

Sierra, Judy. Tasty Baby Belly Buttons. Illus. by Meilo So. 1999. Knopf, $17 (0-679-89369-5). **Y.**

"Belly buttons, belly buttons, tasty baby belly buttons," chant the giant oni of Japanese folklore when they kidnap the village babies, until a tiny heroine comes to the rescue.

Silverman, Erica. Don't Fidget a Feather! Illus. by S. D. Schindler. 1994. Simon & Schuster, $16 (0-02-782685-6); paper, $5.99 (0-689-81967-6). **Y.**

Duck and gander are determined combatants in a "freeze" contest that almost has fatal results in this humorous tale.

Simms, Laura. The Bone Man: A Native American Modoc Tale. Illus. by Michael McCurdy. 1997. Hyperion, $14.95 (0-7868-0089-5). **M.**

A small Modoc boy defeats a terrible giant in this unusual tale made more frightening by stark scratchboard illustrations.

Simon, Seymour. Snakes. 1992. illus. HarperCollins, $16.99 (0-06-022529-7); paper, $6.95 (0-06-446165-3). **M.**

Brilliant proof in the form of eerily beautiful photographs and accessible, informative text that snakes are truly "among the most interesting creatures on earth."

Sís, Peter. A Small Tall Tale from the Far Far North. 1993. illus. Farrar, $17 (0-374-37075-3). **M.**
An Artic odyssey inspired by the tall-tale adventures of a Czech hero is enhanced by original illustrations that delight the eye and excite the imagination.

Sís, Peter. Starry Messenger. 1996. illus. Farrar/Frances Foster, $16 (0-374-37191-1). **M.**
The courage and honesty of a famous scientist are revealed through intricate ink drawings, maps, timelines, and samples of Galileo's own writings in this inventive biography. A Caldecott Honor Book.

Sís, Peter. Trucks Trucks Trucks. 1999. illus. Greenwillow, $14.99 (0-688-16276-2). **Y.**
Time to clean up! Imagination bulldozes Matt into the driver's seat of the trucks, whose yellow bodies litter the floor of the toddler's room.

Sisulu, Elinor Batezat. The Day Gogo Went to Vote: South Africa April 1994. Illus. by Sharon Wilson. 1996. Little, Brown [o.p.]. **Y.**
A 100-year-old great-grandmother proudly exercises her right to vote in South Africa's first free election. Powerful, full-page pastels capture the essence of this poignant story.

Smith, Charles R. Rimshots: Basketball Pix, Rolls, and Rhythms. 1999. illus. Dutton, $15.99 (0-525-46099-3). **M.**
Poems, personal reflections, and photographs bounce and swish across the pages with the energy of a fast pick-up game on the streets or in the gym.

Soto, Gary. Chato's Kitchen. Illus. by Susan Guevara. 1995. Putnam, $16.99 (0-399-22658-3); paper, $6.99 (0-698-11600-3). **Y.**
Chato, a real cool cat from East L.A., expects his mouse neighbors for dinner in this slyly humorous tale.

Spinelli, Jerry. Maniac Magee. 1990. Little, Brown, $15.95 (0-316-80722-2); paper, $5.99 (0-316-80906-3). **O.**
A tale the author describes as "one part fact, two parts legend, three parts snowball." A Newbery Medal winner.

Spinelli, Jerry. Wringer. 1997. HarperCollins/Joanna Cotler, $15.95 (0-06-024913-7); paper $6.50 (0-06-440578-8). **O.**
Palmer LaRue dreads his tenth birthday because it means joining the other boys in killing the wounded pigeons shot at the town's annual Family Fest. A Newbery Honor Book.

Stanley, Diane. Joan of Arc. 1998. HarperCollins, $16.95 (0-688-14329-6); paper, $6.95 (0-06-443748-5). **M**.

Detailed paintings reminiscent of illuminated manuscripts underscore the historical context of this complex story about the fifteenth-century French peasant girl who saved France.

Stanley, Diane. Leonardo Da Vinci. 1996. illus. HarperCollins, $16.95 (0-688-10437-1). **M**.

A stately presentation of Leonardo's extraordinarily productive life featuring watercolor-and-pencil art done in Renaissance style.

Stanley, Diane. Raising Sweetness. Illus. by G. Brian Karas. 1999. Putnam, $15.99 (0-399-23225-7). **Y**.

Rising and shining with homespun humor, Sweetness finds Pa a wife after he feeds his brood of eight too many servings of his favorite pickle and banana pie.

Stanley, Diane and **Vennema, Peter.** Bard of Avon: The Story of William Shakespeare. 1992. illus. HarperCollins, $16.99 (0-688-09108-3). **M**.

Handsome illustrations and fascinating details present a lively account of this "man for all times."

Stanley, Diane and **Vennema, Peter**. Cleopatra. 1994. illus. HarperCollins, $16.95 (0-688-10413-4); paper, $6.99 (0-688-15480-8). **M**.

Mosaic-designed paintings beautifully illustrate this well-researched biography of Cleopatra.

Stanley, Diane and **Vennema, Peter.** Good Queen Bess: The Story of Elizabeth I of England. 1990. illus. Simon & Schuster, $16.95 (0-02-786810-9). **M**.

The eventful reign of England's strong-willed queen is handsomely illustrated with meticulously researched paintings executed in brilliant color.

Stanley, Fay. The Last Princess: The Story of Princess Ka'iulani of Hawai'i. Illus. by Diane Stanley. 1991. HarperCollins, $15.95 (0-688-18020-5); paper, $5.95 (0-689-71829-2). **M**.

Princess Ka'iulani's brief tragic life as the last heir to Hawaii's throne is told in simple narrative illustrated in glowing, jewel-like colors.

Stanley, Jerry. Big Annie of Calumet: A True Story of the Industrial Revolution. 1996. illus. Crown [o.p.]. **O**.

A compelling account of a young woman who stood up for workers' rights in the Michigan mining strike of 1913.

Stanley, Jerry. I Am an American: A True Story of Japanese Internment. 1994. illus. Crown [o.p.]; Random, paper, $12.95 (0-517-88551-4). **O**.

Internment of Japanese Americans during World War II is revealed through personal experiences in this well-documented photo-essay.

Stevens, Janet. Tops and Bottoms. 1995. illus. Harcourt, $16 (0-15-292851-0). **Y.**
Hilarious lessons about work, ingenuity, and resourcefulness are detailed in this traditional southern folktale. Art work graphically extends the humor in the telling. A Caldecott Honor Book.

Stevenson, James. Candy Corn. 1999. illus. Greenwillow, $15 (0-688-15837-4). **M.**
A much-used screen door, a field of daisies, and other everyday objects highlight this playful collection of poetry treats.

Stevenson, James. Don't You Know There's a War On? 1992. illus. Greenwillow, $15.89 (0-688-11384-2). **Y.**
Childhood memories of World War II are vividly recalled through expressive watercolors and a witty, engaging text.

Stevenson, James. Sweet Corn. 1995. illus. Greenwillow [o.p.]; paper, $5.95 (0-688-17304-7). **M.**
Celebrate summer fun with 28 short poems, brought to life by creative designs that stretch, twist, and accent the text.

Stewart, Sarah. The Gardener. Illus. by David Small. 1997. Farrar, $16 (0-374-32517-0); paper, $6.95 (0-374-42518-3). **Y.**
Nostalgic watercolors are a perfect backdrop for the chatty letters that follow the big-city adventures of a small-town girl with a green thumb and a cantankerous uncle.

Stoeke, Janet Morgan. A Hat for Minerva Louise. 1994. illus. Dutton, $13.99 (0-525-45328-8); Penguin/Puffin, paper, $5.99 (0-14-55666-4). **Y.**
Minerva Louise, an enterprising chicken, searches for a hat to keep herself warm but instead finds a pair of mittens fitting both tail and head.

Sutcliff, Rosemary. The Shining Company. 1990. Farrar [o.p.]; paper, $6.95 (0-374-46616-5). **O.**
A survivor recounts his experiences on a doomed seventh-century expedition against the new Anglo-Saxon settlers. A splendidly told adventure based on an epic poem.

Taback, Simms. Joseph Had a Little Overcoat. 1999. illus.Viking, $15.99 (0-670-87855-3). **Y.**
This Yiddish folktale gets new life from bright collage illustrations that catch the warmth and humor of the story. The 2000 Caldecott Medal winner.

Taback, Simms. There Was an Old Lady Who Swallowed a Fly. 1997. illus. Viking, $15.99 (0-670-86939-2). **Y.**

A well-known folk song is funnier than ever, thanks to cleverly designed die-cut pages and silly asides.

Thesman, Jean. Rachel Chance. 1990. Houghton, $16 (0-395-50934-3); Avon, paper, $3.50 (0-380-71378-0). **O.**
Fifteen-year-old Rachel is determined to rescue her little brother, Rider, after he is stolen by a band of campground revivalists.

Tillage, Leon Walter. Leon's Story. Illus. by Susan L. Roth. 1997. Farrar [o.p.]. **M.**
A sharecropper's son recalls his life in the Jim Crow South and during the civil rights movement in an understated memoir.

Tomlinson, Theresa. The Forestwife. 1995. Orchard [o.p.]; Random, paper, $3.99 (0-440-91310-1). **M.**
Mary, niece and ward of her noble uncle, runs away to the forest of Sherwood, rather than become the wife of an old man, and evolves into Maid Marion, the forestwife.

Trivizas, Eugene. The Three Little Wolves and the Big Bad Pig. Illus. by Helen Oxenbury. 1993. Simon & Schuster/Margaret K. McElderry, $17 (0-689-50569-8); paper, $6.99 (0-689-81528-X). **Y.**
Bricks, cement walls, and barbed wire aren't enough to keep the Big Bad Pig at bay in this hilarious take-off on the classic folktale.

Tryon, Leslie. Albert's Alphabet. 1991. illus. Simon & Schuster/Atheneum, $16 (0-689-31642-9); paper, $6.99 (0-689-71799-7). **Y.**
Albert, a carpenter duck, uses limited materials and improvisational genius to construct a unique playground in the form of an alphabet.

Tunnell, Michael O. Mailing May. Illus. by Ted Rand. 1997. HarperCollins, $15.95 (0-688-12878-5); paper, $6.99 (0-06-443724-8). **Y.**
Pa finds a clever way to send May to her faraway grandmother in this heart-warming story based on a 1914 incident.

Turner, Megan Whalen. The Thief. 1996. Greenwillow, $16.99 (0-688-14627-9); Penguin/Puffin, paper, $5.99 (0-14-038834-6). **O.**
Fantastically set in an ancient Greece that might have been, the thief Gen almost loses more than his life when he endeavors to find the mythic Hamlathes's Gift. A Newbery Honor Book.

Van Allsburg, Chris. The Sweetest Fig. 1993. illus. Houghton, $17.95 (0-395-67346-1). **M.**
"Monsieur Bibot, the dentist, was a very fussy man." So begins the tale of a mean dentist who gets his just desserts. The theme is carried into the grainy, fig-color overcast pictures.

Van Allsburg, Chris. The Widow's Broom. 1992. illus. Houghton, $18.95 (0-395-64051-2). **A.**

A haunting and unusual tale of a broom with supernatural powers. Powerful sepia-toned illustrations capture the magic and mystery of the text.

Van Laan, Nancy. In a Circle Long Ago: A Treasury of Native Lore from North America. Illus. by Lisa Desimini. 1995. Knopf [o.p.]. **M.**

Stories, songs, and poems from 21 Native American tribal traditions are handsomely designed in this collection.

Van Laan, Nancy. With a Whoop and a Holler: A Bushel of Lore from Way Down South. Illus. by Scott Cook. 1998. Simon & Schuster/Anne Schwartz, $19.95 (0-689-81061-X); paper, $10 (0-689-84474-3). **A.**

Children will naturally gather 'round this exhuberant collection of stories, poems, sayings, and superstitions from the bayous, mountains, and lowlands of the American South.

Waddell, Martin. Farmer Duck. Illus. by Helen Oxenbury. 1992. Candlewick, $15.99 (1-56402-009-6); Candlewick, paper, $5.99 (1-56402-596-9). **Y.**

The long-suffering duck's barnyard pals rescue him from servitude to a fat, lazy farmer in this hilarious spoof on the story of the Little Red Hen.

Walker, Kate. Peter. 1993. Houghton [o.p.]; paper, $5.95 (0-618-1113-0-1). **O.**

Peter Dawson is a typical 15-year-old Australian, who loves his dirt bike and his camera. But then he meets his older brother's friend David, who is gay, and things will never be quite the same as Peter embarks on a troubled journey of self-discovery.

Walsh, Ellen Stoll. Mouse Count. 1991. illus. Harcourt, $13 (0-15-256023-8); paper, $5.50 (0-15-200223-5). **Y.**

A hungry snake collects 10 mice ("little, warm and tasty, fast asleep"), who awake in time to plan a clever escape. A counting book remarkable for the lovely simplicity of its design.

Walsh, Jill Paton. Matthew and the Sea Singer. Illus. by Alan Marks. 1993. Farrar [o.p.]. **M.**

When the Sea Queen kidnaps Matthew, an orphan boy with a beautiful singing voice, Birdy must find a way to rescue him. A luminously written original fairy tale.

Ward, Helen. The Hare and the Tortoise. 1999. illus. Millbrook, $15.90 (0-7613-0988-8). **Y.**

Slow and steady still wins the race as humor blends with scientific information and dramatic watercolor perspectives in a favorite Aesop fable.

Warren, Andrea. Orphan Train Rider: One Boy's True Story. 1996. Houghton, $17 (0-395-69822-7); paper, $7.95 (0-395-91362-4). **M.**

The true story of Lee Nailling and the early work of the Children's Aid Society in relocating orphans is told in poignant alternating chapters.

Weitzman, Jacqueline Preiss. You Can't Take a Balloon in the Metropolitan Museum. Illus. by Robin Preiss Glasser. 1998. Dial, $17.99 (0-8037-2301-6); paper, $6.99 (0-14-056816-6). **A.**
A balloon chase through the streets of Manhatten and a tour of key muscum treasures parallel each other and then collide in this wacky, wordless picture book.

Wells, Rosemary. Max's Dragon Shirt. 1991. illus. Dial, $15.99 (0-670-88727-7); paper, $5.99 (0-14-056727-5). **Y.**
In a classic department-store confrontation, imperturbable Max gets poetic justice at his bossy older sister's expense.

Westray, Kathleen. A Color Sampler. 1993. illus. Ticknor & Fields [o.p.]. **A.**
A stunning introductory exploration of color, dramatically illustrated through the use of geometric shapes fashioned of classic patchwork quilt designs.

White, Ruth. Bell Prater's Boy. 1996. Farrar [o.p.]. **O.**
When Woodrow's mother, Belle, mysteriously disappears, he moves in with his grandparents and forms a close relationship with his cousin Gypsy. A Newbery Honor Book.

Wick, Walter. A Drop of Water. 1997. illus. Scholastic, $16.95 (0-590-22197-3). **M.**
Clear, stop-action photographs and fine science writing create a sense of awe while introducing the physical properties of water.

Wick, Walter. Walter Wick's Optical Tricks. 1998. illus. Scholastic/Cartwheel, $13.95 (0-590-22227-9). **A.**
Stylishly composed color photographs present 15 intriguing optical illusions to boggle mind and eye.

Wiesner, David. June 29, 1999. 1992. illus. Clarion, $15.95 (0-395-59762-5); paper, $5.95 (0-395-72767-7). **Y.**
When young scientist Holly launches vegetable seedlings into the sky above Ho-Ho-Kus, New Jersey, the results of her experiment are surprising and considerably larger than she had expected.

Wild, Margaret. Our Granny. Illus. by Julie Vivas. 1994. Ticknor & Field [o.p.]; Houghton, paper, $5.95 (0-395-88395-4). **Y.**
Two young children talk about their beloved granny, comparing her to other grannies, all delightfully different.

Williams, Sherley Anne. Working Cotton. Illus. by Carole Byard. 1992. Harcourt, $14.95 (0-15-299624-9); paper, $6 (0-15-201482-9). **Y.**

A powerfully poetic text and expressive acrylic paintings depict a day in the life of Shelan, a young migrant worker in the cotton fields.

Williams, Sue. I Went Walking. Illus. by Julie Vivas. 1990. Harcourt/Gulliver, $16 (0-15-200471-8); paper, $7 (0-15-238011-6). **Y.**
In a beguiling cumulative story, six familiar animals—endearingly depicted in glowing colors—join the young narrator on his walk.

Williams, Vera B. "More More More" Said the Baby: 3 Love Stories. 1990. illus. Greenwillow, $15.99 (0-688-09173-3); paper, $7.99 (0-688-15634-7). **Y.**
Love permeates this book's glorious color artwork and innovative design as three babies are caught up, kissed, and cuddled by their families. A Caldecott Honor Book.

Williams, Vera B. Scooter. 1993. illus. Greenwillow, $17.95 (0-688-09376-0); paper, $10.95 (0-06-440968-6). **M.**
Plucky heroine Elana Rose offers an exuberant view of life in a big-city apartment. Visually delightful, the pages are filled with childlike drawings, acrostics, lists, and borders.

Winter, Jeanette. My Name Is Georgia. 1998. Harcourt/Silver Whistle, $16 (0-15-201649-X); paper, $6 (0-15-204597-X). **Y.**
This diminutive homage effectively draws on the words and painting style of unconventional Georgia O'Keeffe to introduce her unique artistic vision.

Wisniewski, David. Golem. 1996. illus. Clarion, $17 (0-395-72618-2). **M.**
Stunning cut-paper illustrations set a dramatic stage for this disquieting traditional tale about the creation of supernatural clay to protect the Jews in sixteenth-century Prague. A Caldecott Medal winner.

Wisniewski, David. Sundiata. 1992. illus. Clarion, $17 (0-395-61302-7); paper, $6.95 (0-395-76481-5). **M.**
Extraordinary cut-paper illustrations relate the epic story of the man who overcame infirmity to become the savior of his African people.

Wojciechowski, Susan. The Christmas Miracle of Jonathan Toomey. Illus. by P. J. Lynch. 1995. Candlewick, $18.99 (1-56402-320-6). **Y.**
An isolated woodcarver finds healing and hope as he carves a wooden creche for a widow and her seven-year-old son.

Wolff, Patricia Rae. The Toll-Bridge Troll. Illus. by Kimberly Bulken Root. 1995. Harcourt/Browndeer, $15 (0-15-277665-6); paper, $6 (0-15-202105-1). **Y.**
Every time the troll tries to keep Trigg from crossing the bridge to get to school, Trigg outwits him with a riddle—until the troll's mother decides that he, too, should go to school and get smart.

Wolff, Virginia Euwer. Bat 6. 1998. Scholastic, $16.95 (0-590-89799-3); Random, paper, $4.99 (0-8022-8223-5). **O**.

Twenty-one Oregon girls recall a fateful softball game in 1949 when bigotry left over from World War II throws them a curve ball.

Wolff, Virginia Euwer. Make Lemonade. 1993. Holt, $15.95 (0-8050-2228-7); Scholastic/Point, paper, $5.99 (0-590-48141-X). **O**.

Fourteen-year-old LaVaughn takes a job as a babysitter and finds herself part of the poverty-plagued world of a 17-year-old, unwed mother and her two children. A wonderfully readable novel about friendship's power to make lemonade out of life's lemons.

Woodson, Jacqueline. I Hadn't Meant to Tell You This. 1994. Delacorte [o.p.]; Dell/Laurel Leaf, paper, $4.99 (0-440-21960-4). **O**.

Marie forms an unexpected friendship with Lena as they both attempt to cope with loss, discrimination, and abuse.

Wrede, Patricia C. Searching for Dragons. 1991. Harcourt/Jane Yolen, $16.95 (0-15-200898-5); Scholastic/Point, paper, $4.99 (0-590-45721-7). **O**.

When Princess Cimorene and King Mendanbar join forces to rescue the dragon Kazul from the wizards, what follows is adventure sparked with sly wit and romance.

Wynne-Jones, Tim. The Book of Changes. 1995. Orchard/Melanie Kroupa, $15.95 (0-531-09489-8). **M**.

Subtly daffy and inventive stories introduce characters encountering life-changing revelations.

Yep, Laurence. Dragon's Gate. 1993. HarperCollins, $16.95 (0-06-022971-3); paper, $6.99 (0-06-440489-7). **O**.

Otter's dream of leaving China for California, Land of the Golden Mountain, becomes a living nightmare in this story of the building of America's transcontinental railroad. A Newbery Honor Book.

Yolen, Jane. The Ballad of the Pirate Queens. Illus. by David Shannon. 1995. Harcourt [o.p.]; paper, $7 (0-15-201885-9). **M**.

Two of history's proudest and most fearless pirates, Ann Bonney and Mary Read, stand boldly in Shannon's swashbuckling paintings, as a renowned storyteller weaves their legends, old and new, into a vigorous celebration in verse.

Yolen, Jane. Bird Watch. Illus. by Ted Lewin. 1990. Putnam/Philomel [o.p.]; paper, $6.99 (0-698-11776-X). **M**.

Seventeen birds are introduced with disarming touches of humor and unobtrusive wisdom. Lewin's watercolors are outstanding.

Yolen, Jane. O Jerusalem. Illus. by John Thompson. 1996. Scholastic/Blue Sky, $15.95 (0-614-15770-6). **A.**

An evocative collection of poems celebrates the 3,000-year anniversary of Jerusalem—the spiritual home to Judaism, Christianity, and Islam. Dramatic gold-tone acrylic paintings provide a vivid backdrop.

Young, Ed. Seven Blind Mice. 1992. illus. Putnam/Philomel, $17.99 (0-399-22261-8); paper, $6.99 (0-698-11895-2). **Y.**

Truth comes not from knowing part of a thing, but from "running up one side, down the other, and across the top from end to end." A stunning retelling of "The Blind Men and the Elephant," with glowing, gemlike illustrations. A Caldecott Honor Book.

Young, Ronder Thomas. Learning by Heart. 1993. Houghton, $14.95 (0-395-65369-X). **O.**

With the help of a loving family and Isabella, the housekeeper, 10-year-old Rachel struggles with the problems of friendship and racism in a small southern town. An honest, quiet portrayal of a young girl's attempt to learn about life.

Yumoto, Kazumi. The Friends. Tr. by Cathy Hirano. 1996. Farrar, $15 (0-374-32460-3); Random, paper, $4.99 (0-440-41446-6). **M.**

Curiosity about death leads three boys into a surprising friendship with an old man.

Zalben, Jane Breskin. Beni's Family Cookbook for the Jewish Holidays. 1996. illus. Holt, $19.95 (0-8050-3735-7). **A.**

A little bear and his family cycle through the Jewish year in this quietly festive cookbook featuring 50 traditional recipes, each neatly presented with cozy watercolors and informative notes.

Zelinsky, Paul O. Rapunzel. 1997. illus. Dutton, $17.99 (0-525-45607-4); paper, $7.99 (0-14-230193-0). **M.**

Exquisite Renaissance-style paintings illuminate this sophisticated retelling of a classic tale.

Zelinsky, Paul O. The Wheels on the Bus: A Book with Parts That Move. 1990. illus. Dutton [o.p.]. **Y.**

Paper engineering and creative art turn a favorite song into a special treat.

Zhensun, Zheng and **Low, Alice.** A Young Painter: The Life and Paintings of Wang Yani—China's Extraordinary Young Artist. 1991. illus. Scholastic, $17.95 (0-590-44906-0). **O.**

The life and art of China's teenage prodigy Wang Yani is simply told and beautifully illustrated with photographs of her amazing paintings.

Appendix: Theme Lists

by Carolyn S. Brodie and Leslie M. Molnar

Adventure

Adventure, as defined by Webster, is "an undertaking involving danger and unknown risks" or "an exciting or remarkable experience." Applying these definitions to 60 years of Notable Children's Books, adventure can range from a nighttime search for the great horned owl, to hiding out in the Metropolitan Museum of Art, to a struggle for survival alone in the Canadian wilderness. Whatever form the adventure takes in great children's stories, readers are drawn in by unforgettable characters overcoming amazing obstacles in the course of performing thrilling exploits. Try an adventure story, and dare to be an adventurer.

Aiken, Joan. The Wolves of Willoughby Chase. 1963. Illus. by Pat Marriott. **O**.

In the care of Miss Slightcarp, cousins Bonnie and Sylvia are sent to an orphan school. After they escape, they encounter misadventures aplenty.

Almond, David. Skellig. 1999. **O**.

Michael's life is already in turmoil. And now there is a mysterious stranger in the garage, covered in cobwebs and craving flies and Chinese takeout.

Fleischman, Sid. The Whipping Boy. 1986. Illus. by Peter Sis. **M**.

Prince Brat is bad! But Jemmy, the whipping boy, gets whacked instead. When they both run away, frightening and funny adventures change their lives forever.

Fox, Paula. The Slave Dancer. 1973. Illus. by Eros Keith. **O**.

On his way to buy candles, Jessie is kidnapped and forced to join the crew of a slave ship. The 13-year-old must try to survive.

Hamilton, Virginia. The House of Dies Drear. 1968. Illus. by Eros Keith. **M**.

Thomas' family moves from North Carolina to Ohio into the house of Dies Drear, a murdered abolitionist. Strange happenings and hidden passages cause tensions to mount.

Jonas, Anne. The Trek. 1985. **Y**.

To some it may seem to be just a walk through the neighborhood, but to an imaginative child, it's a journey through a jungle inhabited by wild animals.

Keats, Ezra Jack. The Snowy Day. 1962. **Y**.

On his own, Peter has fun making tracks and "angels" in the snow, building a snowman, and trying to save some of the snow for later.

Konigsburg, E. L. From the Mixed-up Files of Mrs. Basil E. Frankweiler. 1967. **M**.

Leaving home and hiding out in the Metropolitan Museum of Art, Claudia and Jamie become involved in a mystery surrounding the new Michelangelo statue.

Paulsen, Gary. Hatchet. 1987. **O**.

Surviving a plane crash in the Canadian wilderness, Brian uses the only tool he has—a hatchet—to help him stay alive until rescued.

Speare, Elizabeth. Sign of the Beaver. 1983. **O**.

Thirteen-year-old Matt's survival in the 1760 Maine wilderness depends upon the friendship and teaching of a reluctant Indian companion.

Williams, Vera B. Stringbean's Trip to the Shining Sea. 1988. **M**.

Scrapbook postcards and photographs chronicle the long journey that Stringbean Coe and his older brother, Fred, take from Kansas to the Pacific Ocean.

Yolen, Jane. Owl Moon. 1987. Illus. by John Schoenherr. **Y**.

One quiet winter night, a little girl and her father go owling, looking and listening for clues that a great horned owl is near.

Animals

Animal stories for children often concern warm relationships between young people and their animal companions—especially dogs. Through such picture books as *Julius* and *Officer Buckle and Gloria*, it is possible for younger children to experience vicariously the love, loyalty, and devotion of both animals and humans. Realistic animal stories for middle and older readers (*Shiloh* and *Sounder*, for example) deal with friendships between people and animals, but they also show instances of great human cruelty.

Armstrong, William H. Sounder. 1969. Illus. by James Barkley. **M.**

A single incident dramatically changes the lives of an African American sharecropper and his family, sending him to prison and gravely injuring the family dog.

Baylor, Byrd. Hawk, I'm Your Brother. 1976. Illus. by Peter Parnall. **M.**

Rudy's dream is to fly freely like the hawks over the Santos Mountains, so he adopts a hawk in hopes that his dream will come true.

Fox, Paula. One-Eyed Cat. 1984. **O.**

Eleven-year-old Ned uses a gun without permission and then must live with the guilt of having shot a stray cat.

George, Kristine O'Connell. Little Dog Poems. 1999. Illus. by June Otani. **Y.**

A little girl narrates her puppy's daily activities from morning until night in a series of small poems.

Gipson, Fred. Old Yeller. 1956. Illus. by Carl Burger. **M.**

An ugly yellow dog protects 14-year-old Travis and his family from danger on the Texas frontier.

Johnson, Angela. Julius. 1993. Illus. by Dav Pilkey. **Y.**

Maya receives a gift from her Grandaddy—an Alaskan pig named Julius who becomes her special friend and protector.

L'Engle, Madeleine. A Ring of Endless Light. 1980. **O.**

Over the course of a summer in which her grandfather is dying of leukemia, 15-year-old Vicky finds comfort and understanding in working with a pod of dolphins.

Naylor, Phyllis Reynolds. Shiloh. 1991. **M.**

Eleven-year-old Marty befriends an abused hunting dog and tries to protect him from his real owner.

Paulsen, Gary. Dogsong. 1985. **O.**

Russell Susskit, an Inuit teenager, travels 1,400 miles across the Alaskan wilderness in search of his own "song."

Rathmann, Peggy. Officer Buckle and Gloria. 1995. **Y.**

Officer Buckle's safety talks are considered boring by the schoolchildren in the audience until his canine partner, Gloria, gets into the act.

Rylant, Cynthia. Henry and Mudge and the Happy Cat. 1990. Illus. by Suçie Stevenson. **Y.**

Henry and his 180-pound dog Mudge make friends with a scruffy cat.

Ward, Lynd. The Biggest Bear. 1952. **Y.**

Johnny brings home a bear cub who becomes a problem as he grows bigger and bigger.

Book Discussions

Book discussions allow children an opportunity to share how they feel and think about a story they have read or heard. Directed by a discussion leader, book discussions often take place in a library or classroom between a predetermined group of individuals who have read or listened to the same book. More formally, book discussions can also take place immediately after a story has been shared with a group. A book discussion leader should stimulate others to think about the book and share their individual responses. The titles listed below offer excellent opportunities for wide-ranging discussion among students in the upper-elementary grades.

Almond, David. Skellig. 1999. **O.**
Do you believe that Skellig might be an angel? In this story of friendship and family, Michael, while exploring the garage in his new home, discovers an unusual character who is filled with mystery.

Avi. Nothing but the Truth: A Documentary Novel. 1991. **O.**
Does the truth prevail? Malloy is suspended from school for humming "The Star Spangled Banner," which attracts the national media and prompts a controversy over whether his civil rights have been violated.

Couloumbis, Audrey. Getting Near to Baby. 1999. **O.**
What does the book's title mean? Two girls try to cope with the loss of their baby sister in an unusual way—by climbing on Aunt Patty's roof and refusing to come down.

Fletcher, Susan. Shadow Spinner. 1998. **O.**
Who is Shahrazad? When Shahrazad begins to run out of new tales to tell the sultan each night, Marjan, a serving girl, begins to supply the stories.

Greene, Bette. Summer of My German Soldier. 1973. **O.**
Is Patty willing to lose her freedom? In a story set in Arkansas during World War II, a 12-year-old Jewish girl befriends an escaped Nazi prisoner of war.

L'Engle, Madeleine. A Wrinkle in Time. 1962. **M.**
Who is the most courageous character? Is it Meg Murry, her brother Charles Wallace, or their friend Calvin O'Keefe—all of whom journey into time and space in spearch of Meg and Charles Wallace's father.

Lowry, Lois. The Giver. 1993. **O.**
How does Jonas confront the hidden truths of his community? Twelve-year-old Jonas is chosen as Receiver of Memories in a futuristic society where stability and security outweigh the need to express feelings, experience beauty, and make personal choices.

Peck, Richard. A Long Way from Chicago: A Novel in Stories. 1998 **O.**
Does Grandma Dowdel tell stories or lies? In this episodic novel set during the Depression, Joey and his sister, Mary Jo, spend summers visiting their eccentric Grandma on her Illinois farm.

Pullman, Philip. The Golden Compass. 1996. **O.**
How is Lyra's world different from our own? Eleven-year-old orphan Lyra and her demon, Pantlaimon, make a fantastical journey to the Arctic in search of magic dust and in hopes of rescuing missing children.

Taylor, Mildred D. Roll of Thunder, Hear My Cry. 1976. **O.**
Why is land so important to the Logans? Cassie Logan and her family maintain their integrity, strength, and self-worth in Mississippi during the Depression, a time of great social injustice.

Wolff, Virginia Euwer. Bat 6. 1998. **O.**
What makes each character unique? Twenty-one sixth-grade girls each share what happened when they played in the fiftieth anniversary baseball game between two Oregon grade schools in 1949.

Boys

Novels that speak to boys typically have male lead characters and plots that are geared to a boy's interests, his need for self-expression, and his competitive spirit. The best novels for boys are those that provide them with good role models that will help foster the men they are to become. Powerful books for boys help them meet challenges, build self-confidence, overcome uncertainty, and find their place in the world.

Cleary, Beverly. Henry Huggins. 1950. Illus. by Louis Darling. **M.**
The humorous story of Henry Huggins, whose life changes dramatically after adopting a dog he names Ribsy.

Collier, James Lincoln and **Collier, Christopher.** My Brother Sam Is Dead. 1974. **O.**
Young Tim Meeker's family is politically divided during the Revolutionary War, and tragedy strikes when Tim's brother Sam, a patriot soldier, is killed in battle.

Curtis, Christopher Paul. Bud, Not Buddy. 1999. **M.**
Set in Depression-era Michigan, Curtis' story follows the perilous journey of 10-year-old Bud, who sets out from his foster home in search of his real father and encounters many memorable adventures along the way.

Curtis, Christopher Paul. The Watsons Go to Birmingham—1963. 1995. **M.**
With humor, drama, and insight into the emerging civil rights movement, Kenny, a 10-year-old African American boy in Flint, Michigan, shares the story of his family, "The Weird Watsons," and their eventful trip to Birmingham, Alabama, in 1963.

Fine, Anne. Flour Babies. 1994. **O.**
When a class of underachievers at an English boys' school embarks on "The Great Flour Baby Experiment," a three-week course in parenting, Simon's six-pound "baby" helps him face crucial issues in his own life.

Forbes, Esther. Johnny Tremain: A Novel for Old and Young. 1943. Illus. by Lynd Ward. **O.**
A dramatic story set just prior to the Revolutionary War. A silversmith's apprentice, who must look for other work after he injures his hand, becomes a messenger for the Sons of Liberty.

Gantos, Jack. Joey Pigza Swallowed the Key. 1998. **M.**
An insightful, humorous novel about one boy's struggle with attention deficit disorder (ADD) and how those around him are affected by his behavior.

George, Jean Craighead. My Side of the Mountain. 1959. **M.**
Spending a year alone in the Catskills, young Sam Gribley builds a tree house and uses his survival skills to deal with his fears, loneliness, and the often-cruel environment.

Isadora, Rachel. Ben's Trumpet. 1979. **Y.**
Isadora's art deco–style paintings in black and white capture the yearnings of a young boy who aspires to play the trumpet like the jazz musicians he hears at the Zig Zag Club.

McClosky, Robert. Homer Price. 1943. **M.**
This episodic novel comprises six humorous stories about a young boy growing up in Centerburg, Ohio. Among Homer's adventures is the story of how he and his pet skunk capture four bandits.

Rowling, J. K. Harry Potter and the Sorcerer's Stone. 1998. **A.**
In this story of courage, identity, and friendship, 11-year-old orphan Harry Potter begins to find his true destiny in the Hogwart's School of Witchcraft and Wizardry.

Spinelli, Jerry. Wringer. 1997. **O.**
Peer pressure abounds in the story of Palmer LaRue, who dreads his tenth birthday because it is at that age that he will be expected to participate in a pigeon slaughter during an annual celebration in his hometown called "Family Fest."

Family

Today's society reflects dramatic changes in family structure and family roles. Families past and present have come in many different shapes and sizes—from two-parent families to all variety of alternative groupings. It is imperative that children from all kinds of families, unconventional as well as traditional, have books that reflect the reality of their daily lives and the world around them and that help them understand family relationships and family issues.

Bunting Eve. Fly Away Home. 1991. Illus. by Ronald Himler. **Y.**

The close bond between a homeless young boy and his father is unmistakable, despite the fact that they live in an airport. Readers will respond to the universal longing for a home of one's own.

Creech, Sharon. Walk Two Moons. 1994. **O.**

This multilayered, multifaceted intergenerational family story follows Salamanca Tree Hiddle on her reflective journey to find the truth about her mother and herself.

Crews, Donald. Bigmama's. 1991. **Y.**

A celebration of the author's childhood memories of summer trips from the city by train to his grandmother's home in rural Florida.

Lomas Garza, Carmen. Family Pictures/ Cuadros de Familia. 1990. **A.**

Brilliantly colored paintings capture moments from the author's own childhood; the accompanying text appears in both English and Spanish.

MacLachlan, Patricia. Sarah, Plain and Tall. 1985. **M.**

In this gently told story, set in the Midwest in the late 1900s, young Anna shares how she came to have a new mother when her father advertised for a mail-order bride.

Paulsen, Gary. The Winter Room. 1989. **O.**

Uncle David's powerful stories, shared in front of a woodstove on frigid winter nights, extend young Eldon's understanding of his heritage and his family in this poetic evocation of life on a Minnesota farm.

Pinkney, Gloria Jean. Back Home. 1992. Illus. by Jerry Pinkney. **Y.**

Watercolor illustrations and an evocative text serve to capture a young African American girl's long train journey and memorable visit with her North Carolina family.

Rylant, Cynthia. The Relatives Came. 1985. Illus by Stephen Gammell. **Y.**

This colorful account of the joyous occasion when the relatives come up from Virginia is marked with lots of kissing, hugging, eating, laughing, and fixing things.

Say, Allen. Grandfather's Journey. 1993. **A.**

Large, formal illustrations reminiscent of a family photograph album combine with Say's text to tell the story of the author's grandfather, a Japanese American who came to California and always felt caught between his new home and the one he left behind.

Taylor, Mildred D. Let the Circle Be Unbroken. 1981. **O.**

Cassie Logan shares the painful yet powerful story of a family friend charged with murder by an all-white jury. This sequel to *Roll of Thunder, Hear My Cry* is set in Mississippi in 1935.

Wilder, Laura Ingalls. The Long Winter. 1946. **M.**

The sixth book in the Little House series concerns the family's courage and bravery during the hard winter of 1880–81 in the Dakota Territory.

Yolen, Jane. Owl Moon. 1987. Illus. by John Schoenherr. **Y.**

The watercolor-wash illustrations set the perfect mood for a father and daughter's magical nighttime stroll in search of a great horned owl.

Famous People

As the written history of the life of an individual, a biography requires extensive research, objectivity, and documentation to ensure accuracy. Familiarity with primary-source materials, such as diaries, journals, and letters, as well as a grasp of the time period during which the subject lived, enables the biographer to write with authority. A fictionalized biography relies on the same level of meticulous research but presents the information more dramatically, making use of invented dialogue. In either format, a person's life story can be enlivened by skillful writing that incorporates rich, descriptive details and fascinating facts.

Blumberg, Rhoda. Commodore Perry in the Land of the Shogun. 1985. **O**.

Closed to the outside world for centuries, Japan was opened to world trade and a new way of life in the 1850s by Commodore Matthew Perry's expedition.

Brewster, Hugh. Anastasia's Album. 1996. **M**.

A collection of photographs, letters, and drawings long hidden in Russian archives reveals the life of Tsar Nicholas II's youngest daughter, Russia's last princess.

Bridges, Ruby. Through My Eyes. 1999. **A**.

Walking through a raging mob in 1960, six-year-old Ruby Bridges becomes the first African American child to attend an all-white New Orleans public school.

Bruchac, Joseph. A Boy Called Slow. 1995. Illus. by Rocco Baviera. **Y**.

Even though he does everything slowly and carefully, a Lakota boy wants a better name—a name that will show everyone his strength and bravery.

Freedman, Russell. Lincoln: A Photobiography. 1987. **O**.

From his birth in a tiny Kentucky cabin to his tragic death by an assassin's bullet, this American hero lived an extraordinary life, captured vividly in Freedman's perceptive text, which is complemented by period photos.

Fritz, Jean. You Want Women to Vote, Lizzie Stanton? 1995. Illus. by Dyanne Disalvo-Ryan. **M**.

Believing that women should have the same rights as men, Elizabeth Cady Stanton became the spokeswoman of the woman's suffrage movement.

Hamilton, Virginia. Anthony Burns: The Defeat and Triumph of a Fugitive Slave. 1988. **O**.

Follow the life of Anthony Burns, a victim of the Fugitive Slave Act of 1850, from slavery through escape and on to his capture and trial.

Lasky, Kathryn. The Librarian Who Measured the Earth. 1994. Illus. by Kevin Hawkes. **M**.

While writing a geography book, Eratothenes, a librarian from the famous library at Alexandria, used geometry to calculate the circumference of the earth.

Martin, Jacqueline Briggs. Snowflake Bentley. 1998. Illus. by Mary Azarian. **M**.

In the late 1800s, the photographs of Wilson Bentley show the world that no two snowflakes are alike, and each is an intricate miracle of nature.

Mochizuki, Ken. Passage to Freedom: The Sugihara Story. 1997. Illus. by Dom Lee. **M**.

In 1940 Lithuania, Polish Jewish refugees are seeking visas. Against Japanese government orders, the consul issues documents, endangering his family but saving thousands.

Provensen, Alice and **Provensen, Martin.** The Glorious Flight: Across the Channel with Louis Bleriot. 1983. **M**.

Flying is Louis Bleriot's dream. Experimenting with all kinds of airplanes, he finally flies across the English Channel in *Bleriot XI*. A daring event in aviation history.

183

Folklore

In every world culture, folklore is passed down orally from generation to generation. Folklore has no single creator; traditional beliefs, songs, myths, and tales are shared, offering caution and motivation. Over time, embellishments occur naturally as the follies and foibles of ordinary people provide a constantly renewing source of material. Folklore reflects a clarity of theme and a comfortable structural pattern: introduction, development, and conclusion. The style and imagery found in folktales are rich, honed through the years. These retellings of old and new favorites, featuring artwork from a variety of outstanding children's-book illustrators, hold a broad appeal for all ages.

The Boy of the Three-Year Nap. Adapted by Diane Snyder. 1988. Illus. by Allen Say. **Y.**

Scheming to continue his lazy lifestyle, a teenage son is outwitted by his widowed mother, who struggles to earn a living. A Japanese folktale.

Brown, Marcia. Once a Mouse. 1961. **Y.**

A hermit changes a mouse from animal to animal to save his life, until he becomes a tiger too proud to remember when he was mouse. An Indian fable.

Ehlert, Lois. Moon Rope: A Peruvian Folktale. 1992. Tr. by Amy Prince. **Y.**

With a grass rope, Fox realizes his dream of reaching the moon, while friend Mole falls back to Earth and is content. A *pourquoi* tale.

Goble, Paul. Buffalo Woman. 1988. **Y.**

A young hunter, rejected by his tribe for marrying a Buffalo woman, must pass a test to join his new family in the Buffalo nation.

Grifalconi, Ann. The Village of Round and Square Houses. 1986. **Y.**

In a small village in Cameroon, women live in round houses and men in square ones. It's the "natural order of things."

Hamilton, Virginia. The People Could Fly: American Black Folktales. 1985. Illus. By Leo and Diane Dillon. **M.**

Celebrating the hope, humor, and imagination of slaves in America, this handsomely illustrated collection of folktales is perfect for sharing.

McKinley, Robin. Beauty: A Retelling of the Story of Beauty and the Beast. 1978. **O.**

To save her father's life, Beauty leaves her home and family and enters the enchanted castle of the beast. A powerful love story.

Sierra, Judy. Tasty Baby Belly Buttons. 1999. Illus. by Meilo So. **Y.**

What do the wicked Oni love to eat? Tasty baby belly buttons, of course! Uriko, the melon princess, rescues the village babies in this Japanese folktale.

Stevens, Janet. Tops and Bottoms. 1995. **Y.**

Planting on lazy Bear's land, Hare outsmarts his adversary by offering him first choice of the crop—tops or bottoms? A trickster tale from the American South.

Wisniewski, David. Golem. 1996. **M.**

To protect the Jews against persecution in the sixteenth century, Rabbi Loew creates a huge clay man—a golem—and brings him to life.

Young, Ed. Lon Po Po: A Red-Riding Hood Story from China. 1989. **Y.**

Disguised as the grandmother of his intended victims, Lon Po Po "invites" himself into the home of three sisters for "dinner," but he is outsmarted.

Zelinsky, Paul O. Rapunzel. 1997. **M.**

Zelinsky's luminous paintings, reflecting the formal beauty of the Italian Renaissance, resplendently illustrate an age-old favorite from the Brothers Grimm.

Friendship

A *friend* is defined as one attached to another by affection or esteem. Children's books often focus on the value of friendship, the supportive role that friends play in daily life. But friendships can also be complicated, engendering strong emotional feelings and considerable conflict. Children's books also address these more difficult issues, showing friends handling disagreements and resolving problems. Often children's authors effectively dramatize the issues of friendship by casting the friends in their stories not as humans but as members of different species: amphibians, hippos, even the most unlikely pairing of a pig and a spider.

Fine, Anne. The Tulip Touch. 1997. **O.**

Though Natalie and Tulip quickly become fast friends, Tulip's uncontrollable and destructive behavior leads to a breakup and, ultimately, to disaster.

Giff, Patricia Reilly. Lily's Crossing. 1997. **M.**

During the summer of 1944, in Rockaway Beach, New York, Lily and Albert become special friends as they share secrets and adventures.

Lobel, Arnold. Frog and Toad Are Friends. 1970. **Y.**

Five brief stories detail the daily adventures in the lives of two amphibians who are genuine best friends.

Marshall, James. George and Martha. 1972. **Y.**

In these five short vignettes, complemented by the author's graceful drawings, two hippopotamuses, George and Martha, endure several true tests of friendship with infectious humor.

Paterson, Katherine. Bridge to Terabithia. 1977. **M.**

Ten-year-old Jess becomes close friends with newcomer Leslie Burke, only to lose her to a tragic accident that takes place in their imaginary secret kingdom.

Polacco, Patricia. Chicken Sunday. 1992. **Y.**

A young Russian Jewish girl and her two African American friends are determined to buy their dear Miss Eula an Easter hat in appreciation of all her wonderful chicken dinners.

Raschka, Chris. Yo! Yes? 1993. **Y.**

With a 19-word text and bold, colorful illustrations revealing lots of body language, Raschka portrays the formation of a friendship between two young boys from different cultures.

Steig, William. Amos and Boris. 1971. **Y.**

When Amos, a little mouse, is saved from drowning in the ocean by a whale named Boris, the pair becomes friends, and eventually, Amos repays his debt.

Taylor, Mildred D. The Friendship. 1987. Illus. by Max Ginsburg. **O.**

In Mississippi in 1933, Cassie Logan and her three brothers go to a store without permission and witness a racist attack that tests the bonds of friendship between two men.

White, E. B. Charlotte's Web. 1952. **M.**

In White's classic story of friendship, loyalty, and joy in the simple things in life, Wilbur the pig is befriended by a spider named Charlotte, whose creativity saves him from a terrible fate.

Woodson, Jacqueline. I Hadn't Meant to Tell You This. 1994. **O.**

Sequential flashbacks retell the story of an unlikely friendship and a shared secret between a black girl and a white girl in Chauncey, Ohio.

Yumoto, Kazumi. The Friends. 1996. Tr. by Cathy Hirano. **M.**

Curious about death, three Japanese schoolboys become friends with an old man in their village, who, they believe, "will probably drop dead soon."

Girls

Books for girls should speak to the creative, independent, and brave spirit of young women in society. Female role models in children's books should be courageous and capable. Their stories should help girls face challenges, solve problems, and resolve conflicts. Girls gravitate toward books with female protagonists dealing with realistic situations in school and family life. In addition to realistic fiction, many girls enjoy reading historical fiction, mysteries, animal stories, and poetry.

Ablelove, Joan. Go and Come Back. 1998. **O.**

Alicia, a young tribeswoman in the Peruvian Amazon, observes two American anthropologist who spend a year in her village.

Blume, Judy. Are You There God, It's Me, Margaret. 1970. **M.**

A coming-of-age novel that describes 11-year-old Margaret's struggles with a move to a New Jersey suburb, with physical changes in her own body, and with the problem of choosing a religion.

Cleary, Beverly. Ramona the Brave. 1975. Illus. by Alen Tiegreen. **M.**

During the summer before she enters first grade, six-year-old Ramona must come to terms with a new bicycle, her mother's new job, and something hiding under her bed.

Grimes, Nikki. Meet Danitra Brown. 1994. Illus. by Floyd Cooper. **M.**

Thirteen original poems describe the special relationship between two African American girls, narrator Zuri Jackson and her best friend, Danitra Brown.

Hamilton, Virginia. Her Stories: African American Folktales, Fairy Tales, and True Tales. 1995. Illus. by Leo and Diane Dillon. **O.**

Hamilton shares 20 tales from the African American storytelling tradition that feature female characters.

Johnson, Angela. Toning the Sweep. 1993. **O.**

Narrated by three generations of females in an African American family, Johnson's novel centers on grieving, hardship, and personal resilience.

Lowry, Lois. Anastasia Krupnik. 1979. **M.**

Ten-year-old Anastasia charts her own coming-of-age by writing down all her important information in a special green notebook, which includes the ever-changing lists of things she loves and things she hates.

McCully, Emily Arnold. Mirette on the High Wire. 1992. **Y.**

In nineteenth-century Paris, young Mirette helps the "Great Bellini" regain his confidence after taking a fall from the high wire.

Naylor, Phyllis Reynolds. The Agony of Alice. 1985. **M.**

Motherless Alice, soon to be a teenager, searches for the perfect role model to help with the process of growing up female.

Paterson, Katherine. Jacob Have I Loved. 1980. **O.**

Feeling unloved and unwanted, Louise leaves home in search of her own self-worth in this novel about the effects of jealousy and the struggle between twin sisters.

Paterson, Katherine. Lyddie. 1991. **O.**

Living in poverty in 1840s Vermont, Lyddie Worthen works six days a week from dawn to dusk in a mill while struggling to gain her independence.

Staples, Suzanne Fisher. Shabanu: Daughter of the Wind. 1989. **O.**

The Pakistan desert is the setting for this contemporary story of courageous 11-year-old Shabanu, a nomad's daughter who has been pledged in marriage to an older man.

Growing Up

The pain of growing up varies in intensity at different times in a child's life. Problems may concern family or friends and can involve such issues as sibling rivalry, peer pressure, conflicts across extended families, divorce, abandonment, and death. The list is long, but it is comforting to know that, through books, children can meet characters like themselves, struggling with the same rites of passage, whether it is Cat, who is abandoned by her parents in *Granny the Pag*, or Bud, who leaves the orphanage in search of the father he never knew in *Bud, not Buddy*.

Bawden, Nina. Granny the Pag. 1996. **O.**

Raised by her Harley-riding Granny after being abandoned by her actor parents, Cat fights in court to remain with the person she loves the most.

Byars, Betsy. The Summer of the Swans. 1970. Illus. by Ted Coconis. **M.**

As she searches for her mentally challenged brother, who gets lost near a lake, 14-year-old Sara learns to be more accepting of herself and others.

Cleary, Beverly. Dear Mr. Henshaw. 1983. **M.**

A 10-year-old boy, who continues to correspond with an author after a class assignment ends, gradually comes to terms with his parents' divorce.

Cleary, Beverly. Ramona Quimby, Age 8. 1981. Illus. by Alan Tiegreen. **M.**

Ramona has some new responsibilities in the family. She takes the bus by herself and helps make dinner. After all, she's in third grade now!

Curtis, Christopher Paul. Bud, Not Buddy. 1999. **M.**

Ten-year-old Bud Caldwell, carrying all his possessions in a cardboard suitcase, leaves the orphanage in search of the father he never knew.

Farmer, Nancy. A Girl Named Disaster. 1996. **O.**

Forced to marry a cruel old man, 11-year-old Nhamo flees her Mozambique home and struggles on her own to survive a treacherous journey to Zimbabwe.

Gantos, Jack. Joey Pigza Swallowed the Key. 1998. **M.**

From poking fingers in pencil sharpeners to swallowing keys, Joey exhibits the impulsive behavior common to those suffering from attention deficit disorder, and he must learn to cope with the frustrations that his condition creates.

Hamilton, Virginia. M. C. Higgins, the Great. 1974. **O.**

After his family refuses to leave their mountain home, 15-year-old M. C. becomes its protector and, along the way, comes to understand himself and his heritage.

Heide, Florence Parry and **Gilliland, Judith Heide.** The Day of Ahmed's Secret. 1990. Illus. by Ted Lewin. **Y.**

Hurrying home after a busy day in the streets of Cairo, Ahmed has exciting news. He has learned to write his name!

Hest, Amy. The Purple Coat. 1986. **Y.**

Every year Gabrielle receives a new navy blue coat, but this year she will convince her grandpa, a tailor, to make her a beautiful purple one.

Keats, Ezra Jack. Whistle for Willie. 1964. **Y.**

Peter has a dog named Willie, and he'd love to be able to call him: "Oh, how Peter wished he could whistle." At first, nothing comes out, but then one day—a whistle!

Yumoto, Kazumi. The Friends. Tr. by Cathy Hirano. 1996. **M.**

Obsessed with death, Yamashita and his sixth-grade friends observe an elderly man who appears to them to be dying. Their "spying" leads to a new friendship.

Historical Fiction

Accuracy of detail and focus on a well-defined period of history are hallmarks of thoroughly researched historical fiction. This genre offers readers the opportunity to experience an age different from their own. In a truly notable piece of historical fiction, the actions of fictional characters make sense within the context of the era, and the plot is so absorbing and well constructed that history and story are united in a seamless whole. Historical fiction for children makes it possible for young readers to step back in time and live history.

Brenner, Barbara. Wagon Wheels. 1978. Illus. by Dan Bolognese. **Y.**

Based on a true account, this story concerns an African American family homesteading in Kansas after the Civil War. Facing starvation and Indian threats, Mr. Muldie moves ahead, leaving his three young sons in charge until he can send for them.

Collier, James Lincoln and **Collier, Christopher.** My Brother Sam Is Dead. 1974. **O.**

The Revolutionary War pits father against son, brother against brother, and Tory against Rebel in a tragic story ending in violence and death.

Curtis, Christopher Paul. The Watsons Go to Birmingham—1963. 1995. **M.**

Growing up in Michigan, Kenny Watson and his family travel to Birmingham, Alabama, in 1963 and are introduced to the pervasive racism and hatred common to the South in that era.

Cushman, Karen. Catherine, Called Birdy. 1994. **O.**

Cunningly thwarting the advances of unwanted suitors, Catherine, a rebellious medieval heroine, observes daily life in a journal recording the events of her fourteenth year.

Erdrich, Louise. The Birchbark House. 1999. **M.**

On an island in Lake Superior, Omakayas, a young Ojibwa girl, chronicles the history of her family in the 1800s.

Fritz, Jean. Shh! We're Writing the Constitution. 1987. **M.**

Wearing woolen clothes and battling bluebottle flies and scorching heat, the Founding Fathers are busy composing and writing at the Constitutional Convention of 1787.

Hesse, Karen. Letters from Rifka. 1992. **O.**

Fleeing to America to escape the persecution of Jews in Russia, Rifka's family outwits suspicious soldiers, survives illness, and copes with long separations. Hesse tells the story through Rifka's letters to a friend.

Lasky, Kathryn. Marven of the Great North Woods. 1997. **M.**

Ten-year-old Marven, sent alone to a logging camp, escapes the winter flu epidemic of 1918 in Duluth, Minnesota.

Lee, Milly. Nim and the War Effort. 1997. Illus. by Yangsook Choi. **M.**

To show her patriotism and win a class contest, Nim ventures outside her Chinatown neighborhood in 1943 San Francisco to collect newspapers. Based on the author's childhood memories.

Lowry, Lois. Number the Stars. 1989. **M.**

Like others in Denmark during the Nazi invasion, 10-year-old Annemarie courageously risks her life to help her Jewish friends escape to safety in Sweden.

O'Dell, Scott. Sing Down the Moon. 1970. **O.**

In 1863, Bright Morning and her Navajo tribe are ordered to leave Arizona and make the "Long Walk" 300 miles to Fort Sumner.

Polacco, Patricia. Pink and Say. 1994. **M.**

A friendship survives the cruelest of tragedies as Pink, a black soldier, rescues Say, a white soldier left for dead on a Civil War battlefield.

Humor

Provoking a quiet chuckle or a loud guffaw, funny stories come in all strengths and across all genres. The source of humor may be exaggeration, nonsense, wordplay, or absurdity, and it may be found in a story's setting, plot, or characters—or in a combination of all three. Illustrations may also add to the fun. Enjoyment, entertainment, and that good feeling that results from having a few ribs tickled are reason enough to try a humorous story or two . . . or three . . . or . . .

Bauer, Joan. Rules of the Road. 1998. **O.**

Laughter and tears abound as sophomore Jenna chauffeurs the president of Gladstone Shoes from Chicago to Texas, preventing a takeover by the "Shoe Rodent."

Cowan, Catherine and **Paz, Octavio.** My Life with the Wave. 1997. Illus. by Mark Buehner. **Y.**

Playing with a wave at the seashore has its ups and downs. But imagine taking it home as a souvenir. Oceans of fun!

Creech, Sharon. Walk Two Moons. 1994. **O.**

Salamanca Tree Hiddle and her eccentric grandparents travel from Ohio to Idaho in hopes of finding her mother and discovering her Native American heritage.

Horvath, Polly. Trolls. 1999. **M.**

Ten-year-old Melissa and her siblings listen spellbound to Aunt Sally's incredulous stories of their father and his sister growing up in Vancouver.

Johnson, Angela. Julius. 1993. Illus. by Dav Pilkey. **Y.**

Meet Maya's new friend, Julius, an Alaskan pig who loves junk food, old movies, loud music, and trying on clothes. Together they share fun times.

Krull, Kathleen. Lives of the Musicians: Good Times, Bad Times (and What the Neighbors Thought). 1993. Illus. by Kathryn Hewitt. **A.**

Enjoy fun and funny "behind the scenes" looks at the lives of 19 famous names in music history.

Marcellino, Fred. I, Crocodile. 1999. **Y.**

Captured in Egypt and shipped to Paris, a crocodile becomes the "Toast of the Tuleries" until Napoleon becomes hungry for Crocodile Pie smothered in Egyptian onions.

Peck, Richard. A Long Way from Chicago: A Novel in Stories. 1998. **O.**

Expecting summers in rural Illinois with Grandma Dowdel to be boring, Joey is pleasantly surprised when his vacations turn out to be filled with memorable adventures.

Rodgers, Mary. Freaky Friday. 1972. **M.**

Wishing for her mother's easier life, 13-year-old Annabel wakes up one morning to discover that she has "switched" lives with Mom for the day.

Sachar, Louis. Holes. 1998. **O.**

How could being hit with a tennis shoe land you in a detention camp digging holes? It's easy if your name is Stanley Yelnats.

Scieszka, Jon. The Stinky Cheese Man and Other Fairly Stupid Tales. 1992. Illus. by Lane Smith. **A.**

Nine familiar fairy tales are hilariously fractured, including "Little Red Running Shorts," "Cinderumpelstiltskin," and "Really Ugly Duckling." A rollicking combination of words and pictures.

Soto, Gary. Chato's Kitchen. Illus. by Susan Guevara. 1995. **Y.**

When a family of mice moves into the barrio, Chato, being the coolest of cats and a charming host, invites them to a welcoming dinner.

Other Places, Other Times

How exciting it is for young readers to travel to other countries and experience different cultures or to visit another time and place in one's own region of the world—all through the pages of a book. Meet Sookan and her family, struggling to live in North Korea during the 1940s; or Surini, saving money for a new bicycle in Tanzania; or Liyanna, leaving her friends behind in America for a new home in Jerusalem. Accurate and authentic portrayals of other locations and eras offer readers a passport to the world, near and far, while at the same time reinforcing the idea that there is a universality in human experience that transcends differences in place and culture.

Choi, Sook Nyul. Year of Impossible Goodbyes. 1991. **O.**

Surviving the Japanese occupation of North Korea, Sookan and her family, in 1945, must flee the Russians and cross the thirty-eighth parallel to safety.

Coerr, Eleanor. Sadako and the Thousand Paper Cranes. 1977. Illus. by Ronald Himler. **M.**

After the atomic bomb is dropped on Hiroshima, Sadako is stricken with leukemia. Today her courage is remembered by folding paper cranes on Peace Day.

Goble, Paul. The Girl Who Loved Wild Horses. 1978. **Y.**

Struggling to find a friend within her tribe, a young girl cares for wild horses and is accepted as part of the herd.

Hall, Donald. Ox-Cart Man. 1979. Illus. by Barbara Cooney. **Y.**

A New England farmer and his family are busy throughout the year gathering and making things for Father to take to New Hampshire's Portsmouth Market.

Hesse, Karen. Out of the Dust. 1997. **O.**

As the dust blows endlessly over her family's Oklahoma wheat farm, 13-year-old Billy Jo witnesses the devastation of the Dust Bowl and its effects on her loved ones.

McCully, Emily Arnold. Beautiful Warrior: The Legend of the Nun's Kung Fu. 1998. **M.**

This story recounts the legend of Wu Mei, daughter of the Ming Dynasty's last emperor, and her devotion to teaching kung fu.

Mollel, Tololwa M. My Rows and Piles of Coins. 1999. Illus. by E. B. Lewis. **Y.**

Needing a bicycle to be able to deliver goods to market, a young Tanzanian boy is disappointed when even his determined saving doesn't produce enough money.

Nye, Naomi Shihab. Habibi. 1997. **O.**

Moving to her father's birthplace is difficult for 14-year-old Liyanna. What with dealing with new relatives and cultural differences, will she ever be able to call Jerusalem home?

Say, Allen. The Bicycle Man. 1982. **Y.**

During school sports-day festivities in a village in occupied Japan, two American soldiers perform tricks on a borrowed bicycle for a cheering crowd.

Staples, Suzanne Fisher. Shabanu: Daughter of the Wind. 1989. **O.**

In present-day Pakistan, 11-year-old Shabanu must choose between marrying an older man for the sake of the family or defying her father.

Williams, Sherley Ann. Working Cotton. 1992. **Y.**

In the cotton fields of central California, a young migrant girl shares with her family the daily events of working from early morning until night.

Picture Books for Three- and Four-Year-Olds

Children obtain meaning and context from illustrations long before they are able to read a picture book on their own. Alphabet books, counting books, concept books, picture storybooks, and wordless books all have much to offer young children as they gradually learn more about the world around them. When selecting picture books to share with younger children, several important criteria should be kept in mind: developmental appropriateness, artistic excellence, and a child's interest. All of those elements are present in this gathering of notable picture books for three- and four-year-olds.

Barton, Byron. I Want to Be an Astronaut. 1988. **Y.**

Bold, brightly colored, and simply drawn illustrations allow the viewer to join a crew of astronauts on a space-shuttle mission.

Carle, Eric. The Very Hungry Caterpillar. 1970. **Y.**

Vividly colored collages depict a newly hatched green caterpillar as he munches his way through the days of the week, spins his cocoon, and ultimately emerges as a beautiful butterfly.

Ehlert, Lois. Color Zoo! 1989. **Y.**

Die-cuts are stacked to reveal boldly colored shapes that create nine different animal faces as the pages are turned.

Fleming, Denise. In the Small, Small Pond. 1993. **Y.**

A subtle introduction to the four seasons as they affect life in and around a small pond. Handmade paper illustrations in seasonal colors make the perfect backdrop for the rhyming text.

Keats, Ezra Jack. The Snowy Day. 1962. **Y.**

The wonder and delight a young child feels on a snowy day is captured in Keats' timeless illustrations, created with torn-paper collage.

Henkes, Kevin. Owen. 1993. **Y.**

Though Owen will be going to school, he will not give up his fuzzy yellow blanket until his mother has an idea that makes everyone happy.

McBrantey, Sam. Guess How Much I Love You. 1995. Illus. by Anita Jeram. **Y.**

Little Nutbrown Hare has the constant assurance of being loved by his father in this softly illustrated bedtime story.

MacDonald, Suse. Alphabatics. 1986. **Y.**

Brightly colored animated letters morph into something new: the A turns into an ark, the B becomes a balloon, and so on through the remaining 24 letters.

Shannon, David. No, David! 1998. **Y.**

Wacky illustrations depict David as he runs amok and must be constantly reprimanded by his mother.

Watanabe, Shigeo. How Do I Put It On? 1979. Illus. by Yasuo Ohtomo. **Y.**

Humorous and colorful illustrations follow a little bear as he runs into problems learning to dress himself.

Wells, Rosemary. Max's Chocolate Chicken. 1989. **Y.**

"No eggs, no chicken, Max," says Ruby, reminding her little brother of the rules for the Easter egg hunt that will decide who wins the chocolate chicken. Max has a plan of his own.

Williams, Sue. I Went Walking. 1990. Illus. by Julie Vivas. **Y.**

In this patterned-response book featuring glowing color illustrations on a white background, a young child encounters six different farm animals while taking a walk.

Picture Storybooks

Picture storybooks are picture books with a narrative thread that has been visualized by the artist through a series of images. Relying on the interdependent relationship between art and story, the best picture storybooks add depth and texture to narrative fiction. Picture storybooks should provide children with understanding about the world and those around them; heighten their aesthetic sensitivity; enhance their curiosity; and increase their communication skills. Important criteria in reviewing picture storybooks include the literary quality of the text, the artistic elements of the illustrations, and the integration of the text and illustrations. Consideration is given for age appropriateness, interest of children, and the intended usage of the book.

Ackerman, Karen. Song and Dance Man. 1988. Illus. by Stephen Gammell. **Y.**

Colored pencils are Gammell's medium of choice for these illustrations, which accompany Ackerman's tale of Grandpa reliving his days on the vaudeville stage for his three young grandchildren.

Bang, Molly. The Paper Crane. 1985. **Y.**

Collages bring three dimensions to Bang's illustrations and provide depth to the theme of an origami crane that comes to life in reward for a poor restaurant owner's kindness.

dePoaola, Tomie. Strega Nona: An Old Story. 1975. **Y.**

Strega Nona entrusts Big Anthony with her magic pasta pot while she goes away to visit a friend. The situation is headed toward disaster when Anthony doesn't follow directions.

Henkes, Kevin. Chrysanthemum. 1991. **Y.**

When Chrysanthemum begins school, she suddenly realizes that her name is not as perfect as she had always believed.

McCloskey, Robert. Make Way for Ducklings. 1941. **Y.**

Mr. and Mrs. Mallard are not discouraged about finding the perfect habitat in which to raise their large family in Boston. How they do it is a delight for all in this classic picture storybook.

Noble, Trinka Hakes. The Day Jimmy's Boa Ate the Wash. 1980. Illus. by Steven Kellogg. **Y.**

A school trip to a farm is mightily upset when Jimmy's boa escapes from its carrier and decides to do some adventuring on its own. With understated humor and action-filled illustrations.

Rylant, Cynthia. When I Was Young in the Mountains. 1982. Illus. by Diane Goode. **M**.

The closeness of an Appalachian family and their simple way of life are shared in this gently told and illustrated story.

Sendak, Maurice. Where the Wild Things Are. 1963. **Y.**

In Sendak's groundbreaking picture book, young Max, after being sent to bed without supper, imagines sailing to the land of the Wild Things, where he becomes king.

Van Allsburg, Chris. Jumanji. 1981. **Y.**

While playing a board game one afternoon, two children are enveloped in a surreal jungle adventure.

Williams, Vera B. A Chair for My Mother. 1982. **Y.**

Having lost all their possessions in a fire, a young girl and her mother and grandmother save their coins in a jar so they can buy a comfortable chair for their apartment.

Yorinks, Arthur. Hey, Al! 1986. Illus. by Richard Eglieski. **Y.**

Al and his dog, Eddie, make a fantastic journey to paradise, where they soon realize that home has its advantages.

Poetry

Poetry is literature at its most compact and imaginative. For children to understand how a poem fuses imagery, sound, and rhythm, they need to hear poetry read aloud and participate in a variety of experiences that reveal the music and rhythm of language: refrains, choral readings, etc. The books on this list—poetry anthologies, single-author collections, illustrated poems, nursery rhymes, humorous verse, haiku, and more—not only offer an excellent introduction to the riches of poetry but also show how poems are an ideal vehicle with which to express cultural diversity.

Adoff, Arnold. All the Colors of the Race: Poems. 1982. Illus. by John Steptoe. **M**.

An eloquent collection of poems written from a child's perspective about growing up with a black mother and a white father.

Adoff, Arnold, ed. My Black Me: A Beginning Book of Black Poetry. 1974. **M**.

This classic compilation for young readers celebrates the strength, hope, and pride of being black. It includes selections from poets such as Langston Hughes, Lucille Clifton, and Nikki Giovanni.

Cassedy, Sylvia. Red Dragonfly on My Shoulder. 1992. Illus. by Molly Bang. **A**.

Intended to be read vertically, this book is made up of 13 examples of Japanese haiku, which serve as the inspiration for clever and creative collage illustrations.

Frost, Robert. You Come Too: Favorite Poems for Young Readers. 1959. Illus. by Thomas W. Nason. **O**.

Frost personally chose these 50 poems from his own work as being appropriate for children. Primarily depicting nature and rural life, the selections include such classics as "Mending Wall" and "The Road Not Taken."

Herrera, Juan Felipe. Laughing Out Loud, I Fly / A Caracajadas yo vuelo. 1999. Illus. by Karen Barbour. **O**.

Twenty-two original poems are filled with a rhythm and vibrancy that celebrate Herrera's own childhood. The poems appear in both Spanish and English.

Kennedy, X. J. and **Kennedy, Dorothy M.** Talking like the Rain: A First Book of Poems. 1992. Illus. by Jane Dyer. **Y**.

More than 100 classic and modern poems make up this timeless and diverse collection, which is made even more memorable by Dyer's glowing watercolor illustrations.

Livingston, Myra Cohn. A Circle of Seasons. 1982. Illus. by Leonard Everett Fisher. **M**.

A 13-stanza poem follows the four seasons through one year. Connections flow throughout between Livingston's words and Fisher's illustrations.

Lobel, Arnold. The Random House Book of Mother Goose. 1986. **Y**.

An essential collection of 306 classic nursery rhymes.

Panzer, Nora, ed. Celebrate America in Poetry and Art. 1994. **O**.

A cornucopia of 50 poems celebrating the American spirit set against the backdrop of paintings and photographs from the National Museum of American Art.

Prelutsky, Jack, ed. The Random House Book of Poetry for Children. 1983. Illus. by Arnold Lobel. **M**.

Prelutsky brings together more than 500 poems in a collection that showcases poetry in its many forms.

Silverstein, Shel. A Light in the Attic. 1981. **M**.

This modern classic of humorous poetry is made even more whimsical by Silverstein's line drawings. A natural for poetry performances.

Read-Alouds

Reading aloud to children of all ages is a special experience. Sharing a good book heightens and satisfies children's curiosity, stimulates their imagination, broadens their knowledge of authors and illustrators, enhances their listening skills, and fosters a love of the written and spoken word. It is important to select books of wide appeal. Always read with expression—use dramatic pauses and modulate your voice. Start at the cover, read chapter by chapter, page by page, and share the joy of and enthusiasm for reading. The discussion and exchange of ideas will continue long after you've finished reading. The following notable titles make perfect read-alouds.

Armstrong, William H. Sounder. 1969. Illus. by James Barkley. **M.**

When a sharecropper is arrested for stealing food for his starving family, his son is left to do his father's work, and his dog, Sounder, is shot and disappears.

Best, Cari. Three Cheers for Catherine the Great! 1999. Illus. by Giselle Potter. **Y.**

It's Grandma Catherine's birthday, but she doesn't want any gifts. Now Sara must find the best "no present" to give her very special Russian grandmother.

Billingsley, Franny. Folk Keeper. 1999. **O.**

Keeping the Folk happy is Corinna's job. Summoned to Cliffside, she discovers her heritage and the source of her unusual powers—a magical, mysterious diary.

Cooper, Susan. The Boggart. 1993. **O.**

An ancient spirit turns a Canadian family's world upside down when 12-year-old Emily finds the mischievous "boggart" trapped in a desk that has just arrived from Scotland.

Fletcher, Susan. Shadow Spinner. 1998. **O.**

After 989 nights, Shahrazad seeks new stories to entertain the sultan and save women's lives. Secretly, the servant girl Marjan must search the bazaar for a story-teller who can giver her tales for Shahrazad.

Lewis, C. S. The Lion, the Witch and the Wardrobe. 1950. **M.**

Playing hide-and-seek, Lucy enters a wardrobe and finds herself in Narnia, an unhappy land awaiting the four children destined to rule it. The first in the classic Chronicles of Narnia series.

North, Sterling. Rascal: A Memoir of a Better Era. 1963. **O.**

The author, who grew up in rural Wisconsin, shares the trials and tribulations of raising a young raccoon. Chapter-by-chapter fun for everyone.

Paulsen, Gary. Woodsong. 1990. **O.**

An award-winning author recounts his life in northern Minnesota, running sled dogs and participating in his first Iditarod. Paulsen's experiences in the wilderness inform much of his writing.

Sandburg, Carl. The Huckabuck Family and How They Raised Popcorn in Nebraska and Quit and Came Back. 1999. Illus. by David Small. **A.**

When Pony Pony discovers a Chinese silver slipper buckle in a squash, it changes the Huckabucks' lives forever. A great introduction to the Rootabaga stories.

Stanley, Diane. Raising Sweetness. 1999. Illus. by G. Brian Karas. **Y.**

When Pa serves his favorite recipe of pickle-and-banana pie one more time, Sweetness and the adopted orphans begin to ask, "Pa, you ever thought about getting' married?"

Van Laan, Nancy. With a Whoop and a Holler. 1998. **A.**

This rich collection of trickster tales, silly rhymes, and bits of folklore from the Deep South is enjoyable for reading and sharing.

School Stories

Going to school can be exciting, challenging, and frightening. Young students must adjust to new faces, surroundings, routines, and rules. The best children's books about going to school reflect the many emotions associated with these experiences. In *Lilly's Purple Plastic Purse*, a young mouse learns the rules of show-and-tell. Shirley Temple Wong, from *In the Year of the Boar and Jackie Robinson*, experiences the pain of being the "new kid," worsened by the fact that she doesn't speak English. *Owl in Love* deals with the issue of a first crush on the teacher. School stories relate universal experiences that are a natural, if often painful, part of childhood.

Brooks, Bruce. The Moves Make the Man. 1984. **O.**

Jayfox, the first African American in his school, knows the moves to survive on and off the basketball court, and he's ready to teach them to his friend Bix, who doesn't like the idea of faking one move before making another.

Henkes, Kevin. Lilly's Purple Plastic Purse. 1996. **Y.**

Mr. Slinger is Lilly's favorite teacher until he takes away the musical purse she's "showing-off" to the class before show-and-tell.

Hoffman, Mary. Amazing Grace. 1991. **Y.**

Classmates tell Grace that, because she is a girl and an African American, she can't be Peter Pan in the class play, but Grace thinks differently.

Houston, Gloria. My Great-Aunt Arizona. 1992. Illus. by Susan Condie Lamb. **Y.**

Born in the Appalachian Mountains and dreaming of faraway places, Arizona remains in North Carolina teaching generations of students in a one-room schoolhouse.

Kindl, Patrice. Owl in Love. 1993. **O.**

Fourteen-year-old Owl Tycho has a crush on her science teacher and uses her special abilities as a shape-shifter to protect him from evil forces.

Konigsburg, E. L. The View from Saturday. 1996. **O.**

Students chosen for Epiphany School's Academic Bowl team win the state championship. But why did Mrs. Olinski select *these* four sixth-graders?

Lord, Bette Bao. In the Year of the Boar and Jackie Robinson. 1984. **M.**

Newly arrived in Brooklyn from China, 10-year-old Shirley Temple Wong doesn't speak English and finds school difficult. Then she discovers baseball and Jackie Robinson.

Naylor, Phyllis Reynolds. The Agony of Alice. 1985. **M.**

As a sixth-grade girl in an all-male household, Alice needs help becoming a teenager! So she turns to her teacher, Mrs. Plotkin.

Scieszka, Jon. Math Curse. 1995. Illus. by Lane Smith. **A.**

When the teacher declares, "You can think of almost everything as a math problem," the narrator becomes obsessed with numbers. It all adds up to great fun.

Slepian, Jan. The Broccoli Tapes. 1989. **O.**

When her father takes a short-term teaching project in Hawaii, 11-year-old Sara knows she will miss her teacher and her classmates. So to keep in touch and to participate in an oral-history project, Sara sends tapes recounting her experiences.

Wolff, Virginia Euwer. Bat 6. 1998. **O.**

During World War II, a sixth-grade girls' softball game in Oregon has everyone on the edge of the bleachers, but bigotry throws a curveball.

Science Fiction and Fantasy

Science fiction and fantasy allow readers to depart from reality as we know it and enter alternate worlds where people cast spells, where animals talk, where the inanimate suddenly becomes animate, or where technological sophistication makes possible unimagined ways of dealing with the world and its problems. Within any alternate world, however, whether in science fiction or in fantasy, characters, setting, and action must remain in sync with one another, creating a harmonious reality that, although very different from our own, is utterly believable on its own terms.

Alexander, Lloyd. The Book of Three. 1964. **O**.

Journey to the mythical land of Prydain as Taran, assistant pig-keeper, finds himself in a fight against the evil Annuvin and his deathless warriors.

Christopher, John. The White Mountains. 1967. **M**.

The ruling Tripods control behavior by "caps." Will must choose between being "capped" or running away to live free in the White Mountains.

Farmer, Nancy. The Ear, the Eye, and the Arm. 1994. **O**.

The year is 2194. The place is Zimbabwe. A trio of detectives with unusual powers track down the kidnappers of 13-year-old Tendai and his siblings.

Fleischman, Paul. Weslandia. 1999. **M**.

In his backyard, Wesley creates a new civilization complete with language, food, and living spaces. Weslandia becomes a neighborhood attraction, and so does its creator.

Levine, Gail Carson. Ella Enchanted. 1997. **M**.

A fairy's gift turned curse haunts Ella's life in this enchanting, retold fairy tale, which includes a wicked stepmother and a handsome prince.

McKinley, Robin. The Hero and the Crown. 1984. **O**.

As the daughter of the Damarian King, Aerin strives to win her birthright with the help of Wizard Luthe and the Blue Sword.

Norton, Mary. The Borrowers. 1953. Illus. by Beth Krush and Joe Krush. **M**.

Lose something? Maybe it's the Borrowers! Living beneath the floorboards of a country house, Homily, Pod, and Arrietty Clock borrow from the "human beans."

O'Brien, Robert C. Mrs. Frisby and the Rats of NIMH. 1971. Illus. by Zena Bernstein. **M**.

With a crow's help, Mrs. Frisby, a widowed mouse, learns her husband's secret past and meets a group of well-read rats who save her son.

Pearce, Philippa. Tom's Midnight Garden. 1959. Illus. by Susan Einzig. **M**.

One night as Tom longs for someone to play with, the old grandfather clock strikes 13, beckoning him into a garden that no longer exists.

Selden, George. The Cricket in Times Square. 1960. Illus. by Garth Williams. **Y**.

A Connecticut cricket is transported to New York in a picnic basket, where he is befriended by Tucker Mouse and Harry Cat, who urge him to put his musical talent to use.

Van Allsburg, Chris. Jumanji. 1981. **Y**.

A mysterious board game played by Peter and Judy plunges them into a wild adventure when every move they make becomes real. Fantastic fun.

Wiesner, David. June 29, 1999. 1992. **Y**.

A science experiment launched from Ho-ho-kus, New Jersey, has seedlings soaring. Soon a mixed medley of veggies circles above the country. But why? How? *Really?*

Survival

Carrying on despite physical or emotional hardship is one aspect of survival. Another is staying alive through hostile or unnatural conditions. Protagonists in survival stories typically survive the perilous situations in which they find themselves—usually not situations of their own choosing—and, in the course of their struggle, come to a greater understanding of self and the surrounding world. For a survival story to succeed, the reader must feel a strong connection with the character or characters in peril. Because they are intrinsically dramatic, usually fast paced, and often feature unusual settings, survival stories have a natural audience in young readers.

DeFelice, Cynthia. Weasel. 1990. **O.**
In this suspenseful novel set in the Ohio wilderness in 1839, 12-year-old Nathan and his younger sister are confronted by a renegade killer known as Weasel.

Eckert, Allan. Incident at Hawk's Hill. 1971. Illus. by John Schoenherr. **O.**
Benjamin, a six-year-old boy, becomes lost in the Canadian wilderness and is taken care of by a female badger. Based on a true story.

Farmer, Nancy. A Girl Named Disaster. 1996. **O.**
After running away from her home in Mozambique, 11-year-old Naomi relies on her survival skills and her strong spiritual beliefs during a year-long journey to her father's family in Zimbabwe.

Fox, Paula. Monkey Island. 1991. **O.**
Eleven-year-old Clay is forced to survive with others in a small city park after his father abandons the family and then his mother disappears.

George, Jean Craighead. Julie of the Wolves. 1972. **O.**
When Miyax, a 13-year-old Eskimo girl, must choose between the old and new ways, she runs away from home and finds herself lost in the Alaskan wilderness.

Holman, Felice. Slake's Limbo. 1974. **O.**
In search of his place in the world, 13-year-old Artemis Slake disappears into a New York City subway tunnel, where he survives for more than 100 days.

Lowry, Lois. Number the Stars. 1989. **M.**
German-occupied Denmark in 1943 is the setting for this powerful novel about how 10-year-old Annemarie helped save her best friend's family from the Nazis.

Napoli, Donna Jo. Stones in Water. 1997. **O.**
Napoli's gripping historical novel is based on the true experiences of a Venetian boy who was forced to work for the Nazis as an indentured laborer during World War II.

O'Dell, Scott. Island of the Blue Dolphins. 1960. **M.**
Karana, a young American Indian girl, survives for years alone on an island by foraging for food, making her own weapons and clothes, and securing her own shelter. Based on a true story.

Paulsen, Gary. Hatchet. 1987. **O.**
The only survivor of an airplane crash, 13-year-old Brian finds himself in the Canadian wilderness with only a hatchet and his wits to keep him from starving. Fifty-four days later, he comes out of the ordeal better equipped to deal with his own life and family problems.

Sachar, Louis. Holes. 1998. **O.**
In this dark and humorous tale of redemption, Stanley Yelnats is sentenced to a nightmarish juvenile-detention facility, where his life is reduced to digging holes in the hot Texas sun.

Steig, William. Abel's Island. 1976. **M.**
A mouse named Abel reflects on his life while marooned on a deserted river island where he is forced to rely on his own resourcefulness.

Author-Illustrator Index

Title Index